THE FIRST BOOK OF DISCIPLINE

The First Book
of Discipline

With Introduction and Commentary

by

JAMES K. CAMERON

*Professor of Ecclesiastical History
in the University of St Andrews*

THE SAINT ANDREW PRESS

EDINBURGH

© JAMES K. CAMERON 1972

First published in 1972
by The Saint Andrew Press
121 George Street, Edinburgh, EH2 4YN

ISBN 0 7152 0212 X

2 85·2
D 631
1 972

200039

FOR EUAN

Printed in Great Britain by
R. & R. Clark Ltd, Edinburgh

Editor's Preface

The First Book of Discipline is one of the primary documents of the Scottish Reformation and one of the most formative writings in the history of the protestant Church. John Knox incorporated it in his manuscript History of the Reformation in Scotland and consequently it appeared in 1848 in the collected works of the reformer, edited by David Laing for the Wodrow Society. It was also included in an appendix by W. Croft Dickinson to his edition of that History in 1949.

The first printed edition, from a different manuscript of which nothing is known, was published on the Continent in 1621 and reprinted in Great Britain in the eighteenth and nineteenth centuries. A separate edition of the text with an introduction and commentary has, however, long been desired. This need was no doubt in the mind of the General Assembly of the Church of Scotland when some years ago it requested its Publications Department to investigate the possibility of publishing some of the Church's historic documents. At the request of this Department I undertook to edit the text of the 1621 edition.

In the introduction, I have briefly sketched the historical background, and then attempted in an analysis of the contents to solve some of the difficult questions posed by the book. In particular I have sought to distinguish the various stages of its development, for undoubtedly the book as we now have it is not the original document that was presented by the reformers to the Great Council of the Realm in May 1560.

I am aware that I have put forward in many cases only tentative solutions, but I have been encouraged to believe that by so doing I am shedding light on the history of the Church during a critical period. In the commentary an attempt has been made to indicate the origin of some of the main proposals and also to illustrate the extent to which it was regarded by the Church as its 'Book of Reformation', despite the fact that it was never accorded equal statutory recognition with the Confession of Faith.

In the preparation of this edition I have received much help from many colleagues and friends which I most gladly acknowledge. To the Librarian and staff of the University Library, St Andrews, I am indebted for their unfailing helpfulness and courtesy. Professor Gordon Donaldson of Edinburgh University has afforded me encouragement and helpful criticism. Mr R. N. Smart of the manuscript department of the University Library of St Andrews is to be thanked for his keen interest and help especially in my study of the section on the reform of the universities. My greatest debt is to my former teacher and now my colleague, Mr R. G. Cant, Reader in Scottish History in St Andrews. In discussing with him the varied problems of editing a sixteenth-century text Mr Cant has given unsparingly of his time and of his intimate knowledge of the period. He has also shared in the reading of the proofs.

August 1972   JAMES K. CAMERON
St Mary's College
St Andrews

CONTENTS

INTRODUCTION

THE HISTORICAL BACKGROUND

The Compilation of the First Report

In the history of the Scottish Reformation Movement the spring of 1560 marked the beginning of a crucial stage. The throne of England was now occupied by one to whom Scottish affairs were a matter of real concern. In her own interest Queen Elizabeth could not but be sympathetic towards the outcome of the politico-religious struggle. With the presence of an English fleet in the Firth of Forth and an English army united with the Scottish Protestant forces on Scottish soil, victory, although not yet within sight, could not be long delayed. The time had come for the Protestant leaders to unite in their last solemn band and to look to the future settlement of the country's religious troubles and to the reorganisation of the Church. On 27th April 'all the Nobility, Barons and Gentlemen professing Christ Jesus in Scotland' contracted to 'set forward the Reformation of Religion according to God's Word . . . that the truth of God's word may have free passage within this realm' and to recover their 'ancient freedoms and liberties'.[1] Two days later the Great Council of the Realm, which had been seeking to exercise authority within the country since the 'deprivation' of Mary of Lorraine of the regency in November 1559, commissioned the 'ministers of Christ Jesus' within the realm 'to commit to writing' their 'judgements touching the reformation of Religion'.[2] Sharing their leaders' confidence those ministers who were with them in Edinburgh set to work and at the end of three weeks presented their report.[3]

The text of the ministers' proposals, which must have been put together somewhat hurriedly, has not survived in its original form. Of the *Book of Discipline* which John Knox incorporated in the manuscript of his *History* only the Preface and Conclusion can with any degree of certainty be regarded as belonging in their present form to this early document. However, these two sections provide an indication of the main topics on which the ministers gave their judgments 'for the observance of common order and uniformity of religion'. According to the Preface their proposals dealt under several 'heads' with Doctrine, the administration of the Sacraments, the ministry, discipline, and 'policy' (ecclesiastical administration),[4] and from the Conclusion we are able to deduce

[1] Dickinson, *Knox's History*, 1.314ff; Laing, *Knox's Works*, 2.61ff; *CSP Scot.*, 1, no. 751.   [2] *Infra*, p. 85.   [3] *Infra*, p. 209.   [4] *Infra*, p. 85.

that these heads also contained proposals about the maintenance of the ministry which the authors realised would cause the Lords some concern.[5] An attempt to recover parts of this original text, which may still be extant within the body of the work preserved by Knox, will be made later in this introduction.[6]

The names of the ministers who were commissioned in April 1560 have not been recorded in any part of the surviving documents. They must, however, have been drawn from those who had accompanied the Lords of the Congregation in their recent campaign. Of these reformers John Knox and John Willock were the most prominent; John Spottiswoode and John Row may also have been present, but of this there can be no certainty or of the presence of John Douglas and John Winram from St Andrews. All six 'Johns' were, according to another account, later commissioned to 'draw in a volume the Policy and Discipline of the Kirk'.[7]

Of the reception given to the reform programme in May we have again no precise information, but it would appear that it commanded only general approval. On 25th May, five days after the date affixed to the Conclusion, Maitland of Lethington informed Cecil that the Lords were preparing to have the Estates assembled in Parliament on 10th July at which he thought 'ane uniform order' would be taken 'by a common agreement'.[8] When, however, the Estates met and, contrary to the conditions of the Treaty of Edinburgh, took up the question of religion, they contented themselves with the adoption of the *Confession of Faith*, the prohibition of the Mass, and the abolition of the jurisdiction of the Pope. Almost three months had passed since the presentation of the ministers' report on the organisation of the Church, but the 'Book of Reformation was not at this time presented to the Lords of Articles'.[9] Instead, it was being translated into Latin in order that it might be sent to Calvin, Viret, and Beza in Geneva, and to Martyr, Bullinger, and others in Zürich. Randolph, who has provided this information, was of the opinion

[5] *Infra*, pp. 208f.

[6] *Infra*, pp. 16f, 20, 23, 26, 31, 34f, 40, 45, 48f., 55, 57. Donaldson, *Scottish Reformation*, 62 n.2, has suggested on the basis of the preface 'that the original "book of reformation" included only the heads concerning doctrine, sacraments, discipline and "policy of the kirk", that is, the heads now numbered 1, 2, 7, 8, and 9, and that all the remainder was inserted later'.

[7] Dickinson, *Knox's History*, 1.343; Laing, *Knox's Works*, 2.128.

[8] *CSP Scot.*, 1, no. 799.   [9] *CSP Scot.*, 1, no. 891.

that the ministers would not be prepared to accept the judgment of England although they would not refuse to 'commune' with any of the learned among them.[10] A Protestant Doctrine had met with the full approval of the great majority of those who had attended the Parliament but for the time being at least the matter of ecclesiastical polity was still under discussion and undecided.

However arrangements for 'the equal distribution of ministers', which the original report had requested,[11] had already been taken in hand in mid July and entrusted to 'the Commissioners of the Burghs with some of the Nobility and Barons'.[12] This committee, perhaps the embryo of the later General Assembly, would appear to have met and carried out its remit. John Knox, who earlier had been 'elected' minister of Edinburgh, was 'appointed' to that city, John Willock to Glasgow, and Christopher Goodman to St Andrews. All three had considerable experience in England and of the reformed churches on the Continent and were consequently chosen for important centres. If Knox's account of what took place at this time can be relied upon when not corroborated by other evidence, then Adam Heriot, who had been minister in St Andrews probably since early in 1559, was appointed to Aberdeen, John Row to Perth, William Christison to Dundee where he must have been well known and where his links with Scandinavia would be valuable, Paul Methven to Jedburgh, David Ferguson to Dunfermline, and David Lyndsay to Leith. Knox also informs us that at the same time some superintendents were nominated, but there is no strong supporting evidence that this was done at this stage.

The fact that the Parliament of July–August 1560 arrived at no decision in the matter of organisational reform may be due to several considerations. The plans that were put forward may have been of too radical a nature, more adapted, perhaps, to the organisation of small politically independent communities such as the Swiss Protestant cities than the needs of a kingdom which was above all anxious to foster and maintain the political and religious advantages to be gained from internal unity and co-ordination. In the immediately preceding period the Protestant faith had developed in the important coastal towns and cities of Angus,

[10] CSP Scot., 1, no. 891.　　[11] Infra, pp. 105f, and Introduction, p. 21.

[12] Dickinson, Knox's History, 1.334; Laing, Knox's Works, 2, 87; CSP Scot., 1, no. 891. Knox may be in error in placing this distribution before the reassembling of Parliament in August as Randolph's dispatch is dated 25th August.

Fife, Lothian, and Ayrshire; and centres such as Dundee, Perth, Ayr, and St Andrews had, so far as can be ascertained, followed the Genevan city pattern which resulted in the election of elders and deacons from the community and whenever possible the election of a minister. In other towns where the support of the whole community was neither so united nor so forthcoming, as in Edinburgh, the reformed congregation, while it sought to have its own independent organisation, for some time lacked 'the public face of a kirk'.[13]

A second consideration, which with some was undoubtedly of primary importance, was the practical one of providing adequate financial support for the ministers required by such an organisation. Of this difficulty the authors in their Conclusion were deeply conscious. 'If blind affection rather lead you to have respect to the sustentation of these your carnall friends . . . then that the zeale of Christ Jesus his glory provoke and move you to set his oppressed Kirk at freedome and liberty we feare . . . that the glory and honour of this enterprise be reserved unto others.'[14] Many of those who had been most zealous in furthering the cause of the Reformation had been enriched at the expense of the decaying Church. Could they be expected to allow so much of what they had so recently acquired to be taken so soon from them even in the interests of the cause they themselves had brought to so successful an issue?

Further, what was to become of those bishops who had supported or were likely to support the movement for reform? One of the Archbishops, James Beaton of Glasgow, had set his face definitely against the Protestant cause and had left the country for France,[15] but the other Archbishop, John Hamilton of St Andrews, half-brother of the titular head of the Protestant nobility, was as yet undecided and might still, some thought, be won over.[16] Similar hopes, but with very little foundation, were entertained in some influential quarters about William Chisholm of Dunblane and Robert Crichton of Dunkeld. Maitland wrote to Cecil on

[13] Dickinson, *Knox's History*, 1.148ff; Laing, *Knox's Works*, 1.300ff.

[14] *Infra*, p. 209.

[15] Donaldson, 'Scottish Episcopate', *EHR*, 60 (1945), 353; *DNB*, 4.19ff; *infra*, p. 121 n.16.

[16] Donaldson, *Scottish Reformation*, 55ff; Herkless and Hannay, *Archbishops of St Andrews*, 5.130ff. On 7th October Randolph reported to Cecil that Arran had written 'that bishop of St Andrews is like to become a good protestant – has already given over his Mass, and received the common prayers', but Randolph was not hopeful of his conversion (*CSP Scot.*, 1, no. 911, p. 486).

18th August when he reported the passing of the *Confession of Faith* by Parliament: 'It is true that the Archbishop of St Andrews, the bishops of Dunkeld and Dunblane, and two of the temporall lordes did excuse themselffes that they were not ready to speake theyr jugement, for that they wer not sufficiently avysed with the book. This far they did liberally profes, that they wold aggre to all thing myght stand with Gods Word, and consent to abolish all abuses crept in in the Churche not agreable with the Scriptures – and asked longar to deliberat on the book propounded, wherby they did in a maner conferme our doctrine, wheras they, having liberte to speake what plesed them, durst not impugn it, and uterit theyr aune ignorance to thyr confusion.'[17] Alexander Gordon, Bishop-elect of Galloway, had, on the other hand, taken a leading part in the final stages of the conflict on the Protestant side; he had signed the last band, and had voted for the *Confession* and other reforms in the Parliament.[18] James Hamilton, Bishop of Argyll, was also present at the Parliament but appears to have been of little significance.[19] Adam Bothwell, Bishop of Orkney, had spent some time abroad and although he is not recorded as having taken any part in the proceedings of the summer of 1560 he is found early in the following year actively engaged in the work of reformation in his diocese.[20] Henry Sinclair of Ross, although hostile to Knox, may at this time have given some indication that he was favourably disposed towards reform for later he was described by Knox as 'a perfect hypocrite'.[21] Of the remaining two bishops (three of the sees were vacant) William Gordon of Aberdeen was to show 'no enthusiasm for the Romanist cause'[22] and there is 'no evidence that Patrick Hepburn of Moray had any interest in the religious developments one way or the other'.[23]

A considerable problem quite clearly faced those who proposed the reorganisation of the Church – a problem which, if the earlier trend of organising the Church round important burghs was to continue, could not readily be solved. It must not be forgotten that there were, or might be, others of high rank in the Roman Church, such as Winram, Sub-prior of St Andrews, who would have to be fitted into any new ecclesiastical polity. And what was

[17] *CSP Scot.*, I, no. 885.   [18] *Infra*, p. 121 n.17.
[19] Donaldson, *Scottish Reformation*, 59; *infra*, p. 117 n.10.   [20] *Infra*, p. 116 n.8.
[21] Dickinson, *Knox's History*, 2.90; Laing, *Knox's Works*, 2.398; *infra*, p. 117 n.9.
[22] *Infra*, p. 118 n.11.   [23] *Infra*, p. 117 n.9.

perhaps of even greater importance, some may have held that the wishes of England in the matter could not be completely ignored. Randolph had in fact talked with the leading ministers and had impressed upon them the need 'to search their opinions how uniformity might be held in religion in both realms', but he had found them 'so severe in that theie professe, and so lothe to remytte any thyng of that that theie have receaved' that he entertained little hope of success.[24] More time was obviously required as well as further and more detailed discussion of the needs of the whole country which had now declared itself Protestant in Parliament.

The 'Second' Commission

Among the unfinished tasks of the Parliament of July–August 1560 that of ecclesiastical reorganisation for the whole country must have been uppermost in the minds of many. Despite the fact that the text of the Book of Discipline which Knox incorporated in his *History* assigned the commissioning and completion of the work, as we have seen, to the end of April and the beginning of May, Knox did not in his account of the events of those months mention it. 'The Parliament dissolved,' he wrote, 'consultation was had how the Kirk might be established in a good and godly Policy, which by the Papists was altogether defaced.'[1] The following sentence states that only then was 'commission and charge given to Mr John Winram, Sub-prior of Saint Andrews, Master John Spottiswoode, John Willock, Mr John Douglas, Rector of Saint Andrews, Master John Row and John Knox, to draw in a volume the Policy and Discipline of the Kirk, as well as they had done the Doctrine'. It may well be that we have here one of Knox's not infrequent lapses in the recording of precise details, and that he has confused the earlier commissioning with a subsequent request of the Protestant leaders to the ministers to take up the matter once again in preparation for the reassembling of the Estates in January. Or it may be that the Lords having been fully satisfied with the *Confession of Faith* which had been drawn up in accordance with their command and in an amazingly short time[2] considered that the ministers who had served their cause so well were the most worthy to be entrusted with this further urgent responsibility. Whatever the truth may be – and it can

[24] *CSP Scot.*, 1, no. 981.
[1] Dickinson, *Knox's History*, 1.343; Laing, *Knox's Works*, 2.128; cf. Keith, *History*, 3.15.   [2] Dickinson, *Knox's History*, 1.388; Laing, *Knox's Works*, 2.92.

probably never be known – there is evidence in the text which has been preserved of much revision which could only have taken place in the comparatively more stable situation of the autumn and early winter of 1560–61. An attempt will be made in the course of this introduction to indicate the main lines of this revision, which resulted in the incorporation of some repetitions, but also the inclusion of three major 'interpolations', in length and detail out of all proportion to the rest of the work.

On these undoubtedly important discussions and on the progress of the work of revision Knox is tantalisingly silent. John Row the historian, son of the Reformer of the same name, whose account although late ought not lightly to be set aside, has provided some interesting details which seem to confirm conclusions suggested by the study of the text itself. He wrote that

> When the Ministers did putt their hands to work, the Assembly of the Kirk laid some Heads of the Policie of the Kirk upon everie man who wes thought meetest for the same; and after they had given in their travells, to be considered by the Brethern, they were either approven in that whilk they had done, or els their inlaiks were supplied and doubtes opened up to them, that they might sett doune the head appoynted to them more perfitelie; whilk by great pains, much reading, prayer and meditation, earnestle incalling the name of God, in end was finished, and by the allowance and approbation of the whole General Assemblie, after that some articles whilk were thought too long were abridged, the wholl Policie of the Kirk wes put in writ in a book, and presented to the Nobilitie and Great Councill of this realme in the end of the same yeare 1560.[3]

That the main work of revision took place in the months immediately following the rising of the Parliament in August cannot seriously be contested. The members of the commission recorded by Knox in all probability revised the original report during this period and in preparation for the Assembly which met in Edinburgh between the 20th and 27th December 1560.

Of this December meeting, which is normally styled the first General Assembly, the extant records refer only to sessions held on the 21st and the 27th;[4] nothing is known of what took place on the intervening days, but it is likely that the discussions to

[3] Row, *History*, 16.   [4] *BUK*, 1.3ff; Shaw, *General Assemblies*, 14.

B

which Row referred occurred at this time; the detailed compilation of the several sections must, however, have been a prior and more lengthy affair. It is arguable that some of the marginal comments as well as some decisions attributed or attributable to the Church belong to this period. Row's statement that some of the topics were assigned to those 'thought meetest for the same' is not only in accordance with common sense, but is also borne out by an examination of the text itself. Later it will be argued, for example, that the section on education is almost certainly the result of two people, or two groups, working independently, and this may also be true for much of the material in the fifth and sixth heads.[5] Row's final point that the Book was approved by the whole General Assembly before it was presented to the nobility is without explicit confirmation in the records but is supported by the facts that the ministers repeatedly sought to have the Book given statutory recognition, that subsequent general assemblies sought to have its regulations enforced, and that kirk sessions obeyed its injunctions.[6]

The Discussion by the Lords

On 29th August 1560 Randolph wrote to Cecil that the Parliament had been prorogued 'till it seem good to the Lords to reassemble'.[1] Nothing further was to be attempted by the Estates until the envoys sent to inform the Queen of what had taken place had returned. In the meantime the government of the country was in the hands of the Duke of Châtelherault and a small number of prominent Protestant lords who acted as a Privy Council. The names of Arran, Lord James, Morton, Glencairn, Ruthven, Menteith, Rothes, Boyd, and Ochiltree, together with that of the Secretary, Maitland, appear most frequently on official documents which the Council issued.[2]

The return of the ambassadors in December coincided with the arrival of the news of the death of the Queen's husband, Francis II of France. This unexpected event aroused considerable anxiety amongst those of the nobility who had been most active in the

[5] *Infra*, pp. 57f, 22ff, 27ff.

[6] Dickinson, *Knox's History*, 1.373, 2.27; Laing, *Knox's Works*, 2.181, 297; *BUK*, 1.8, 15, 17, 25, 26, 41; *StAKSR*, 75, 85, 215, 220; Calderwood, *Kirk of the Canagait*, passim.

[1] *CSP Scot.*, 1, no. 893 p. 474.

[2] Cf. *CSP Scot.*, 1, no. 896 p. 437, no. 953 p. 508, no. 955 p. 509, no. 957 p. 509, no. 959 p. 516.

cause of the Reformation and the English alliance and gave considerable encouragement to the lukewarm and to those who were hostile towards the recent changes. With the possibility of the return of the widowed Queen in the spring or early summer the time was opportune for the reassembling of the Estates. Châtelherault and his Council summoned them for 15th January.[3] Of this impending Convention all who attended the Assembly in December had been fully aware and, in the hope that it would seize the opportunity to carry further forward the work of reformation, they had, as we have seen, revised and agreed upon a final form of the Book of Discipline.[4]

At the meeting of the Estates, which was thinly attended, the religious cause was, Randolph again informs us, '"fyrste sett forwarde. . . . The self same Booke of Dyscipline (or at the leaste not farre alteryde from that you sawe wrytten as your honour remembrethe by whome)" was presented by its authors to the Lords. Six whole days were spent in examination and reasoning thereon, the matter well debated, divers well satisfied, and in the end approved by common consent.'[5] A similar account was written at the same time by Maitland. 'In religion many things are determined for the policy of the Church, and order taken for establishing religion universally.'[6] Knox, writing with the advantage of later experience, with perhaps a deeper realisation of what had taken place, and with no need to put the best construction upon events for the benefit of English hearers, recorded that the nobility 'perused' the book many days, that it was read in public audience and 'by the space of divers days the heads thereof were reasoned', that some approved of it and some (especially those who feared that their own 'worldly commodity' would be adversely affected) disapproved of it, that it was subscribed by a great part of the nobility, and that no one was required to subscribe what he had not understood.[7]

Of the discussion some evidence is preserved in the marginal comments of Knox's text. They consist of a small number of *additiones* and indications of agreement or consent, and are noted as they occur in the course of the analysis of the various sections.

[3] *CSP Scot.*, 1, no. 933 p. 498.   [4] *Supra*, pp. 8f.

[5] *CSP Scot.*, 1, no. 959 p. 511; described by the writer of the *Diurnal*, p. 63, as 'sum greit disputation'.

[6] *CSP Scot.*, 1, no. 958 p. 509.

[7] Dickinson, *Knox's History*, 1.343f, 2.27; Laing, *Knox's Works*, 2.128, 297.

In one of the *additiones* there is an indication of an attempt to alter or modify what had been proposed;[8] in one a decision to discharge certain teinds is taken;[9] and in one a disagreement among the Lords over the extent of glebes is recorded;[10] but for the most part the marginal comments register agreement with what is being proposed or grant consent to what is being petitioned. Knox gives some details of a debate that took place at this time on the Mass and in which an attempt was made to oppose the reformed teaching. The reformers, however, maintained their ground and re-asserted their willingness to agree with their opponents if they could establish their doctrine 'by God's Scriptures'.[11]

Much of the interest, as the reformers had foreseen, in fact centred round the financial aspects of the programme, and what was to happen to ecclesiastical revenue that was under lay control or still in the hands of those who remained loyal to the Roman Church. It was debated 'whether it were better to reject all Papists that ever had enjoyed "benefyte of the Churche" or admit and restore to their possessions such as willingly will subscribe and accord to the Book of Discipline'. After much reasoning 'to and fro', it was resolved to admit all 'of what estate somever theie were' who submitted by 25th February. Those who did not were to be rejected and reputed as enemies of God's truth.[12]

In the course of his narrative Knox listed the names of those who subscribed and 'approved of the Book of Discipline' in the Tolbooth of Edinburgh on 27th January 1561, and records the terms of this 'approbation'. The statement together with a similar but not identical list of subscribers was appended to the text of the Book of Discipline which was inserted in the *History* and is entitled 'Act of Secret Council, 27th January, 1560'.[13] It was also printed in the 1621 edition.[14]

The subscribers 'think' that the Book of Discipline with the notes and additions which have been made, conforms 'to God's word in all points' and promise to do all in their power to have it followed, but with one major provision: all the prelates and benefice holders who have already joined the reformers are to be allowed to retain the revenues of their benefices during their life-

---

[8] *Infra*, pp. 107ff.   [9] *Infra*, pp. 157f.   [10] *Infra*, p. 163 textual note h.
[11] Dickinson, *Knox's History*, 1.352ff; Laing, *Knox's Works*, 2.138ff.
[12] *CSP Scot.*, 1, no. 959 p. 513.
[13] Dickinson, *Knox's History*, 1.344f, 2.324f; Laing, *Knox's Works*, 2.129f, 257ff.
[14] *Infra*, pp. 210ff.

times on condition that they make provision out of these revenues for 'upholding the Ministry and Ministers', that is to say, for the preaching of the Word and the administration of the sacraments.

The 'Act of Secret Council' must be the edict of the Convention of which Randolph had written. Whether it had been first passed as an act by the Privy Council must in the absence of the Council's register for this period remain uncertain. It may well have been that after the lengthy discussion in the Convention the 'Act' or 'edict' had been drawn up by those who formed the core of Châtelherault's Privy Council, for the first signatures are from the pens of those who were among the most prominent members of that body. There are, nevertheless, some noteworthy omissions, particularly that of Lord Erskine, who, according to Knox,[15] was the backbone of opposition to the reformers' financial proposals, and that of Maitland of Lethington. Those who according to the *Diurnal* had been present in July–August and in January–February but did not sign also included Crawford, Cassillis, and Somerville.[16] Even of those who signed some are later found as ardent supporters of the Queen in the ensuing struggle.[17]

From the outset the authors of the Book of Discipline had expected that their claim that the reformed Church should inherit the patrimony of the old Church for the three traditional purposes would arouse considerable opposition and strain the loyalty of a number of their supporters. Nevertheless they persisted in their demands, and were not mistaken in their calculation. There can be little doubt that the somewhat sweeping financial proposals had been the cause of much discussion and had aroused considerable hostility towards the reformers. In the eyes of so many of the most ardent supporters of religious change there could be no question of allowing the Reformation programme to 'impair' their 'worldly commodity'.[18] Everything else could be accepted, but as Knox so well understood, adequate provision for the ministry was of the essence of the programme. If this was not granted, if so many who were mere titulars continued to enjoy the greater part of the Church's financial resources, there could be little hope of the establishment of the Church in its 'liberty and freedom'.[19]

[15] Dickinson, *Knox's History*, 1.344; Laing, *Knox's Works*, 2.128f.
[16] *Diurnal*, 63, 281f.   [17] *Infra*, pp. 210ff and notes.
[18] Dickinson, *Knox's History*, 1.343; Laing, *Knox's Works*, 2.128.
[19] *Infra* p. 159, cf. p. 209.

By insisting upon the condition which they inserted in their subscription the supporters of the Reformation among the nobility were taking a realistic, if somewhat selfish, attitude; the unscrambling of the various sources of ecclesiastical revenue could not so easily be accomplished as the ministerial reformers envisaged. But further, with the death of Francis II and the impending return of the Queen, wholesale change, even if it were within the realm of possibility, was not in the eyes of the 'lay' element politically expedient. Little wonder that the astute Maitland had his reservations. He reported to Cecil that what had been determined was 'something more vehement' than he 'at ane other tyme would have allowed', but he was fully aware of the political advantage of an 'ernest embracing off religion' in order to 'joyne ws straitly togidder'.[20] Randolph, too, saw difficulty ahead; despite the 'great advancement' of God's word, he could not be sure what root it had taken in men's hearts, but trial would soon be taken 'If this discipline be universally embraced and all points observed'.[21] The reformers had hoped that their programme would have been set forth 'by an Act and public Law';[22] in the unsettled situation they had to rest content for the time being with a severely limited approval.

GENERAL OUTLINE AND DEVELOPMENT OF THE BOOK

The Preface

The Preface begins by recalling the immediate cause of the compilation of the Book, namely the necessity of having a programme for the reformation of religion, and then goes on to claim for the proposals that follow the warrant of 'God's plain word'. In terms closely paralleled in the *Confession of Faith* the authors state that Scripture is the ultimate authority by which their plans must alone be judged and if need be amended.[1]

In the Laing text[2] six topics or 'heads' are mentioned: Doctrine, Sacraments, Election of Ministers, Provision for them, Ecclesiastical Discipline, and Policy; but in the final form of the Book these heads are expanded to nine.

[20] *CSP Scot.*, I, no. 958 p. 509.   [21] *CSP Scot.*, I, no. 959, pp. 511f.
[22] Cf. Dickinson, *Knox's History*, 1.373; *Knox's, Works*, 2.181.
[1] *Infra*, p. 86.   [2] *Infra*, Introduction pp. 75ff. and text pp. 85f.

Heads I, II, and III are concerned with the preaching of the Word and the right administration of the sacraments, the two primary notes or distinguishing marks of the Church.[3] From these topics it was logical for the authors to take up the question of the ministry, and to outline their proposals not only for the election and maintenance of ministers but also for the provision that would have to be made to meet the needs of every parish including the education of those who in due time would succeed them in the ministry. These subjects form the principal themes of Heads IV, V, and VI. The third note or mark of the Church was, according to the *Confession of Faith*, the exercise of ecclesiastical discipline,[4] and to this topic Heads VII and VIII are primarily devoted. 'Policy' or ecclesiastical administration, that is the ordering of both public and private religious practice throughout the country, is covered in Head IX, which also includes sections on the repair of Church buildings and the punishment of those who sought to exercise any of the functions of the ministry without a 'lawful' calling.

The Conclusion, more than twice the length of the prefatory paragraph, is in the nature of a brief apology. The writers are aware that some of their 'petitions' will appear 'strange' at first sight; nevertheless it was their primary responsibility not to offend God, even if by such action they should incur the displeasure of men. It is therefore obvious that from the outset the reforming ministers were aware that their plans would encounter strong opposition, but it is equally obvious that they were prepared to take a bold stand, for they did not hesitate to warn the lords of 'just punishment from God' if following their 'own corrupt judgements' they 'contemne his voyce and vocation'.[5]

The First Head[1]

This section, entitled 'Of Doctrine' and comprising a single sentence, urges the necessity of having the Gospel freely preached throughout the realm and of having all teaching opposed to the Gospel suppressed as hostile to man's salvation. Here the situation in which the reformers found themselves in the late spring of 1560 and while as yet no Confession of Faith had been established is clearly reflected. Hence it was considered necessary to add an explanation. By the 'Evangel' or Gospel is understood the

---

[3] *Infra*, p. 87 n.1.   [4] *Infra*, p. 165 n.1.   [5] *Infra*, p. 209.
[1] *Infra*, pp. 87ff.

Scriptures of the Old and New Testaments, 'inspired of God' and expressing sufficiently all things required for the instruction of the Church; points which form an essential element of Reformed Protestantism and which were given further elaboration in the *Confession*. By all opposing teaching was understood in effect those parts of the Canon Law and theology of the mediaeval Church which had been imposed on the Christian conscience without the express warrant of Scripture. A number of examples are cited; the taking of special vows, the wearing of distinctive dress, the superstitious observance of fasting days and saints' days, the feasts of the Christian year. Again these topics are more carefully elaborated in the *Confession*, and in particular the attitude of the reformers to the decisions of the Councils of the Church. The final sentence of the explanation makes clear that by suppression was understood the punishment of obstinate upholders and teachers of such doctrine by the civil magistrate.

The contents of this head together with the 'explication' of it clearly indicate that we are here dealing with an essential and, in all probability, the initial section of the original report of May 1560.

The Second Head[1]

The second note or mark of the Church, according to Protestant teaching, was the administration of the Sacraments, and to this topic the second head is consequently devoted. The Sacraments are the seals and visible confirmation of the promises contained in the Word. Two only are admitted, Baptism and the 'Holy Supper of the Lord Jesus'. In order that they may be administered aright these sacraments must be celebrated by a 'lawful Minister' and given to those who have been instructed in the promises of the Gospel in their own language. The preaching of the Word and the administration of the Sacraments are held to be necessarily connected, but while there may be preaching without the administration of the Sacraments there can be no administration which has not been preceded by preaching and instruction.

The manner of administration, it is maintained, must follow strictly the New Testament accounts of the institution by Christ and of the apostolic practice. It is recognised that some congregations are already following the 'Order' used by the English congregation at Geneva of which Knox had been for some time one

[1] *Infra*, pp. 90ff.

of the ministers, but for the sake of others it was considered necessary to add some practical instructions in order that 'an uniformity' be kept.

There is no evidence of revision and consequently this section may also be regarded as part of the original work.

The Third Head[2]

This section, entitled 'Touching the Abolition of Idolatry', is in the nature of a corollary from the two which have preceded it in that it requires the removal of all that is not in accordance with the reformers' doctrine of the Word and Sacraments. The exercise by the Lords of their responsibility for the well-being of the nation by enforcing the utter 'suppression' of all abbeys, monasteries, friaries, and similar institutions, except where the buildings are being used as parish churches or schools, is 'required'. The authors of the Book are in no doubt that God has armed the Lords with the power to remove 'idolatry' from the presence of all persons without exception, and that neglect on their part would incur the divine wrath.

The absence of any reference to the legislation of the Parliament of 1560 against the Mass would seem to indicate that this section antedates and perhaps in part prepared the way for that legislation. It may also be regarded as providing the formal justification of the ministers, if such were needed, for any iconoclasm that had already taken place.

The Fourth Head[1]

If the preaching of the Gospel and the administration of the sacraments may be said logically to lead to a demand for the abolition of all contrary doctrine and practice, then it may also be said that logic demands that consideration be next given to the constructive work of regulating and providing for the 'lawful Ministry' required for the fulfilment of these ecclesiastical functions. To this topic the authors of the Book of Discipline direct their attention in the fourth head. In the matter of the ministry the Reformation movement on the Continent had departed most radically from mediaeval doctrine and practice; it was therefore natural that considerable attention should be given to it in a work compiled for those who had no such first-hand knowledge by some who had been actively engaged in the work of the reformed ministry.

[2] *Infra*, pp. 94f.   [1] *Infra*, pp. 96ff.

It is, however, necessary to remember that at the time when the Book of Discipline was being drawn up, the Protestant faith had been most securely rooted in a number of towns and cities and that these centres had for some time prior to the Reformation been taking greater hold over their burgh churches. The burghs had been tending to increase their independence and to that trend Protestantism had brought added impetus. In particular, towns such as Dundee, St Andrews, Perth, Montrose, and Ayr had already carried through the reformation of the local church[2] with full civic support and had erected an ecclesiastical organisation closely parallel to that of the reformed towns and cities on the Continent – as for example Zürich, Basel, Bern, Geneva, Strasbourg, Frankfurt and Emden.[3] Further, it should be noted that the ecclesiastical organisation of these centres on the Continent exercised more than a local influence. It was, for example, the practice in Geneva and Lausanne of the church of the city to take an active part in providing for the needs of the smaller congregations that were emerging in the surrounding rural districts and in exercising spiritual oversight of them.[4] Similar development was also taking place in many parts of France where, despite a hostile central government, the Reformed faith had been making remarkable progress, and had already claimed some important towns. It was therefore for many reasons a natural development in the Scottish situation that the 'best reformed Kirk' in an area should in the important matter of ecclesiastical reorganisation be given a prominent place and that the evangelisation of the surrounding country should be regarded as a primary responsibility of its church court. It is against this contemporary background that the reformers' plans for the ministry must be examined.

Three elements are held to comprise a lawful ministry, namely, election, examination, and admission. In the matter of election the right of the individual congregation to choose its minister is asserted, but this right is soon seen to be hedged about with restrictions. If it is not exercised within forty days it devolves upon the 'best reformed kirk' of the area, which has also the responsibility through its 'men of soundest judgment' of carrying

[2] Donaldson, *Scottish Reformation*, 50f; Dickinson, *Knox's History*, 1.159f; Laing, *Knox's Works*, 1.316.

[3] Courvoisier, *La Notion*, 22ff; Vuilleumier, *Histoire*, 1.241ff, 388ff; MacGregor, *Scottish Presbyterian Polity*, 26ff.

[4] Vuilleumier, *Histoire*, 1.207ff, 241ff.

out the principal elements of the examination of those elected or to be presented by itself for election. In the examination stress is placed upon the ability of the candidate to interpret a passage of Scripture, to engage in controversy on matters of doctrine, and to preach. This latter part of the examination is to take place before the congregation which is without a minister, for a congregation cannot be compelled to accept as its minister one in whose examination it has not had a part, but the congregation on the other hand is not held to possess the right of 'unreasonable' refusal.

At this point the grounds on which a person might not be admitted to the ministry are explicitly stated. They are public infamy, inability to edify the church by wholesome doctrine and the fact that a person is known to be of 'corrupt judgment'. As the second and third points had already been discussed, it was only necessary to explain what was intended by the first. Public infamy arose when a person was found guilty of crimes which according to Scripture ought to carry with them the death penalty. Even when the guilty person is penitent and is pardoned by the state the stigma of infamy is not and indeed cannot be removed; consequently that person is held to be ineligible for election and admission to the ministry. In order that all scandal be avoided and the life and conversation of the person presented or to be elected may be known edicts are to be sent for publication to all places where he has spent any considerable time and a strict injunction made that those guilty of concealing information will be considered as if they did 'communicate' with the sins of the unworthy person. Although the moral requirements are shown here to be rigorous, it is noteworthy that 'common sins and offences' which had been committed before a person had accepted the Protestant faith and of which he has by his subsequent life shown himself penitent are not to be taken into account.

After successfully completing the requirements for election and examination, the candidate is ready to be admitted to the office of the ministry of Word and Sacraments. It is considered expedient that this admission be held in public and in the presence of the congregation to which the minister-elect is to be appointed. In a sermon, preached by 'some especial minister' the duties and responsibilities of both the minister and congregation towards each other are to be set forth, and in particular the people are to be reminded that the commandments which ministers pronounce 'from God's mouth and book' are to be obeyed by them as 'they would obey God himself'. Two points are regarded as essential in this service of admission, namely, the public approbation of the people and the declaration of the 'chief minister' (by which, in all probability, was understood the minister who was presiding at the service) that the minister presented is appointed to that charge. The laying on of hands is stated to be unnecessary.

The minister and the congregation are by this service held to have entered into a mutually binding contract; the minister cannot at will leave the flock nor the flock reject him unless he be found worthy of deposition. This contract, however, is not binding in all circumstances, for the right is reserved to 'the whole Church'[5] on 'just considerations' to translate ministers to other parishes where better use may be made of their ability. Men who serve in the ministry in a voluntary capacity ('of benevolence') may be drafted for full-time service in the Church in any part of the country.

At this point the authors of the Book of Discipline, mindful that they are presenting a report to the Lords, thought it appropriate to defend the high standards which they were wishing to impose and which could not but lead to a great scarcity of suitable candidates for some time. Nevertheless they affirm that the dangers that would result from the acceptance of unqualified men are much greater than those that would result from the lack of adequately qualified persons. Remedy is to be sought in prayer and in the exercise by the Lords of their authority in conjunction with the Church in compelling those with the requisite gifts to bestow them where the need is greatest.

This head has the appearance of early compilation and as will be seen from the notes supplied to the text closely follows the Continental reformed practice and in particular the ecclesiastical ordinances of Geneva. The following points should be noted as lending support to an early date of composition. (a) The opening phrase 'In a Church reformed or tending to reformation'[6] suggests that the enemy has not yet been overthrown by act of Parliament. (b) There is no specific reference to any particular responsibilities of the superintendent as such in the examination or admission of ministers. Indeed in this entire section while there are references to 'some especial minister' and 'the chief Minister' the word 'superintendent' is not used to describe him and the responsibility is always said to rest with the 'best reformed kirk' or with 'the men of soundest judgment' in 'some principal town next adjacent to them'.[7] It is significant that it was thought necessary to interpret these phrases by adding a gloss. In the first example the 'best reformed kirk' is explained as 'the Church of the Superintendent with his council' and in the second as 'the city of the Super-intendent'. (c) The areas of which St Andrews and Edinburgh are regarded as the nearest 'principal' town do not correspond to the areas assigned later in the Book to the Superintendents of St Andrews or Lothian.[8] It would therefore appear that at the stage when this head was compiled no detailed thinking, or at least no detailed plans for the appointment of superintendents and the allotting to them of dioceses, had been undertaken; it may even be doubted if the office as it later developed had as yet been clearly envisaged. This line of argument will be resumed when the sections which deal specially with the office of superintendent are discussed.[9]

At this juncture, it should, nevertheless, be noted that in the final paragraph of the sub-section on the admission of ministers there is an indication that the minds of the authors were moving in that direction when they request the Lords that they 'with the consent of the church assign unto your chiefest workmen, not onlie townes to remaine in, but also provinces, that by their faithful labours churches may be erected and order established where none is now'.[10] This paragraph is an expanded restatement of the pre-vious one and is in almost the same words; it may therefore be of a later date, but the point should not be pressed. What is of greater significance is that the Lords may have acted, as has been indicated previously,[11] upon this request after the great service of thanksgiving in July. At that time 'the Commissioners of the Burghs with some of the Nobility and Barons' were appointed to 'see equal distribution of Ministers and to change and transport as the most part should think expedient'.[12]

Of the dearth of suitable qualified ministers the authors of the Book of Discipline were fully conscious and that awareness must have become increasingly acute in the summer and autumn of 1560 as they were faced with the problem of providing for all the parishes of the country when religious observance of the old form

[7] Infra, pp. 97ff.   [8] Infra, p. 97 and n.7, pp. 119f.
[9] Infra, pp. 49ff.   [10] Infra, p. 105.   [11] Supra, p. 5.
[12] Dickinson, Knox's History, 1.334, Laing, Knox's Works, 2.87, and supra, p. 5 n.12.

had been prohibited by law. It was to meet this situation that the final short section entitled 'For readers' was added, in all probability during the revision following the close of the Parliament in August. The section clearly reveals that the office of reader is regarded as an expedient in the face of an emergency, and there is no indication that the office is expected to become a permanent feature of the ministry.

Those who can read the Common Prayers and the Scriptures are expected to continue their education and develop any ability they might have 'to persuade by wholesome doctrine' and within a relatively short time be able to pass through the regular processes of examination and admission from their present position to that of ministers of Word and Sacraments. Further, some who could be accepted as ministers, because they have 'of long time' been Protestants and have the moral qualifications and educational ability but 'content themselves with reading', should be encouraged to comfort their brethren by some exhortation so that they may qualify themselves for full admission as ministers. In this way the reformers were prepared to allow for a progression from the position of reader to that of exhorter and finally to that of a minister, who alone was authorised to administer the sacraments. It seems possible that they would at first have been concerned not to have made the distinction between reader and exhorter a rigid one. Discussion obviously took place on this matter with the Lords in January 1561 for their decision is contained in the first *additio*. None, they think, should be allowed to preach but those that are qualified and by that they mean only those who have been found qualified by the superintendent. It should be noted that it is in this *additio* that for the first time a specific responsibility of the superintendent is stated.[13]

The Fifth Head[1]

Having outlined the way by which the reformed Church should obtain for itself a 'lawful' ministry, it was logical for the authors of the Book of Discipline to take as their next topic the matter of adequate material provision for those who would be elected and admitted to office in the Church. The contents of this head, however, suggest that it has been subjected to considerable revision. As has already been pointed out, there is evidence in the Conclusion of the Book for maintaining that something must

[13] *Infra*, p. 107; Introduction, pp. 64f.   [1] *Infra*, pp. 108ff.

have been said in the original report on this subject, but exactly
how much is difficult to ascertain. A detailed analysis may,
nevertheless, assist us in forming our ideas about the original
content of this section of the document. Such an endeavour is not,
it should be added, without encouragement from the arrangement of the text itself.

There are three clearly marked *additiones*.[2] None of these is
attributed to the Lords. The second and third may with a considerable degree of certainty be atttributed to the revision by the ministers themselves in the autumn or early winter of 1560. Further
internal evidence suggests that some *'additiones'* may have been
incorporated without any external indication.

At the beginning the authors state that they have, on the basis
of Scripture, the best authority for requiring that 'honest', *i.e.*,
honourable or decent, provision be made for every minister and
for his wife and family in the event of his death in the service of
the Church. The earlier 'heads' all begin with similar general
statements and there is therefore no reason for considering that
this statement is not original. There follows the first *additio* of the
section, which merely contains the decision that provision for the
widows of ministers 'be remitted to the discretion of the Church'.
There is no indication by whom it was taken, but the probability
is that it came from the Lords.

The next paragraph states that the needs of every minister will
vary according to the nature of his charge and, if he is married,
the size of his family. Some ministers will be permanently resident
in their parishes but others, if they have charge of several
churches, will have to travel and change their dwelling place.
There is therefore difficulty in appointing a 'several', *i.e.*, particular, stipend to every minister when their charges 'are so unequal'. Again there is no apparent reason for not accepting this
paragraph as from the original report, for it is in full agreement
with the previous statement that the 'chiefest workmen' have not
only towns to remain in but provinces where they are to be
engaged in erecting churches.[3]

There follows a marked *additio*[4] beginning with the words 'We
judge' and going on to detail what, it was considered, every
minister needed for the support of himself and his family and

[2] *Infra*, pp. 108 and n.*b*, 109 and n.4, 110 and n.*x*.

[3] *Infra*, p. 105 and Introduction *supra*, p. 21.

[4] *Infra*, p. 109.

which was to be taken from the rents and treasury of the Church 'where he serveth at the discretion of the Congregation, conforme to the qualitie of the person and the necessity of the time'. A minister ought to have sufficient to maintain a house and to provide for the daily necessities such as food, clothing, books, fuel and so forth. This sentence provides the first indication of the source from which the ministers were to be supported. Such a claim, for the reason stated above[5] was almost certainly in the original report, and on that account this part of the paragraph may be original or may replace another of similar import. The remaining sentences of the paragraph, however, which give precise details in quantities of meal and malt, and which assign the 'modification' to the 'judgment of the Kirk at the annual election of elders and deacons', are in effect the essentials of the *additio* and are clearly the result of later discussion which was taking place at a time when those working on the Book were already familiar with the plans for the organisation of the local churches.

The next sentence returns to the subject of the provision for those ministers who travel from place to place for the establishment of the Church and states that in their case 'further consideration must be had'. Again this sentence is of similar import to that which referred in general terms to the requirements for ministers and suggests by its wording that details will have to be worked out at some later date. However, there immediately follow the precise details of the quantities of grain and malt and money that these ministers should receive, but in this connection all is to be arranged 'at the discretion of the Prince and Councell of the Realme'. This sentence, like that at the end of the previous paragraph, suggests that this decision arose out of later discussion; in all probability it belongs to the period of the second revision.

It should be noted that the term 'superintendent' in this section is employed in the same way as it has been employed earlier in the text and is in the nature of a gloss.[6]

It is impossible to date the next paragraph which returns to the provision for a minister's family which has been rendered fatherless. As it is somewhat out of place it may belong to one of the periods of revision as does the *additio* which follows and which requires that daughters of deceased ministers be 'honestly' dowered .[7]

---

[5] *Supra*, p. 6.   [6] *Infra*, p. 109, cf. pp. 96f.   [7] *Infra*, p. 110.

The authors maintain, in conclusion, that the provision for ministers and their families is required not so much for their own sake as for the increase of virtue and learning and the benefit of posterity. They are sufficiently realistic to point out that men are not to be expected to dedicate themselves and their children to the service of God and the Church and to look for no worldly benefit. Thereafter they explain that they have not dealt with the stipends of readers because, if they can only read, then they are not 'judged true ministers'. Such a person should only be given a modest amount in order to encourage him to seek further advancement and not sufficient for him to be tempted to remain a reader. As in the three previous examples where similar statements are made there follow again, somewhat unexpectedly, precise details of the provision that is to be made for readers and a number of regulations for both readers and exhorters, which one would have expected to have found in the earlier section on readers, and which is appended to the previous head.

In addition to his reading of the Scriptures and the Common Prayers the reader is to teach the children of the parish, and if after two years he is unable to 'exhort' he is to be removed from his office and another person given the opportunity to advance in knowledge whereby he may edify the Church. It is clear that by the time these specific requirements were being drawn up the authors were aware that there would be considerably more candidates for the office of reader or exhorter than that of minister and that they would have to be careful that they did not allow men who in the long term would not be able greatly to benefit the Church to be settled in its livings. At the end of the paragraph a sentence that was probably directed against any conforming incumbent who might have considered that he had a right in virtue of his previous admission to remain in possession was added; readers are to be 'put in by the kirk and admission of the Superintendent'.[8] There follows a short paragraph to which attention is drawn by a marginal 'nota', and which gives details of the stipend to be provided for exhorters. It should be noted that the stipend for both readers and exhorters is, unlike that for ministers, stated as a sum of money and that within the terms expressed (forty marks more or less for a reader and a hundred or more for an exhorter) the final decision is left to the local congregation in agreement with the person concerned.

[8] *Infra*, pp. 111f.

C

The remainder of this head begins with a brief statement about the other calls that are to be met out of the 'patrimony of the Church', namely the support of the poor and the furtherance of education. These claims had traditionally been met by the Church and no general alteration is suggested. In the sentences that follow provision for the poor is discussed. The care of the genuine poor of a parish is held to be the responsibility of that parish, but not that of those 'stubborne and idle beggars who running from place to place make a craft of their begging'.[9] Such people ought to be punished by the civil magistrate. A number of regulations, which can hardly have been drawn up at the same time as the earlier part of the paragraph, complete the treatment of the topic. All who want to beg must not be allowed to do so, the strong must be compelled to work, those who cannot work must be compelled to return to their native place, a register of the poor of the parish must be compiled, and only then stipends appointed for those so registered. Here again is further evidence of the growth and development of the document, and although it is impossible to be dogmatic, one may not be far wrong in seeing in the first half of the paragraph the original proposal and in the second half the result of the discussion which took place in the autumn and early winter of 1560.

At this point one would have expected a section on education but instead what appears to be a completely new section is found which in the first printed edition of 1621 is given the dignity of a separate head and from its opening sentence it will be realised that it is in the nature of a digression. The authors now wish to explain why they have appointed a larger stipend to those 'that shall be superintendents' and why they have made 'a difference betwixt Preachers at this time'.[10] The 'head' is of considerable length and detail; it will be discussed later;[11] at this juncture it will be sufficient to point out that even a very cursory glance at the analysis will show that it breaks the continuity of development and is an obvious interpolation inserted in the report. A section on education does follow thereafter[12] but, as will be seen from the analysis, it is again far out of proportion to that given to any other single subject in the book, and, as in the section on the superintendents, puts forward a detailed programme which can hardly

[9] *Infra*, pp. 112ff.   [10] *Infra*, p. 115.
[11] *Infra*, Introduction pp. 49ff.
[12] *Infra*, pp. 129ff, and Introduction, pp. 54ff.

have been prepared in the month of May in 1560. The scope of the provisions and the nature of the political situation which they presuppose, as will become clearer when these sections are discussed in detail, reflect that of the autumn of 1560 rather than the uncertainties of April and May, and in the case of the section on education in particular reveal an intimate knowledge of the universities and especially of St Andrews.

Of the revision and amplification of the original section on the providing of material support for the ministers there can be little doubt; to go further than to illustrate this fact from the text itself is, however, hazardous procedure, and any attempt to indicate the limits of the original draft report must remain conjectural and subjective. Nevertheless, it may with a fair measure of safety be concluded that it contained the following topics. (*a*) Proper financial support for ministers and their wives and children if left widows and fatherless was to be derived from the 'rents and treasury' of the local congregations – a claim made despite the knowledge that much of this revenue had been appropriated or leased in recent years for interests other than the purely ecclesiastical. (*b*) Additional provision was to be allocated to meet the needs of those ministers whose responsibilities would involve them in extra travelling and living expenses. (*c*) Such claims were put forward as realistic, for the prospect of poverty which would discourage men from entering the ministry must not be allowed. (*d*) The costs of caring for the genuine poor and for furthering education were to continue as charges upon the income of the Church.

The Sixth Head[1]

The theme mentioned at the beginning of the last paragraph of the fifth head, provision for the poor and the teachers of the young, is resumed at the beginning of what is styled the sixth head. The first sentence reads, 'These two sorts of men, that is to say, Ministers and the poore, together with the Schooles, when order shall be taken thereanent, must be susteyned upon the charges of the Kirk.'[2] It will be obvious how naturally such a sentence follows the first half of that last paragraph, and indeed the sixth head hardly introduces a new topic, but rather continues the treatment of the rents and possessions of the Church and gives special attention to outlining the way by which the sums necessary

[1] *Infra*, pp. 156ff.   [2] *Infra*, p. 156, cf. p. 112.

for the furtherance of the Church's responsibilities are to be lifted.

Before, however, the authors of the book take up the subject they address themselves to the Lords and indeed to all those who have in any way obtained possession of a right to raise levies that are by their nature 'ecclesiastical'. If such persons are to expect to further the Reformation then they must have compassion on those who labour and till the soil by appointing them to pay 'reasonable' teinds. They must not continue the oppressive exactions of the papists, as some 'Gentlemen' are doing. 'The Gentlemen, Barones, Earles, Lords and others' – everyone without exception who is raising revenue from the land – 'must be content to live upon their just rents' and to 'suffer the Kirk to be restored to her liberty', that is to the right to have from those who work the land the teind of its produce, 'that in her restitution the poore . . . may receive some comfort and relaxation'.[3]

It was the opinion of the reformers that the possessing of the teinds, that is the acquiring of the right to collect them, should not belong to any private individual who had secured it by means of a lease or tack; the farmer alone and without the activity of a middleman should be answerable for what is justly owed to the Church from the produce of his labour directly to 'the Deacons and Treasurers of the Kirk'. At this point an *additio* is indicated and it is accompanied by the marginal comment, 'The Lordis agreis with this heid of the reseaving of the deaconis.' The *additio* explains that the deacons are to receive the 'rents' and not the ministers because the poor and the schools are to be sustained from the same source; it continues it 'is expedient that common Treasurers: to wit Deacons, be appointed from yeare to yeare, to receive the whole rents appertaining to the Kirk'; and that commandment be given that no man be permitted to deal with these matters except 'such as by common consent of the Kirk are thereto appointed'.[4]

This sweeping demand would have had the effect of removing altogether a considerable amount of income from an entire group of people who had for some time been acquiring from the Church, for the payment of a fixed sum, the right to collect the ecclesiastical dues from those engaged in tilling the soil. The reformers were prepared to face opposition to their proposals. They realised that many who had bought or entered into contracts for the collection of teinds would, if faced with this pro-

[3] *Infra*, pp. 157ff.   [4] *Infra*, pp. 158f.

posal, be deprived of recovering what they had spent in acquiring their leases. Nevertheless the acquiring of the right to collect ecclesiastical revenues in this way was declared 'no possession before God' because it had not been within the power of the ecclesiastical authorities in the first place to alienate the patrimony and common good of the Church.[5] However, the reformers realise that 'just recompense' would have to be made to those who had acquired such leases by payments made to the pre-Reformation incumbents, provided that it could be shown that such transactions had not been recently and hurriedly carried through ('done of plain collusion') in order to deprive the Church of its rightful income. For this purpose a thorough examination of these contracts would have to be made so that the Church in the end may 'recover her libertie and freedom, and that onely for the reliefe of the poore'.[6]

These demands are defended by emphasising that they are made in the interests of the labourers who have been so cruelly oppressed and defrauded by the priests and their collectors. One can detect something of the reformers' revolutionary zeal when they complain that the labourer has been required to maintain both the churchman and his hired collector, the labourer is 'debter' only to the Church and the Church is bound to sustain on her charges the ministers, the poor, and the teachers.[7]

This scheme of reorganisation was, it need hardly be said, totally unrealistic. The employment of middlemen and the leasing of the collecting rights had gone on for many years, despite the fact that it had caused concern in the councils of the Church. The reformers were seeking the simplification of something which was impossible of a simple solution. In innumerable cases the various sources from which the Church derived its income had become inseparably linked and in order to facilitate collection the Church authorities had been willing to assign their entire rights to some collectors for an agreed payment. To seek to unravel the tangle, had such an attempt been made, could not but have alienated a large number of the gentlemen and barons from whom the Reformation had derived so much support and upon whom it would have to depend for the furtherance of its programme and its defence.

These sentences addressed to the Lords form, as has already been

[5] *Infra*, p. 159. Alienation of ecclesiastical property was contrary to canon law.
[6] *Infra*, p. 159.   [7] *Infra*, p. 160.

stated, a digression or aside. Thereafter the attention of the reader is directed to the main subject of the head, the patrimony of the Church and the way in which the revenue is to be collected. The patrimony is the teinds but when these are 'reasonably' taken it is realised that there will not be enough for all purposes and therefore the reformers lay claim to other endowments that had been made for pious purposes to the Church.[8] Further it is claimed that for the upholding of the universities and the sustentation of the superintendents the whole revenue of the temporality of the bishops', deans' and archdeans' lands, and all rents pertaining to cathedral churches would be required.

According to this programme little or nothing would be required from the merchants and craftsmen of the burghs, who did not pay such teind; it was therefore thought that they should make some provision for the upkeep of the burgh churches and this suggestion would in fact be in line with developments that had been taking place over a number of years.[9] A marginal note indicates that the Lords expressed their agreement.

Parish priests and their vicars were by canon law required to be provided with manses and glebes. These properties in many parishes had been alienated or were occupied by tenants of the benefice holders. The reformers request that they be restored to their former use and made available for the ministers. Six acres is regarded as all the land that should be returned meantime if the glebe were larger than that size, and to this proposal a marginal note indicates the approval of a number of the Lords and records the withholding of consent by four earls.[10]

Having stated what they regarded as the patrimony of the Church and the inalienable source of its revenue, it was considered necessary to explain the way whereby these 'rents and duties' were to be uplifted. The collectors are to be the annually elected deacons or treasurers of the local congregations who are held responsible to the ministers and elders and are required to distribute the income in accordance with their directions. If, however, controversy arises, the matter in dispute is to be settled by appeal to the 'whole Kirk' (the local congregation) and the 'judgment of the Kirk with the Ministers consent shall prevaile'. Further details follow, which make it clear that the reformers were anxious to avoid corruption or misappropriation and we

[8] Infra, pp. 160f.   [9] Infra, p. 162 and n.40.
[10] Infra, p. 163 and textual note h; cf. Introduction supra, p. 12.

note that the 'Superintendents in their visitation' play an important role in this respect, as does 'the great Councell of the Kirk'.[11]

How much of this head can be attributed to the original period of compilation? That the subject, as has been said,[12] follows naturally upon the conclusion to the fifth head is in itself no argument that it did in fact follow. Indeed it could be argued that all that is original may be no more than the opening sentence of this head and that in the original report it may well have formed the final sentence of the fifth head. Further it is conceivable that in their original report the reformers had not discussed the method of collecting the ecclesiastical revenue but had contented themselves with laying claim to the patrimony for the support of the traditional ends. In those early days the reformers were perhaps only anxious to state their claim and to leave the practical arrangements until more stable times.

This hypothesis would lead to the conclusion that practically all of this head belongs to the autumn or early winter of 1560–61. It is, in this connection, not without significance to note that it does not begin with a brief general introduction to the subject as is the case in all the foregoing heads and in the one that immediately follows. Further the content and tone of the digression, in which the authors complain that 'some Gentlemen are now as cruell over their tenants as ever were the Papists, requiring of them whatsoever they afore payed to the Kirk',[13] suggests that the overthrow of the old Church had already taken place.

Difficulties, however, remain, which seem to defy solution. The digression requires that teinds be paid to the deacons and treasurers; as we have seen an *additio*, to which the Lords gave their consent, states that the authors, or rather the revisers, require that this be done and explains that they think it 'most expedient' that the treasurers or deacons be annually appointed; then in the section that follows the digression, the duties and responsibilities of the deacons are repeated, including the statement that they are to be appointed annually by free election.[14] As the office of the deacons is again discussed in another head along with the eldership,[15] it is difficult to account for all that is stated here about it, unless it is assumed that during the revision in the autumn a different group was responsible for this section from that which was responsible for the later section on the election of elders and

[11] *Infra*, pp. 163f.   [12] *Supra*, pp. 27f.   [13] *Infra*, p. 156.

[14] *Infra*, pp. 163f.   [15] *Infra*, pp. 173ff.

deacons, and that in the final form of the document no attempt was made to remove statements that were being repeated.

The Seventh Head[1]

In the *Confession of Faith* prefixed to *The Forme of Prayers and Ministration of the Sacraments* drawn up and used by the English Congregation at Geneva in 1556 ecclesiastical discipline is defined as the third note or distinguishing mark of the Church.[2] Discipline had become, particularly in the forties and fifties, an ever increasing component in the life of the Genevan Church, one for which Calvin was prepared to abandon everything and retire from the city if the right to exercise it were not unquestioningly granted and guaranteed.[3] It was, in fact, during the period of Knox's residence in Geneva that Calvin finally secured this freedom for the Church, and Knox in a frequently quoted extract from one of his letters has recorded his thorough and complete approval of the achievements of the Geneva reformers in this matter.[4] It is therefore not surprising to find in the Book of Discipline an entire head devoted to the subject, or to have 'ecclesiastical discipline uprightly ministered' stated in the *Confession of Faith* of 1560 as one of the 'Notes of the true Kirk of God'.[5]

The head begins by defining in general terms the need for discipline in any organised community or 'commonwealth' and by analogy in the Church. Without the reproving and correcting of faults which the state has neglected to punish or may not punish because of their nature the Church cannot be brought to purity or retained in it. Crimes such as blasphemy, adultery, murder, perjury and the like ought to be punished by the civil sword; but offences such as drunkenness, fornication and oppression of the poor ought to be punished by the Church 'as God's word commands',[6] that is in accordance with the injunction of St Matthew 18.15–18. Nevertheless as the 'accursed Papistry' has brought such confusion in this matter the Church is compelled to take action against both classes of offenders and punish them with excommunication until evidence of repentance is made manifest.

[1] *Infra*, pp. 165ff.   [2] Laing, *Knox's Works*, 4.172ff.
[3] McNeill, *History*, 138ff, 165ff, 188ff.
[4] Laing, *Knox's Works*, 4.240.
[5] Cap. XVIII; Dickinson, *Knox's History*, 2.266; Laing *Knox'sWorks*, 2.110.
[6] *Infra*, pp. 166f.

At this point a marginal note indicates the approval of the Lords of the suggestion.

The procedure to be adopted in the case of those who are guilty of offences which the Church ought because of their 'ecclesiastical' nature to punish follows. It conforms in every detail to the practice of established Calvinist congregations on the Continent. The authors regard the matter as one of supreme importance; every opportunity is to be given to the offender to repent, even on the final Sunday when excommunication is about to be pronounced 'by the mouth of the minister, with the consent of the Ministry and commandment of the Kirk'. The person 'pronounced excommunicate from God and from all society of the Kirk' is cut off from all communication with anyone not of his own family in the hope that 'seeing himself abhorred of the godly and faithful' he 'may have occasion to repent and so be saved'.[7] The sentence is to be published throughout the realm and any children begotten thereafter are to be refused baptism till they become of age or they are presented by their faithful mother or some special friends and members of the Church.

A new and at first sight somewhat confusing sub-section entitled 'The Order for Public Offenders' follows.[8] The opening paragraph states that those who commit crimes such as murder and adultery ought, as was indicated at the outset, to be punished with death by the civil sword, but if they are permitted to live they ought to be subjected to the same 'order' or procedure that has already been outlined for impenitent offenders against ecclesiastical discipline, and to the same ecclesiastical penalties, and be required to submit themselves when penitent to public repentance. Both the 'obstinate impenitent' ecclesiastical offender and the civil offender are thus regarded alike as 'public offenders'. It thereafter becomes clear that the section is not, as might have been expected, concerned with the disciplining of civil offenders but rather the 'order' or procedure that is to be followed in receiving again into the fellowship of the Church both classes of offenders. A marginal note indicates that the section was 'consented to by the Lords'.

Four paragraphs outline the procedure involved in public repentance. The congregation must be forewarned, the penitent assigned a day on which to make his public confession to the Church, the minister must examine him to discover the sincerity

[7] *Infra*, pp. 168ff and n.17 and 18.   [8] *Infra*, pp. 171ff.

and genuine nature of his repentance, the Church must decide to
have him restored to fellowship, and finally there must be a
public reception of the penitent brother in which he is to be taken
by the hand by 'the Elders and chief men of the Kirk'[9] and
embraced by one or two representatives of them. If it should be
found that the penitent is ignorant of the principles of religion he
is to be instructed before he is received by the Church.

The head concludes with a brief paragraph which is given the
title 'Persons subject to Discipline'[10] and which has a marginal
note indicating the consent of the Lords. All estates are, it is stated,
to be subject to discipline, the rulers, the preachers and 'the
poorest with the Kirk', but especially the ministers because
they form 'the eye and mouth of the Kirk'. This matter,
however, is to be left over until the election of elders and deacons
has been treated.

Throughout this head there is repeatedly emphasised the 'congregational' nature of the Church. In every part of the procedures
outlined the final word is always seen to be with the whole
congregation, and the fellowship of the congregation is always
jealously guarded. Neither minister nor elders are ever allowed to
take the final decisions. It is also to be noted that in this all-
important matter of ecclesiastical discipline no mention whatever
is made of the office or function of the superintendent. He is, in
fact, conspicuously absent.

It has already been noted that the Preface stated that Ecclesiastical Discipline formed one of the original heads of the report of
May 1560.[11] There is in the contents no evidence to lead one to
believe that this head is not in its original form. Reference is made
to the confusion that 'this accursed Papistry has brought'[12] and to
the possibility that the state may permit civil offenders, guilty of
receiving the death penalty, to live, statements which would tend
to support an early rather than a late date, and as has recently been
noted the absence of the superintendent should not be overlooked
in this matter. There are no *additiones*, but three indications of
agreement on the part of the Lords.

The Eighth Head[1]

According to the Preface the original Book of Reformation does
not appear to have included a separate head with this title:

[9] *Infra*, p. 172.   [10] *Infra*, p. 173.   [11] *Supra*, p. 14; cf. *infra*, p. 85.
[12] *Infra*, p. 167   [1] *Infra*, pp. 174ff.

'Touching the Election of Elders and Deacons'.[2] At first sight this absence is somewhat surprising as the office of the elder had been one of the most significant developments in the Reformed Church,[3] and we know that elders and deacons quickly appeared in the reformed congregations that were set up in the months immediately preceding the summer of 1560 and had been playing an important part in the development of these early congregations, if the only surviving Kirk Session Register for the period, that of St Andrews, can be taken as typical evidence.[4] The fact, however, that a separate head is not mentioned need not necessarily mean that nothing was said in the original draft report about elders and deacons.

We have noted that those heads dealing with the election of ministers and the arrangements for their maintenance naturally followed upon the elaboration of the first two notes or marks of the Church, the preaching of the Word and the administration of the Sacraments, and that these titles were in fact mentioned as separate heads in the Laing text. Further we have argued that there are grounds for believing that these topics were discussed in the original report, but perhaps not so completely as they are in the final form of the document. In similar fashion a section on the election of elders and deacons could be regarded as naturally following upon the elaboration of the third distinguishing mark of the Church, as, in this matter, these officers necessarily have an important function. The exercise of discipline needs a kirk session in the same way as the preaching of the Word and the administration of the sacraments need a lawfully admitted ministry. The question, therefore, would seem to be, not whether there was a section on elders and deacons, but rather how much there was on this topic, and how much, if any, has been added to it or altered in the course of the revision of the autumn and winter of 1560–61.

The head is one of the most disorganised in the entire book and yet it has only one marginal comment providing evidence that it had probably been discussed by the Lords.[5] It may, therefore, be fairly safe to regard any revision that took place as occurring during the Church's discussion of the book.

The first sentence begins bluntly by stating the moral qualifications required of those who are to be nominated for the offices of

---

[2] *Supra*, pp. 15f; cf. *infra*, p. 85.
[3] See for example Henderson, *Scottish Ruling Elder*, 11ff.
[4] *StAKSR*, i.xxiii f.   [5] *Infra*, p. 175.

elder and deacon. It does not state by whom the nomination is to be made, but adds that if any man knows others of better qualities they may be nominated in order that 'the kirke may have the choyce'. The freedom of the local congregation to nominate and elect both elders and deacons is thus seen to be a basic principle, although the lack of precise detail might suggest that the nomination could perhaps be carried out (as this was to be an annual event) by the retiring body and added to if thought necessary by anyone else. This was the procedure followed in the annual burgh elections and it is conceivable that a similar method would be employed by the Church.[6] There is in this paragraph nothing that is inconsistent with what we know of the practice of the Protestant congregations in Scotland in 1559–60.

A short paragraph states that churches which are 'of smaller number' may be joined to the 'next adjacent' as the 'plurality of kirks [i.e., congregations] without ministers and order [i.e. organisation] shall hurt rather than edify'. Two points call for attention. There is introduced in place of the word 'elder' the alternative term 'senior' which was also used in this connection on the Continent. It is impossible to attach any significance to the use of the term here. Of importance is the marginal note 'What churches may be joined let the policy judge'. If this remark emanated from the Lords it could be taken as evidence that in the matter of local organisation the Church was at liberty to make the necessary changes in parish boundaries.

The annual election of elders and deacons, which is intended to prevent anyone from presuming 'upon the liberty of the kirk', is the subject of the next paragraph. The authors are not against re-election provided there is every year a free election. Deacons cannot be re-elected for 'the space of three years'. The matter of voting is left to local arrangement.

On election the elders must be 'admonished of their office' which consists in assisting the minister 'in all publike affaires of the kirk'. They are (a) determining and judging causes', by which it is suggested that the minister and elders replace the old ecclesiastical courts – as was in fact done in St Andrews in the matter of divorce; (b) admonishing the licentious liver; and (c) taking into consideration the 'manners and conversation' of everyone within their charge.

Several paragraphs concerned with the oversight of the conduct

6 Marwick, *Records*, 3.

of the ministers follow and these contain some inconsistencies. A good example is found in the first paragraph, which on examination appears to be a conflation of two separate statements. The paragraph begins by noting that the

> seniors ought to take heed to the life, manners, diligence, and study of their ministers. If he be worthy of admonition, they must admonish him; of correction, they must correct him; and if he be worthy of deposition, they with the consent of the kirk and Superintendent, may depose him, so that his crime deserve so.[7]

This is a compact embodiment of all that was required. The remainder of the paragraph, however, repeats much that has been said but with significant variation:

> If a Minister be light of conversation, by his Elders and Deacons he ought to be admonished. If he be negligent in study, or one that vaikes not upon his charge or flock or one that propones not faithfull doctrine, he deserves sharper admonition and correction. To the which if he be found stubborn and innobedient, then may the Seniors of the kirk complain to the ministry of the two next adjacent kirks, where men of greater gravitie are. To whose admonition if he be found inobedient, he ought to be discharged of his ministry till his repentance appeare, and a place be vakand for him.[8]

It will be immediately clear that the two parts of the paragraph reflect different ecclesiastical organisation. The first part confines the matter to the seniors and finally to them along with the 'kirk and Superintendent'. The latter phrase is difficult; it may have been intended to refer to the local congregation with the help and advice of the superintendent, or to some superior court of the Church – possibly the superintendent's court. The second part is unaware of the existence of the superintendent, and reflects the situation already exhibited in the section dealing with the examination of candidates for the ministry and which emphasises the importance of adjacent congregations and their responsibility for helping their neighbours. It is with the assistance of 'the men of greater gravity' which these congregations can supply that the unworthy and disobedient minister can be discharged and replaced.[9]

---

[7] *Infra*, p. 176; cf. p. 123, and Introduction, p. 53.
[8] *Infra*, pp. 176f.   [9] *Supra*, pp. 17ff, and *infra*, pp. 96ff.

As is argued elsewhere the ascription of a responsible personal oversight to the superintendent is a development that took place in the autumn of 1560;[10] we may therefore regard the first part of the paragraph as belonging to the period of the first revision (and perhaps the paragraph which requires a report on the minister to be presented by one elder and one deacon once in the year to the 'ministers of the Superintendents kirk'), but the remaining part which emphasises the place of the neighbouring churches and of the local congregation we may regard as belonging to the initial report.

The oversight of the wives and families of ministers form the topic of the next paragraph. They are to be subject to the same discipline as are the ministers, who in the management of their households must neither be needlessly extravagant nor avaricious.

The authors next stress that a minister's responsibility is supremely to the Church; he must not frequent the 'Court', that is to say be engaged in public administration, unless he is sent there by the Church or called by 'the Authority for his counsell' but he may 'assist the Parliament if he be called'. These statements represent a complete break with the past. The reformers realise that much harm had come to the Church by many of its most important officers being given responsible places in the government of the country and decide, despite the fact that Alexander Gordon, bishop-elect of Galloway, for example, had used his position on the Council to favour the Protestant cause, to suggest the incompatibility of the two offices and responsibilities. This decision, which on several occasions General Assemblies sought to have put into effect, was to provide the cause of much trouble in later years.

A short paragraph defines the duties of the deacons in which reference is made to one or other of the earlier statements about the office. It may be worth noting that in the earlier statements[11] nothing was said about the responsibility of the deacons for the gathering in of the 'alms of the Church'. Indeed this is the first occasion on which alms are mentioned. The paragraph also indicates that the deacons 'may assist in judgment with the Ministers and elders, and may be admitted to read in the assembly if they be required and be found able'. From the St Andrews Kirk Session Register it would appear that elders and deacons served

[10] *Supra*, p. 26, Introduction, pp. 49ff, and *infra*, pp. 115ff.
[11] *Infra*, pp. 163f.

together on the Session from the beginning and it is interesting to note that the first reader at St Andrews was also one of the deacons. The wives of elders and deacons and their households are to be subject to the same discipline as were the families of ministers. Compared with the duties of the ministers those of elders and deacons are considered much less demanding and hence it is not thought necessary to provide them with a stipend.

It is extremely difficult to date the various paragraphs which treat of the offices of the elders and deacons. It has already been suggested that what was said about the office of deacon in the sixth head may belong to the revision that took place in the autumn of 1560 and that the duplication is to be accounted for by assuming that a different group was responsible for each section, and that in the final form no attempt was made to remove the repetition. As has, however, been stated there is ground for believing that a separate head on the election of elders and deacons, such as we now have, was not included in the plan of the first report and that the origin of this head is to be found in the Church's exercise of discipline, and in particular of the responsibility of the elders and deacons in the oversight of the conduct of their minister.[12] It may therefore be claimed that, while this eighth head is the result of considerable revision and extension, originally it did little more than state their disciplinary duties, namely that elders and deacons must be elected by the local congregations every year, that the elders assist the minister in the exercise of discipline, that the elders watch over the conduct of the minister, that the deacons collect the 'rents' and gather the alms, and distribute them as they are instructed, that they be permitted to assist the minister and elders in the exercise of discipline, and that they may read the lessons and prayers at the services when required and if they are able to do so.

The Ninth Head[1]

The original report included a head on the Policy of the Church.[2] To that topic the ninth head of the final text is devoted. It is to be expected that this important subject of ecclesiastical administration would be of lively concern and that it would be subject to careful examination at the hands of the Church and of the Lords. Of such revisionary activity, as shall be seen, the text provides

[12] *Supra*, pp. 34f.

[1] *Infra*, pp. 180ff.   [2] *Infra*, p. 85, and Introduction, p. 15.

some evidence. Again, the difficulty of the task and the subjective and tentative nature of any suggested reconstruction must be emphasised. In its final form this head has six separately titled subsections, but how many or how much of these sections can be affirmed original with any degree of certainty, must always remain an open question. Some parts, as shall be pointed out, can with a measure of certainty be regarded as belonging to the comparatively more stable period of the first revision.

The word 'policy' is defined as embracing those matters which are required for retaining good order in the Church; some of these are essential, such as the preaching of the Word, the administration of the Sacraments, the public offering of prayer, the instruction of little children in religion, and the correcting and punishing of offences. Other matters, such as the public singing of Psalms, the reading of the Scriptures, and the saying of prayers when there is no sermon, are regarded as 'profitable, but not meerly necessarie'. With regard to the second group a definite order cannot be established and the individual congregation must make its own decision. Nevertheless, certain proposals are laid down for the cities and towns.

In the 'great towns' it was thought expedient that there be sermon or common prayers with the reading of Scripture every day. On the day of sermon it was not thought advisable to have common prayers as this service might come to be regarded as a superstitious performance as had happened with the Mass. In 'notable towns' it was 'required' that one day in addition to Sunday be appointed for sermon and prayers. Smaller towns are left free to make their own arrangements for week-day services.

Strict observance of morning and afternoon services on Sunday is ordered in all towns. On Sunday mornings in addition to the preaching of the Word, the Sacraments are to be administered and marriages solemnised. The afternoon service was to be of an educational nature at which the young children were to be publicly examined in the portion of the Catechism assigned for that day; it was also permitted to celebrate baptism when the forenoon service was considered an inconvenient time. If, however, there was no preaching or catechism 'prayers' were to be used, by which is no doubt intended an afternoon service of lessons and prayers similar to that of the week-days. All these arrangements are in line with Reformed Continental practice and there is no reason to suppose that they were not suggested in the initial report.

The next paragraph begins by asserting the principle that 'it appertains to the Policy of the Church to appoint the times of the Sacraments', by which statement the reformers would appear to wish to indicate that this was a matter for decision by the individual congregation. One would not, therefore, have expected detailed regulations to follow, but this is in fact what happens. Baptism, which has just been mentioned, may be administered whenever the word is preached, and that would normally mean on Sundays or on the day of the week when a sermon is preached. Two reasons are given on doctrinal and on practical grounds; the need to remove the 'error' that children who die unbaptised are damned, and the need to encourage the people to be present and 'assist the administration . . . with greater reverence than they do'.

The Sacrament of the Lord's Table is to be administered four times a year, and in such a way as to avoid 'the superstition of the times'. Again the reason is doctrinal; the superstition that 'the time gave virtue to the sacrament' was to be resisted. Specific dates are mentioned, but the authors recognise that 'any several Kirk' may for 'reasonable causes' change the time and may even administer the sacrament more often, but the danger of a superstitious association should be avoided. It was for the same basic reason that the reformers go on to emphasise that only those of understanding are to be admitted to the Lord's Table. Not only must the intending communicant be able to say 'formally' the traditional requirements, *i.e.*, the Lord's Prayer, the Creed, and the Ten Commandments, but the ministers must be admonished to instruct and examine them. Indeed it was the opinion of the reformers that there should always be an examination, especially of those whose knowledge and understanding was suspect, before every celebration.

How much of these two paragraphs can be regarded as from the original report? There is nothing in the contents taken by themselves that requires a date later than May 1560. Three factors should, however, be taken into account. (*a*) As has already been mentioned the opening sentence does not lead one to expect the detailed arrangement that follows. (*b*) The time for the celebration of baptism has already been mentioned. (*c*) The following paragraph once removed, which deals with the responsibility of the master of the household to attend to the instruction of his

D

family before they are to be admitted to the Lord's Table, ordains a yearly examination by the minister and elders of everyone within the parish, and therefore they are not in strict harmony. Any attempt to assign any priority to the one rather than the other would be hazardous in the extreme. In favour, however, of a later date for the section 'Baptism . . . Law'[3] it may be suggested that by the specific nature of its recommendations, it reflects the more favourable conditions of December rather than those of May 1560.

There follows a provision which one might have expected somewhat earlier: the requirement that every church obtain a Bible in English, and that the people be commanded to attend to 'hear the plain reading or interpretation of Scripture, as the Church shall appoint'. The importance of the section lies in the injunction that the Books of the Old and the New Testament be read orderly to the end. This practice had been popularised by Zwingli in Zürich and had been followed by the Reformed Churches in general; it underlies the decision of the Scottish reformers to obliterate all trace of the religious observance of the Christian year even to the following of a lectionary. There are no good grounds for assigning this paragraph to one period of the composition of the book rather than to another.

Religious instruction in the home and family worship form the topics of the concluding paragraphs. Common prayers are to be used morning and evening for the 'comfort and instruction' of the members of the household. At this point we have a rare indication of the contemporary political situation: 'For seeing that we behold and see the hand of God now presently striking us with divers plagues . . . which now for our iniquities hang over our heads' and of the need for 'repentance of our former unthankful-nesse' and of 'earnest invocation of his name'.[4] It is suggested that we have here a reference to the uncertainties and rebuffs of March and April of 1560, which the forces of the Lords of the Congregation had sustained following upon the successes of the previous year rather than the more favourable situation of the autumn and early winter and before the news of the illness of Francis II of France.

An important feature of the ecclesiastical life of the Continental reformed cities and in particular of Geneva was the weekly meeting of ministers for the interpretation and discussion of the

---

[3] *Infra*, p. 182 line 10 to p. 184 line 18.   [4] *Infra*, p. 187.

Bible.[5] By the late fifties these occasions had become not only popular sessions for mutual instruction and correction of the brethren but also opportunities for discussing the needs of the expanding Reformed Church in France by examining and providing candidates for the work of the ministry. The practice of holding such meetings had been followed in Frankfurt among the English-speaking congregation and at an earlier date in the exiled reformed congregation in London over which John à Lasco presided. It was, therefore, natural for those familiar with the Reformed Church organisation to propose such meetings or 'prophesyings' for the Reformed Church in Scotland. The subsection that follows in the ninth head is an elaboration and justification of the practice.[6]

The educational purposes of such regular meetings is stressed in the opening sentence; that the Church 'may have tryall of mens knowledge' and that 'such as have somewhat profited in Gods word may from time to time grow to more full perfection to serve the Kirk, as necessitie shall require'. Throughout the section care is taken to prevent the interpretation of the prescribed passage of the Bible becoming either a sermon or a discussion of one of the *loci* or common places of theology. Again, it is to be noted that these exercises or prophesyings are to be held in 'every town where Schooles and repaire of learned men are' and the ministers and readers of rural parishes within six miles of the 'chief town' are to attend and take part. In addition – and at this point an earlier statement[7] is reaffirmed – 'men in whom is supposed to be any gift which might edifie the Church, if they were well imployed, must be charged by the Ministers and Elders to join themselves with the session and company of interpreters' in order that the Church may know whether they can 'profit the Kirk in the vocation of ministers or not'. In this way it is seen that every effort was to be made to provide the Church with suitably qualified ministers and that no one whom the Church regarded as qualified was to be permitted 'to live as best pleased him within the Kirk of God', but was with the concurrence of the civil magistrate 'to bestow his labours when of the Kirk he is required'.

To what date can this sub-section be assigned? The contents suggest that it is original. Prominence is given to the place of the

[5] *Infra*, p. 187 n.30.   [6] *Infra*, pp. 187ff.
[7] *Infra*, p. 104.

chief town, and there is no reference whatever to the super-intendent; those who bring in strange doctrine are to be admonished by the 'Moderator, Ministers and Elders'; further those who are thought to have gifts that might be employed in the service of the Church are to be 'charged by the Minister and Elders' to attend and take part and be disciplined if they refuse. We notice that a practice that was essentially reformed was being suggested and in the form in which it is presented no effort is being made to adapt it in order to provide for the functioning of the superintendent.

It has frequently been pointed out that 'The Exercise' as it came to be known in Scotland, so far as can be discovered from extant records in its initial stages, met with little support, that in some prominent centres it at times almost ceased to exist, and that on more than one occasion General Assemblies passed measures intended to enforce attendance. By the end of the seventies, however, in some areas these meetings were more or less regularly held and formed the basis for the development of presbyteries in the following decades.[8]

The third sub-section of this head entitled 'Of Marriage' is virtually a separate head. On account of the contempt into which marriage had been brought by the late mediaeval Church and in order to avoid further confusion the authors of the Book of Discipline considered it necessary, as Calvin had done in the *Ordonnances* of 1541, to set forth their 'judgments' on this topic.

The proposals amount to a thorough revision, or rather replacement, of the existing law and practice by new laws in conformity with Scripture. The rights of parents and guardians are safeguarded in that those 'under the power and obedience of others' are prohibited from entering secretly into marriage, but at the same time parents and guardians are not permitted an unreasonable exercise of their rights and in such cases where this impediment is alleged the intending couple can appeal to 'the Minister or to the Civil Magistrates' to further their interest or even to 'enter in the place of the parent' and consent to 'just requests'. Sexual offences – fornication, whoredom, and adultery – are to be punished in accordance with the Levitical Law. The permitted ages at which marriage could be entered remain, unlike Geneva, those prescribed by Canon Law, fourteen for the man and twelve at least for the woman. The ancient practice of proclaiming banns

[8] See further p. 187ff and n.30 and Donaldson. *Scottish Reformation* 204ff, 211.

is likewise retained and clandestine marriages are forbidden. Divorce is only permitted in the case of adultery, and while the innocent person is permitted to remarry, it is intended that the guilty person be punished by death. If his life is spared he is to be excommunicated and reputed a dead member. Nevertheless, if 'the fruits of repentance of long time appear' in the excommunicated person, he may be restored to the fellowship of the Church, and may in order to prevent further offence be allowed to remarry. If a reconciliation can be effected with his former wife, the offender is not permitted to marry any other person. At this point the reformers, aware that they were likely to encounter difficulties 'in so doubtsome a case', restated their desire that the law of the land be brought into conformity with the Levitical Law. As will be seen from the notes to the text many problems were to arise and although the church courts were active for some time in determining matters of divorce the subject was reserved by statute to a civil court in 1563 in which the precepts of Canon Law rather than any new laws based on Scripture were regarded as normative.

The sub-section on marriage defies precise dating. It contains nothing that could not have been in the initial report, and indeed the form in which the subject is presented with its repeated appeals to 'your Honours' to 'prefer his [God's] express commandment' to their own 'corrupt judgments' may suggest that much of the section does belong to May 1560. Further we know that the Kirk Session of St Andrews was already dealing with matrimonial offences and requests for divorce. On the other hand it may be doubted whether in the unsettled period of the early summer of 1560 it would have been considered necessary to provide such a detailed programme.

As in the *Ordonnances* of Geneva this sub-section on marriage is followed by one on burial. In the period immediately prior to the Reformation considerable emphasis had been placed on the ceremonies that centred round death and burial. To the reformers, who, it need hardly be said, shared the contemporary belief 'that the body committed to the earth should not utterly perish', many of these practices were superstitious, were connected with idolatry or 'advantage', and were consequently to be avoided. Prayer for the dead in any form was contrary to Scripture and therefore inadmissible. For these reasons burial was to be carried out with the utmost simplicity, without either singing or reading or any kind of ceremony previously used, and the body committed to the grave with such gravity and sobriety 'that those present may seem to fear the judgments of God, and to hate sin which is the cause of death'.

An *additio*[9] indicates that the proposals of the reformers were too narrow and some considered that individual congregations ought to have the liberty to make use of reading and singing provided they have 'the consent of the Ministerie of the same' and that they will be able to 'answer to God, and the Assemblie of the Universall Kirk gathered within the Realme' – one of the undoubted references to the General Assembly in the document.[10]

The paragraph that follows takes up the subject of funeral sermons and argues against their employment on the grounds that the ordinary sermons ought to be sufficient to remind people of their mortality; and that because so many sermons would be required ministers might feel compelled to preach for some and not for others and this in turn might result in there being funeral sermons for the rich and honourable and none for the poor. Such differentiation could not be made 'with safe conscience'. With a splendid notion of equality of all men in the sight of God it is declared that the pastor's ministry 'appertaineth to all alike; whatever they do to the rich in respect of their Ministry, the same they are bound to do to the poorest under their charge'.

The section concludes with a brief paragraph which prohibited interment within buildings used for public worship, and recommended that burials be in some convenient place in an open area, walled and reserved for the purpose.

The same difficulties which are encountered in attempting to date the section on marriage are encountered in this section. Apart from the *additio*, which may have been made during the discussions held by the General Assembly in December 1560, there is no ground for regarding it as a result of the process of revision.

Contrary to popular belief the reformers, far from requiring the destruction of all ecclesiastical buildings, were anxious that those necessary for the preaching of the Word and the administration of the Sacraments be repaired, preserved, and suitably furnished. There is ample evidence that in the years immediately prior to the Reformation the fabric of many parish churches had

9 *Infra*, p. 200.
10 Introduction, pp. 69ff, and *infra*, p. 200 n.*b*.

been allowed to fall into disrepair and even decay.[11] Little surprise should be aroused on finding in this head a sub-section on the repair of churches.

The honour of the Word of God, and the administration of the Sacraments, require that the churches be kept in a good state of repair. It is regarded as the duty of the civil authority to see that 'strait charge' be given to those responsible to fulfil their obligations within a specified period, and in the event of default to impose penalties.

There follows a second paragraph which repeats and elaborates some of the points already made. The repairs are to be carried out according to the ability and number of the congregation; furnishings essential for every church are listed; and in the larger churches where the congregation is 'great in number' provision is to be made for the 'quiet and commodious receiving of the people.' The cost of such repairs and furnishings are to be borne partly by the people, in all probability by some form of 'stenting', and partly from the teinds in agreement with the local church court.

On examination it might appear that the two paragraphs of this sub-section are of different origin. The first is more general than the second, lacks the detailed specification, concerned with the principle that the buildings be put into a proper state of repair, and is anxious to point out that the ultimate responsibility lies with the state. The second is also concerned with what should be done but indicates the way the money is to be raised. The responsibility of the Lords is not mentioned, but as is pointed out in the notes the mediaeval procedure whereby the congregation and the person who possesses the teinds are jointly responsible for the upkeep of the church is advocated. The different emphasis of the two paragraphs should not be stressed; they are not mutually exclusive; both may belong to the same period. It is not possible to assign to them with any certainty a specific date of composition.

The concluding sub-section of the ninth head draws attention to those who 'profane the Sacraments' and to those who 'presume' to minister them without a lawful calling. There have always been those who have attributed to the Sacraments a virtue which they did not possess and those who have no proper regard for them at all. These two groups are still to be found. Not long ago none would have presumed to have said Mass save priests,

[11] *Infra*, p. 202 n.78.

but now some men without any calling dare to administer what they suppose are the true Sacraments in open assemblies, and others imitate in their houses what the true ministers do in open congregations, without reverence, without sermon and without minister. Clearly there existed those who maintained that private individuals could administer the Sacraments, and there were some who were doing so. The authors of the Book of Discipline must have been aware of the presence of an extreme Protestant radicalism which had so often on the Continent accompanied the spread of the reformed teaching, but little evidence seems to have survived of its activities.[12] The reformers desire that without delay 'strait laws' be made against both the despiser and the profaner of the Sacraments and against those who dare presume to minister his sacraments, not orderly called to that office. Indeed the death penalty is suggested and the Lords are warned against the danger of incurring by default the divine displeasure.

Thus far the authors have not specifically mentioned the position of priests of the mediaeval Church, although they may have been included in the general denunciation, and it is possible that some former priests who had conformed had thought that they had in virtue of their previous ordination and without a new 'admission' the right to continue to administer the Sacraments but according to the reformed manner. To any who were of this mind the authors make their position clear. 'Papistical priests' have as such no power or authority to administer the Sacraments 'because that in their mouth is not the sermon of exhortation'. Their former ordination with its ceremonies did not make them 'true ministers of Christ Jesus'. What makes a minister (and for the first time in this document an important element in reformed theology is stated) is the inward working of the Spirit in the heart of the individual, the nomination of the people, the examination of the learned, and the service of public admission. All these elements combine in providing an 'ordinary vocation'; but the reformers do not rule out an extraordinary vocation when God by himself 'raiseth up to the Ministrie such as best pleaseth his wisdome'.

The difficulties already encountered in attempting to assign dates of composition to the various sub-sections of this head are again encountered in this one. The situation depicted could fit any period of 1560, but the fact that the authors are petitioning that

[12] *Infra*, p. 205 n.92.

laws be made against those former priests and individuals who are administering the Sacraments suggests that the period of composition is prior to the Act of Parliament prohibiting the Mass. This act, it should be noted, condemns any manner of persons who in any way in time coming administer the Sacraments secretly or publicly, other than those admitted for that purpose, and then goes on to condemn those who say or hear Mass. It is, on this ground, suggested that this sub-section belongs to the original report.

The Conclusion[1]

In the brief conclusion the authors acknowledge that in fulfilling the commission given to them they have put forward some 'petitions' which will appear strange at first sight, but this has been necessary for they must take care that they do not offend God. They are aware that the liberty they require for the Church from maintaining 'idle bellies' or supporting the former 'tyranny' will not please many. However, they restate their readiness to bring their requests into conformity with Scripture if it can be shown that they have erred, and they warn in stern language those who would let 'blind affection' lead them to support 'carnal friends', and who do not set God's 'oppressed Church at freedom and liberty', that they will be inviting divine punishment.

This section, which bears the date 'the 20 of May 1560' has considerable internal evidence to support its early composition. The Church has not been set at liberty, and there is still some danger that the glory and honour of this enterprise will be reserved for others.

THE THREE INTERPOLATIONS

Of the Superintendents[2]

The opening sentence begins by stating the grounds for the inclusion of this section. A larger stipend has been appointed to 'them that shall be Superintendents than to the rest of the Ministers' and it is to be expected that the Lords will require to know the reasons for making a 'difference betwixt Preachers at this time'; how many will be required, 'their bounds, office, election, and causes that may deserve deposition'.

The reasons for making the difference are practical ones: the

[1] *Infra* pp. 208ff.   [2] *Infra*, pp. 115ff.

scarcity of ministers and the extent of the country to be evangel-
ised. If the best-endowed ministers were appointed to particular
centres and restricted in their activity to these places 'the greatest
part of this Realme should be destitute of all doctrine'. The authors
have, therefore, thought it 'a thing most expedient for this time'
that is to say, most suitable or advantageous in the present situation,
that from the 'whole number of godly and learned men . . . ten
or twelve' be selected and charged to 'plant and erect kirkes, to set
order and appoint Ministers' in those provinces assigned to them
'where none are now'. The Lords are reminded of their responsibilities for the whole country and of the consequences if they
neglect to carry them into effect.

It has already been argued that the assigning of particular
stipends to ministers in the fifth head was undertaken during the
revision that took place in the autumn and early winter of 1560;[1]
that the majority of earlier references to the superintendents are
in the nature of glosses;[2] and that although the petition, that some
of the 'chiefest workmen' would not only have 'towns to remain
in' but also 'provinces that by their faithful labours kirks may be
erected . . . where none is now', was made in the original report,[3]
there is no convincing evidence that in drawing up the other parts
of the Book of Discipline which can be assigned an early date the
existence of the superintendent was given further serious consideration. In addition it has been pointed out that there is no con-
clusive evidence that any of the five superintendents was appointed
before the spring of 1561.[4]

That a plan to exercise a form of superintendence, centred in
the chief town of the neighbourhood, existed in the scheme of the
reformers from the earliest days is clearly evident; it would in
fact have been strange if it had not. Superintendence was by 1560
a well established principle not only in Lutheran Churches, with
which the Reformation in Scotland had for some time close relations, but in sections of the reformed Church on the Continent,
and in England particularly in the reign of Edward VI many of
those English reformers who had been most closely influenced
by the reformed Churches on the Continent had sought to
establish, in the interests of evangelisation, a reformed episcopacy.[5]

---

[1] *Supra*, p. 24.   [2] *Supra*, pp. 21ff, 24.
[3] *Supra*, pp. 21f; *infra*, p. 105.   [4] *Supra*, pp. 20ff.
[5] *NSH*, 11.166; Dunkley, *Reformation in Denmark*, 77ff, 84ff; Donaldson,
Scottish Reformation, 115ff; Donaldson, 'The Example of Denmark' *SHR*, 27

Further, three of the six authors, Willock,[6] Spottiswoode,[7] and Knox, had experience of the reformed churches outside Scotland. When faced with the practical problem of providing for the establishment of Protestant congregations throughout the country it would have been surprising if the reformers had not, as Cecil advised them, looked at what had been done elsewhere in similar circumstances.[8]

Their problem, however, was not a simple one. The existing bishops had not, with one notable exception,[9] been actively engaged at this stage in the work of Reformation; the Reformation was already well established in certain prominent city centres and had provided itself with a constitutional organisation in accordance with the pattern of cities such as Geneva, Bern and, Lausanne. Further, the old ecclesiastical organisation of the country must have seemed to many to be ill suited to the demands of the new faith, for the dioceses were of very unequal size; some were much too large for effective oversight by one person, others too small. The practical needs of the country faced with a problem of evangelisation and a great scarcity of suitably qualified ministers demanded that some distinction of function be made between ministers, and consequently that some differences be made in their remuneration to meet their requirements, and further that there be a reorganisation of the ecclesiastical structure of the country around as far as possible certain prominent cities where there could be a lively church and which would be reasonably accessible from all parts of the diocese. The problem which therefore faced the revisers of the original Book of Discipline in the autumn of 1560 was considerable; it was that of adapting a reformation scheme, that had grown up largely in the burghs and been determined by the Genevan programme, to suit the requirements of the whole country. In that reorganisation the superintendent, it was envisaged, would occupy an important position; hence the lengths to which the revisers must go in order to outline and justify the 'difference betwixt ministers' and all that it involved. Hence this long section that is so out of proportion to much else in the Book.

(1948), 57ff; Donaldson, 'The Polity of the Scottish Church', *RSCHS*, 11 (1955), 212ff; Macgregor, *Scottish Presbyterian Polity*, 42ff; Shaw, *General Assemblies*, 75ff.

[6] Shaw, *Reformation and Revolution*, 42ff.

[7] *DNB*, 53.411ff. [8] *CSP Scot*, 1, no. 506 p. 234.

[9] Alexander Gordon, elect of Galloway, see *infra*, p. 121 n.17.

In the second section the areas of ten dioceses are briefly outlined. It will be seen that although they correspond in name with many of the mediaeval dioceses, they represent a complete reorganisation or rather a complete replacement of the mediaeval scheme in which an attempt has been made in accordance with the contemporary geographical knowledge of the country to designate areas that are roughly comparable in size, that can be seen to follow natural geographical boundaries, and that have in all but one case a main town as a recognised centre of the area.[10]

In the remaining paragraphs the writers are anxious to make it absolutely clear that the superintendent is not to be allowed to live as 'your idle Bishops have done heretofore'. They must first and foremost be preachers and must be almost continually engaged in travelling through their dioceses till their churches be planted and provided with ministers or readers. A residence of three or four months at most in their chief town is all that is to be permitted before the recommencing of a tour of visitation in which they will have to examine the life, diligence and behaviour of the ministers,[11] the order of the churches and the behaviour of the people, the provision for the poor and the instruction of the youth. Further, they are to note 'such crimes as be heinous' in order that they may be corrected by the censure of the Church.

The superintendent was, clearly, intended to lead a most active life and as the last paragraph indicates was himself to be subjected to oversight and discipline, but it is not at this stage stated by whom such correction was to be exercised.

Having decided upon the dioceses and the responsibilities of the superintendents, it was natural to outline the procedure that was to be adopted in order to fill these posts. The contemporary situation and its exceptional circumstances were recognised as requiring a particular procedure, which was, nevertheless, not to be regarded as normative for the future. Nomination was to be carried out either by the Lords or a committee commissioned by them, and those nominated, were to be called to appear before the Lords or their commission (to whom it was suggested should be added some of the gentlemen and burgesses of every diocese to bring the Church into some practice of her liberty) to accept appointment to their provinces. If the required number of suitably qualified men could not be found, it was considered that the

[10] See contemporary map reproduced on p. 78.
[11] cf. *supra*, pp. 37f, and *infra*, pp. 122 and 176ff.

positions should remain unfilled for the time being.

If after the lapse of three years a vacancy were to occur, the ministers, elders and deacons with the Provost and Town Council of the chief town, were stated to have the power to nominate by public edict within twenty days two or three from amongst the ministers of the realm and to inform the neighbouring superintendents and two or three provinces. In the event of failure to nominate the responsibility is said to fall upon the three neighbouring provinces to make nominations to the chief town. At the same time the churches of the diocese may add their nominations. After the nomination and the publication of edicts thirty days are to be allowed for the raising of objections. The examination of the nominees was to be carried out by three or more superintendents and 'the whole Ministers of that Province' and they should be required to preach. The election was confined to 'all them that convene' but it was considered that the ministers should bring with them the votes of the members of their parishes. As in the admission of ministers, no other ceremony than the examination and approval of the ministers and superintendents with the consent of the elders and the people present was to be permitted.

Already it had been stated that the superintendent was to be subject to discipline; it is now noted that he is, as are other ministers, subject to the censure of the ministers and elders of his chief town and of his whole province, and if they fail to act when the occasion arises the responsibility falls upon the neighbouring dioceses. Further, nominations are to be restricted to those ministers who have laboured in the ministry of some church for at least two years, and any subsequent translation of a superintendent can only be effected with the consent of 'the whole Counsell of the Kirk'[12] and for 'grave causes and considerations'.

The section concludes with a warning to the Lords that in making appointments they do not deprive the chief towns 'where learning is exercised' of such ministers who may be more profitably employed by remaining in one place and in particular by providing the profound interpretation of the Scriptures so essential for the education of the young people in those places.

It need hardly be pointed out that there is in these sections a real attempt to combine two types of ecclesiastical organisation.

[12] Introduction, pp. 69ff.

In order to provide for effective evangelisation and supervision of areas that otherwise would have been without an effective ministry the power of *episkope* is assigned to a responsible minister who would be actively engaged in fulfilling his task. At the same time in order to avoid any hierarchical tendency and to uphold the doctrine that those who exercise the ministry of Word and Sacraments are all alike preachers it is carefully stated that the differences between them are of function and extent of responsibility and that both superintendents and ministers are equally subject to the same system of ecclesiastical discipline.

Sufficient emphasis has, perhaps, been given to the importance of practical considerations in the preparation of these proposals. What long-term future, it has often been inquired, did the authors envisage for the office of superintendent? Was it proposed merely as a solution to a practical problem? Did the authors envisage a time when there would be sufficient ministers for every parish and a sufficient number of towns from which there could be an easily exercised supervision by fellow-ministers, and when superintendents with large dioceses would no longer be required? To these questions the reformers do not in the Book of Discipline address themselves. They were, within the terms of their commission, planning for the foreseeable future, a future which they knew to be full of uncertainties. They must have realised that it would take a considerable number of years to provide all the parishes with men of the high educational standard they were setting. The fact that, as the footnotes to the text indicate,[13] the General Assemblies continued to request the appointment of able superintendents, and that they appointed commissioners to plant kirks, and regularly reappointed them to fulfil superintendents' duties, and the ease with which an episcopal scheme was reintroduced in 1572, would all suggest that the reformers would probably have continued to uphold for some time at least a strictly controlled form of personally exercised *episkope* as expedient. The allied theological question of an episcopal order as essential to the structure of the Church does not arise in the Book of Discipline.

For the Schools[1]

In the final paragraph of the fifth head it is stated that the 'poore and teachers of the youthead' are to be sustained upon the

---

13 *Infra*, pp. 117 n.9, 118 n.11, 120 n.15, 121 nn.16 and 17.   1 *Infra*, pp. 129ff.

patrimony of the Church;[2] some details are given about the provision to be made for the poor in the rest of the paragraph but nothing is said about the teachers; there follow, as we have seen, the sections on the superintendents. Thereafter we find a number of sections on education which contain the parts of the Book of Discipline most frequently mentioned by writers of Scottish history.

The first three sections are of a more general nature, the remaining six deal exclusively with the universities and are on account of the detailed nature of their provisions more suitably treated as a separate topic.

The opening sentence of the sixth head runs: 'Their two sorts of men, that is to say, the Ministers and the poore, together with the Schooles, when order shall be taken thereanent, must be susteyned upon the charges of the Kirk.'[3] The phrase 'when order shall be taken thereanent' would seem to indicate that at the time it was written the programme of educational reform, although envisaged, had not been produced.

The first brief section entitled 'For the Schooles' states that it is the responsibility of the 'godly Magistrate' to provide for the continuance of the Church in purity and liberty,[4] and that on this account it is necessary for the reformers to offer to them their 'judgments' in this matter. A much longer section follows entitled 'The Necessity of Schooles', the first paragraph of which merely re-states in slightly more elaborate form the necessity 'that your Honours be most careful for the virtuous education and godly upbringing of the youth of this realme'. These two paragraphs in all probability represent the opening paragraphs of two original draft programmes of which only one, or one compiled from the two, remains.

It is considered that 'every several kirk' should have a schoolmaster. If the town is 'of any reputation' he must be able to teach the rudiments and the reading of Latin, if the church is in a rural area the reader or minister must teach the children the catechism and the elements of Latin grammar. Every 'notable town, specially the town of the Superintendent', should have an arts college and a sufficient number of masters to teach 'Logic and Rhetoric and the Tongues', i.e., Latin, Greek, and possibly Hebrew, and one in which provision would be made for the education of the poor. In this way the young would be educated in the presence of

[2] *Infra*, p. 112f.   [3] *Infra*, p. 156.   [4] Introduction, pp. 62ff.

their friends, the 'inconveniences' which can arise from the education of the children away from such home influences would be avoided, the examination of the children in the churches would be helpful in instructing the older members, and the universities would be 'replenished with those that shall bee apt to learning'.

As is indicated in the notes to the text, the programme thus briefly outlined is not original. The Lutheran Churches had from the outset laid considerable emphasis on the education of children, and they in turn were followed by the Swiss reformers. In those Swiss cities especially where there were no mediaeval university foundations there emerged under the new religious and educational influences which were spreading as a result of the work of Sturm in Strasbourg, the arts college.[5] Such a development was taking place in Geneva when Knox was minister of the Congregation of English exiles there, and it is important to note that in Geneva at that time there resided the educational reformer of Nîmes, Claud Baduel, whose work did so much to further the ideas of Sturm among the Reformed Churches of France where the development of arts colleges was most conspicuously successful in the latter half of the sixteenth century.[6] It is not surprising that a similar 'ideal' programme was envisaged for Scotland.

Education was to be provided for all. With more than an echo of the celebrated 'Education Act' of 1496,[7] the reformers state that the rich must be 'compelled' to dedicate their sons 'by good exercise to the profit of the Church and of the Commonwealth' if found suitable. Such schools were to be visited every quarter by the ministers and elders and the best learned men in every town.

The final paragraph of this section briefly summarises the various stages of the educational course; it does not detail the length of time to be spent in them, but emphasises the necessity of laying a basis for everyone in religious knowledge. A more explicit programme of instruction is contained in the separate section entitled 'The Times appointed to every Course', which follows. It is an outline of the familiar progressive educational programme that emanated from Strasbourg and Nîmes, with some minor differences which are indicated in the footnotes to the text. It is highly probable that these two paragraphs represent,

[5] Vuilleumier, *Historie*, 1.394ff; Junod and Meylan, *L'Académie de Lausanne*; Gaufrès, *Claude Baduel*, 11ff; Dunkley, *Reformation in Denmark*, 84f; *infra*, notes to pp. 129ff.   [6] Gaufrès, *Claude Baduel*, 278ff.   [7] *Infra*, p. 132 n.17.

as we have suggested above for the two similar opening paragraphs, two original draft programmes.

Is it possible to assign a date to any part of the educational programme so far provided? There is nothing to indicate that in its essentials the suggested programme could not have been represented in the original report. And its dependence upon the ideas of Sturm and Baduel would suggest that Knox was probably the main author. On the other hand the phrase 'when order shall be taken thereanent', as has been remarked, must be taken into account. There is probably too much uncertainty to allow the assigning of any part of the plan to a particular period, but it may be suggested that in the process of revision the general topic of education was given serious attention for the first time and handed to Knox and Row, who soon became engaged in educational work in Perth,[8] and that the subject of university reform was at the same time entrusted as was most natural to Douglas and Winram, whose entire lives had been spent in university circles.[9]

Unlike the sections which follow on the reform of the universities, there is in those which we have briefly outlined above nothing about the existing educational provisions throughout the country. It must not, however, be concluded that the reformers planned to ignore them. In the later Middle Ages there had been established a number of burgh schools, which had achieved a considerable measure of distinction, there was also a number of elementary or 'sang' schools attached to religious foundations, and proposals had been made for the provision of higher education in Edinburgh and elsewhere. Our knowledge of the burgh schools indicates that they were being influenced by Renaissance educational ideals and that in some of them Greek and possibly Hebrew had been introduced.[10] In these ways a basis already existed for the furthering of the reformers' proposals. Nevertheless, a comprehensive scheme for the whole country and providing for the needs of everyone capable of benefiting from education was lacking and it is primarily such a scheme that the authors of this section of the Book of Discipline provide.

[8] *DNB*, 49.328.

[9] John Douglas was principal of St Mary's College, St Andrews, from 1547 to 1574, and JohnWinram was closely connected with St Leonard's College from his student days in 1513 (along with Douglas) until his death in 1582.

[10] *Infra*, pp. 130f. and notes.

E

The Erection of the Universities[1]

In the sections devoted to university reform a complete reorganisation of the existing three universities is planned. The scheme for St Andrews is given in considerable detail. The three colleges are to be retained, but instead of each offering the same syllabus of courses, as they had been doing, they are to be allocated to different branches of study. Thus the first college is to be responsible for providing the instruction in Dialectic, Mathematics, and Physics in a three-year course leading to graduation in Arts. This course is to be followed by everyone who entered the University. The first college was also to provide for the five-year course in Medicine. The second college was to be responsible for instruction in Moral Philosophy and in Roman and Statute Law. The Moral Philosophy course, which encompassed the study of Ethics, Economics, and Politics, extended to one year, but that in the Laws to four years. The third college was to be responsible for the teaching of Hebrew and Greek and the theological exposition of the Scriptures. Four years of study led to graduation in Laws, and five years of the study of theology to graduation in Divinity.

The arts course which is outlined is that which was normally followed in the universities and which in essentials had remained unchanged in the reformed programmes at Nîmes and Geneva. The significant change is not so much in what was to be taught as in the way it was suggested that the teaching should be conducted. The old system whereby a regent took his pupils through the successive stages of the course leading to examination and graduation was to be replaced by the employment of 'specialist' readers who would be responsible for the particular study of one year only. A development of this nature had been taking place in university education generally, and it is probable that Douglas and Winram, although reared on the old system, were, on account of the humanist influences that had been suggested in the founding of St Mary's College,[2] in favour of the general change.

It is, however, in the suggestions for the third college that the programme is, as was to be expected, most radical. As is indicated in the notes to the text the *Leges* of the recently established Academy at Geneva appear to have been the chief source of inspiration, with their emphasis on the study of the biblical languages and the theological exposition of the Scriptures.

[1] *Infra*, pp. 137ff.   [2] Cant, *University of St Andrews*, 34f.

In the regulation governing entry into the arts college, and to the subsequent stages of higher education, the contemporary regulations of the university provide the pattern of the proposals.

The University of Glasgow, which had been organised around one college from its inception in the middle of the fifteenth century, is, it is suggested, to have two colleges, an arts college as at St Andrews, and a college for the study of Moral Philosophy, Roman and Statute Law, Hebrew, and Divinity. Greek is not mentioned but this is most certainly an oversight. This college was to combine the functions of the second and third colleges at St Andrews. The University at Aberdeen, which had also been organised around one college, was to conform to the plan proposed for Glasgow.

It will be seen that the plans of the reformers would, if carried out, have led to the organisation in Glasgow and Aberdeen of an arts college, on the same lines as that which has been suggested in the previous general section on the reform of education for 'every notable town, and especially in the town of the Superintendent',[3] and that instruction in the higher faculties would have been concentrated in a 'post-graduate' college. The position in St Andrews would have been the same had it not been suggested (probably for the sake of maintaining a balance of studies in the three colleges) that the first or arts college be responsible for the study of Medicine, which, it will be noted, was not to be provided at the other centres.

The remaining paragraphs of the section on the courses of study outline the constitution of the colleges, and of the university. It will be seen from the notes supplied to the text that the existing arrangements in St Leonard's and St Mary's were very much in the minds of the authors, and that their suggestions vary very little from what is known of the statutes and regulations of these colleges, and of the university. There are, however, some surprising omissions; nothing whatever is said of faculty organisation, but this may be accounted for by the assumption that in the new arrangement the Masters of the College would form the 'faculty', and in the same way the absence of the office of the deans may be explained. There is in the final paragraph one sentence which may refer to the faculties. There the authors state that they have said nothing about 'the books to be read in each class and all particular affairs' which they 'refer to the discretion of the

[3] *Infra*, pp. 131f.

Masters, Principals and Regents, with their well-advised Councils'.[4] Decisions about books had certainly been a faculty matter.

The sub-section, entitled 'Of the Stipends and Expenses necessary', in which is detailed in sums of money the amount to be paid to everyone in the university, is one of the most difficult in the entire book on which to comment. A considerable part of the endowment of the colleges in all three centres came from the appropriated teinds of parishes. These sources would no longer be available as the reformers were claiming the return of teinds to their original purpose of supporting the parish ministry. To offset this considerable loss it is suggested that the universities be endowed with the 'rents and revenews of the Bishopricks temporalitie, and of the Kirkes collegiat so far as their ordinary charges shall require'.[5] In the sixth head it is, however, suggested that for 'the upholding of the universities and the sustentation of the Superintendents, the whole revenue of the temporalitie of the Bishops, Deanes and Archdeanes lands and all the rents of lands pertaining to Cathedral kirks' be employed.[6] The two statements are not incompatible, and obvious differences may be explained by the fact that the sections were drawn up by different persons. The main line of argument seems fairly straightforward.

When faced with the problem of providing for the superintendents and the universities the reformers would have to turn to those sources of ecclesiastical revenue which were not being claimed for the support of the parish ministry, and the obvious source was the temporality, that is to say the revenue derived from the leasing or renting of land that had been given in endowment of non-parochial ecclesiastical offices. Those authors concerned with the fixing of the stipends of the superintendents had produced their proposals and had suggested that the actual amounts paid to the superintendents be left to 'the discretion of the Prince and Council'.[7] The reformers concerned with this section on university stipends would have no wish to see the universities impoverished, but it is extremely difficult to compare the stipends proposed for the teaching members of the colleges with that which their predecessors had been receiving under the old order.

The sub-section concludes with statements of the various fees which students who were not bursars would be required to pay

[4] *Infra*, p. 155 and n.76. [5] *Infra*, p. 150.
[6] *Infra*, pp. 161f. [7] *Infra*, p. 110.

to the beadle, an important official in the mediaeval universities, whose office was to continue, and also the fees which would be required from students for the maintenance of the fabric of the buildings. It is noteworthy that the scale of fees differed as they had done in the late Middle Ages in accordance with one's social status.

In mediaeval society the universities shared along with the Church a considerable number of privileges, particularly in juris- diction and in taxation, but the sixteenth-century Protestant reformers on theological grounds had consistently objected to all forms of clerical privilege. It is not therefore surprising to find in this part of the Book of Discipline's educational programme a section on the privileges of the university. No special protection is sought for members of the university if accused of criminal offences, but they could have the services of the rector as an assessor, when summoned before the civil magistrate. In civil action, if the matter was one between members of the university, it could be heard before the rector and his assessors, otherwise the general practice of pursuing in the court of the defender was to be followed. In the matter of exemption from taxation and general civil impositions such as 'charges of war' and the acceptance of responsibilities such as curatorships which would distract them from their function as teachers of the youth, the ancient privileges granted by successive sovereigns from the foundation of the uni- versities were claimed for the rector and 'all inferior members of the University'.

This long and elaborate section on 'the Erection of the Uni- versities' ends with an appeal to the Lords to 'set forward letters in the sort prescribed' and thus bestow upon posterity a treasure of wisdom and learning that would be worthy of greater esteem than any earthly treasure. The ultimate responsibility is laid upon the civil power in exercising what the reformers regard as the 'authority' committed to their charge.

It has already been pointed out that the consideration given to the reform of education and in particular the reform of the uni- versities far exceeds in length and detail that given to almost any other single topic in the Book of Discipline. It need not be argued further that this section as it is found in the final text can hardly have been composed in the brief three weeks at the end of April and the beginning of May in 1560. It could not have been com- posed earlier than the late summer and autumn and could only have been compiled with the knowledge and co-operation of those of the 'revisers' most intimately connected with the University of St Andrews.

THE CIVIL POWER AND THE CHURCH

A Protestant country, according to the reformers, is one which agrees to live in conformity with the Gospel, one which agrees to organise both its civil and its religious life in accordance with the same beliefs. The acceptance of such an understanding is implicit in the action of the Parliament in July–August 1560 in approving of the *Confession of Faith* and thereby agreeing to govern the country in conformity with the exposition of the Christian faith contained in that document. The responsibility towards the Church which such an acceptance places upon the civil government is expressed in the following terms:

> Moreover to Kings, Princes, Rulers, and Magistrates, we affirm that chiefly and most principally the conservation and purgation of Religion appertains; so that not only are they appointed for civil policy, but also for the maintenance of true Religion, and for the suppressing of idolatry and superstition whatsomever, as in David, Jehoshaphat, Hezekiah, Josiah, and others highly commended for their zeal in that case, may be espied.[1]

In this light the authors of the Book of Discipline understand and seek to fulfil their commission. They acknowledge, as we have seen, in the opening lines of the Preface that the Great Council has power to require and command them 'in the name of the eternall God'[2] to set down in writing their proposals for the reformation of religion. They accept that the government has a responsibility for the establishment of true religion, for providing for its maintenance, and for removing all that is held to be contrary to it.[3]

In effecting a religious reformation this executive power is, nevertheless, strictly limited. The Lords have no power to admit 'anything which God's plain word shall not approve', or to reject 'such ordinances as equitie, justice and Gods word do specifie'.[4] In the eyes of the reformers this submission to the Word of God would undoubtedly act as a guiding force upon the exercise of civil power and at the same time would require

---

[1] Cap. XXIV; Dickinson, *Knox's History*, 2.271; Laing, *Knox's Works*, 2.118f.
[2] *Supra*, p. 3, and *infra*, p. 85.   [3] *Infra*, p. 94.   [4] *Infra*, p. 86.

co-operation between the civil power and the ministers as the interpreters of the Scriptures – a fact admitted in the granting to them of the charge to draw up the Book of Discipline. The language used is at times that of petitioners, anxious that their requests be granted, but without any trace of servility. Indeed, frequently the Lords are reminded that certain things are 're-quired' by the reformers, and they are warned in language that may seem somewhat strong for 'humble servitors' that unless they fulfil their responsibility they will bring down upon themselves and upon the country the vengeance of God. It was the fact that in the eyes of Knox the civil power did not remain true to the reformers' understanding of its godly responsibility that led to so much trouble and caused him to insert the Book of Discipline in his *History*.[5]

In line with the statement quoted from the *Confession of Faith* the reformers 'require' the civil power to ensure that Christ Jesus be truly preached, and his sacraments administered throughout the country, that the monuments of idolatry be suppressed, and that the practice of idolatry be removed from the presence of all persons without respect of estate or condition. It is further stated that the Lords have in these respects a responsibility in conjunc-tion with the Church to take steps to remedy the scarcity of ministers. They are required 'in God's name' and by the authority which they have of God to compel men, accepted as suitably qualified by the Church, to undertake the ministry, 'if called by the Church'.[6] In the important matter of electing, examining and admitting of ministers the civil power has, however, no direct or immediate responsibility. These concerns, which pertain to the ecclesiastical government, are handled by the ecclesiastical courts and regulated by them. For example in judging the moral requirements of ministers the Church is not bound to take notice of a civil pardon for a criminal offence by a minister.[7] Neverthe-less it is clearly recognised that in seeking to establish the ministry throughout the country the reformers cannot 'prescribe' to the Lords a 'rule' for distributing the ministers and learned men, but can require them to use their power and authority 'with the consent of the Church' to assign towns and provinces to their 'chiefest workmen'.[8] In thus providing for the needs of the country

[5] *Supra*, pp. 11ff, and *infra*, p. 69; Dickinson, *Knox's History*, 1.373f; Laing, *Knox's Works*, 2.181f.

[6] *Infra*, p. 105.   [7] *Infra*, pp. 100f.   [8] *Infra*, p. 105.

both the civil power and the Church through its courts are seen to exercise complementary functions. Both must be engaged in exercising their respective responsibilities.

At the end of the section on readers there occurs the first marked *additio* inserted as a result of the discussion that took place in January–February, 1561.[9] The Lords 'think' that none be allowed to preach but those found qualified, and that those that are already preachers and not found qualified by the superintendent are to be placed as readers. At first sight it may seem that this suggestion of the Lords was only intended to prevent readers from becoming exhorters without examination by the superintendent, but it is capable of a wider application in that it sought to give to the superintendent a personal responsibility and power in the examination of candidates for admission as ministers. If this broad interpretation is what the Lords intended then their suggestion must be regarded as inconsistent with the earlier statements about examination which was to be conducted by the 'men of soundest judgment' in 'the principal town next adjacent' to them. In support of this broad interpretation is the statute passed by the 'Superintendent and holl ministrie, wyth consayll of the Provest of Sanctandrois, Rector and chief members of the Universitie' on 25th April 1561, empowering the superintendent in his visitation to try every minister, exhorter and reader already placed, and declaring that in future the examination be appointed by the superintendent.[10] It is to be noted that the addition qualifies what the authors have already proposed and provides evidence that the Lords considered that it was within their power to make such a modification of their programme.

As the protector of the Church, it is held to be the responsibility of the civil government 'to set the oppressed Church at freedom and liberty' by assuring to her the full enjoyment of her traditional income. The authors, therefore, 'require' that adequate provision be made for the maintenance of the ministry, for the support of the poor, and for the furtherance of education 'out of that which is called the patrimony of the Church'.[11] The reformed Church, it is claimed, should be put in direct possession of the patrimony, much of which had been secularised or appropriated for other than ecclesiastical uses, and should have, through the locally elected 'Deacons and Treasurers', control over its use

---

[9] *Infra*, pp. 107, and *supra*, p. 22.

[10] St *AKSR*, 1.75.   [11] *Infra*, pp. 108, 112, 156.

and distribution. To this latter proposal the agreement of the Lords is recorded.[12] It was not envisaged at this stage that the civil power would be directly involved in the financial affairs of congregations. The Privy Council was to be responsible for the fixing of the stipend of the superintendent.[13] Further, it is interesting to find that some of the Lords supported the 'return' of manses and glebes to ministers,[14] although these, so far as has been discovered, were not guaranteed to the Church by statute, but by canon law.[15] The objection of four of the earls is noted in an addition, which provides the first indication of opposition. The section also indicates that the Lords by 'concluding' that a number of the small teinds and exactions which had been particularly oppressive should not be taken, considered it within their power to determine the range of ecclesiastical dues.[16] The local Church was also to be responsible for the care of the poor and the provision of education as these were universally recognised charges upon the patrimony of the Church. In making arrangements for fulfilling both of these commitments the civil power was expected to attend to the advice of the ministers and make legally binding arrangements.

In the eyes of the reformers the acceptance of the authority of Scriptures puts the civil power under an obligation to bring civil law and civil penalties into conformity with the requirements of Scripture,[17] but at the same time requires the exercise of discipline by the Church. Open transgressors of God's law, such as those guilty of blasphemy, adultery and murder should be punished with death, but the punishment of less serious offences is held to 'appertaine to the kirk of God'.[18] Such punishment, carried out in accordance with a detailed procedure, is to be meted out to offenders whatever their 'estate' and leads to excommunication pronounced by the minister at the command of the Church. It is also to be pronounced upon offenders whom the civil power has neglected to punish. Both types of offender, however, can if repentant be received back into the fellowship of the Church.

The exercise of an independent ecclesiastical discipline had been a matter of considerable concern and controversy on the Continent and lines of demarcation had been difficult to define. The authors of the Book of Discipline make it clear that in this matter

[12] *Infra*, p. 158 n.x.   [13] *Infra*, p. 110.   [14] *Infra*, p. 163 n.h.

[15] *Infra*, p. 162 n.41.   [16] *Infra*, p. 157 n.m.

[17] *Infra*, pp. 165ff.   [18] *Infra*, pp. 166f.

the Church has its rights and the Lords by their consent which is noted in the margin give them the assurance of their support.[19]

In the matter of ecclesiastical administration or policy considerable freedom is claimed for the local Church, and the function of the civil power is again thought of as lending official support to the suggested arrangements, for example by enjoining strict observance of Sunday.[20] It is not envisaged that the state should be actively engaged in these matters except where the Church fails, for example, in requiring that parents educate themselves and their children in the faith,[21] or in securing that men with suitable qualifications attend the Exercise.[22]

Throughout the Book of Discipline the reformers stress the responsibility of the state to God to bring the laws of the country into conformity with the law of God as revealed in Scripture, and to support the worship of God, and at the same time uphold the right of the Church to make such demands. This aspect of the reformers' understanding is, perhaps, most clearly seen in the concluding sections of the Book. The state must uphold and maintain the divine ordinance of marriage; it must act with the Church in the best interests of those who wish to marry, and if need be, be prepared after examination of the case to support one side against the other if there is a conflict between children and parents. The state must punish adulterers with death, but if in this matter it fails in its responsibility, the Church must proceed to excommunication.[23]

The state must see that churches are kept in good repair and that those responsible fulfil their obligations in these matters;[24] and that severe penalties be provided for those who in any way profane the sacraments.[25]

In the three digressions or interpolations the areas of responsibility of the civil power are again clearly marked. The Lords' responsibility for the evangelisation of the country is furthered by nominating certain preachers as superintendents and assigning them to their dioceses.[26] It is, however, envisaged that in time the nomination by the civil government will give way to local nomination and a freer election. Those nominated to this office are subject to ecclesiastical discipline and are not independent of the church courts and can only be transferred from one area to

---

[19] *Infra*, pp. 167, 171.   [20] *Infra*, p. 191.   [21] *Infra*, p. 186

[22] *Infra*, p. 191.   [23] *Infra*, pp. 191ff.   [24] *Infra*, pp. 202ff.

[25] *Infra*, pp. 210f.   [26] *Infra*, pp. 123f.

another, or relieved of their responsibility, by ecclesiastical authorisation. It is clearly anticipated that ultimately the Church and not the state should select and control its 'chiefest workmen'.[27]

State support for education is also part of the godly magistrates' office and is to be given in the interests of both the Church and the Commonwealth. In this matter the Church expects the state to support it in its efforts to provide a suitable education for every child according to his capacity to learn and irrespective of the child's social or economic background. 'If God shall move your hearts to establish and execute this order and put these things in practice', the authors continue, 'your whole Realm, we doubt not, within few years, will serve itsself of true preachers, and of other officers necessary for the commonwealth.'[28] Similarly in the detailed plans for the university reform the Lords are expected to further by their 'authority' what is proposed.[29]

In the attitude which they adopt towards the state and in their understanding of the civil government's responsibilities to the Church the authors of the Book of Discipline are in full agreement with the teaching of many of the Continental reformers and in particular with those of the Reformed Churches. Their ideal is the establishment of a Christian commonwealth in which both the civil and the ecclesiastical powers co-operate in the cultivation of true religion. Given this understanding of the relation between the two powers it is not difficult to understand why Knox and his fellow reformers repeatedly requested the acceptance of the Book of Discipline by the Estates in the same way as the *Confession of Faith* had been accepted. It is also easy to understand today why he found it impossible to accept Queen Mary as long as she retained her Roman Catholic faith. The inconsistency of supporting the Catholic Queen as sovereign and maintaining at the same time the Reformed Church, although an essential deduction from the doctrine embodied in the Book of Discipline, was but tardily recognised.

THE CHURCH AND CHURCH COURTS

The word 'church'[1] is used in the Book of Discipline, as in Christian terminology generally, to signify the Christian com-

---

[27] *Infra*, pp. 125ff.   [28] *Infra*, 135.   [29] *Infra*, p. 154.
[1] From the use of the words 'Church' and 'Kirk' in both the Laing MS and the 1621 edition no satisfactory conclusion can be drawn. See *infra*, p. 85 n. *f*.

munity at the parochial or congregational level, and to refer to
the collective Christian community of a larger area, extending to
the whole country but possible also of a still wider application.

In the reformers' scheme the congregation, or local manifesta-
tion of the wider Christian community, is of fundamental
importance. It possesses the true notes or marks of the universal
or catholic Church, the preaching of the Word, the administration of the Sacraments, and the exercise of godly discipline, and
for their exercise must be provided with a 'ministry'. This term
is sometimes used in a restricted sense referring only to the
ministers of Word and Sacraments, but frequently it is employed
to denote the local ecclesiastical administration or organisation or
court, and consists of the minister or ministers and the elders and
deacons.[2] The part played by the congregation in electing those
who exercise this ministry is given considerable attention and,
while the congregation may have a minister presented to it, it is
given unqualified freedom to elect annually its own elders and
deacons by whatever method it decides to adopt.[3] Further, whenever important issues arise, for example, the final decision in a
matter of excommunication or the settlement of some local
financial problem, the congregation is required to assume responsibility and the ministry is compelled to act as the executive of the
congregation's wishes.[4]

Extensive as the powers and responsibilities of the congregation
are, it is never regarded as independent of its neighbouring congregations and in particular of the church of the most notable
town of the district. In its relation to this 'greater' church the
local church is sometimes spoken of as the 'inferior' church.[5]

The church of the most important town, the 'best reformed
church' of the area, although itself a parochial church with its own
locally elected ministry and congregational responsibilities, is also
the 'church of the superintendent', and as such exercises with him
through its 'council' a measure of oversight of the other churches
of the area.[6] In the examination of candidates for the ministry of
Word and Sacraments, whether they be first put forward by the
congregations or are to be presented to them by the superintendent
and his council, it plays a prominent and determinative part.
Every year this council is to receive reports on the life and work
of the ministers of local congregations through one elder and one

---

[2] See *StAKSR*, I.xxiii ff, and *infra*, p. 179.   [3] *Infra*, pp. 174ff.

[4] *Infra*, pp. 170, 163.   [5] *Infra*, pp. 99f, f. 177   [6] *Infra*, pp. 97ff, 177.

deacon elected for the purpose.[7] Indeed, it would appear that the 'greater church' was expected to provide through its ministry an area or diocesan court for the assistance of the superintendent in the exercise of his duties. Such a court, however, should not be confused with the pre-Reformation synod, although we may here detect, as has been pointed out, the embryo of the later synod.[8] Synods had been by this time successfully introduced into the reformed Churches of Switzerland and were beginning to occupy a place of considerable importance in the reformed Church of France, therefore it is a little surprising that there is no specific mention of this court in the Book of Discipline.

As the Scottish reformers were asked to provide plans for the whole country it is also surprising to find that no attention is given in their report to the composition and organisation of an ecclesiastical court at the national level. The first indication of the existence of such a body is encountered in the section of the fourth head which deals with the admission of ministers. There it is stated that a minister once admitted to a charge cannot be transferred at will but that 'the whole Church, or the most part thereof, for just considerations may transferre a minister from one Church to another'.[9] The same phrase occurs again in the designating of the areas proposed for the various superintendents. A change was effected in one of the dioceses 'by the consent of the whole Kirk'.[10] The phrase receives amplifications in the following section where it is stated that superintendents cannot be transferred from one diocese to another 'without the consent of the whole counsell of the Kirk'.[11] Still further light is shed when it is stated that the superintendent must present the audited accounts of the congregations of his diocese to 'the great councell of the Kirk'.[12] This 'great council' is again mentioned in an *additio* to the section on burial which permits to congregations some liberty to follow a different procedure from that laid down, provided they are ready 'to answeir to God, and [the] Assemblie of the Universale Kirk gathered within the Realme'.[13] The Book of Discipline has, however, nothing further to say of this court or of its relation to the civil government. As will have been noticed the references to it are all of an incidental character.

Of the later graded system of ecclesiastical courts, with the

[7] *Infra*, p. 177. [8] *Infra*, p. 177, n.17. [9] *Infra*, p. 103.
[10] *Infra*, p. 120. [11] *Infra*, p. 127. [12] *Infra*, p. 164.
[13] *Infra*, p. 200 n.*b*; Donaldson, *Scottish Reformation*, 136f, 149ff; Shaw, *General Assemblies*, 19ff.

exception of the kirk session, the Book of Discipline presents but a dim foreshadowing. In 1561 the reformation of the Church in Scotland was only beginning to emerge as a national movement. Having proposed that the old episcopal administration be largely discarded it had no ready-made organisation at hand to meet the needs of the country as a whole. The emergence of such a new scheme would depend to a considerable extent on developments in the civil government. Certain principles can, nevertheless, be discerned in the Book of Discipline which were to prove normative and which were to receive a more detailed elaboration at later stages in the course of the Church's history. A considerable measure of freedom is given to the local congregation through its ministry to exercise a wide range of responsibilities. Secondly, a prudential oversight of a reasonably sized area is entrusted to the superintendent, who in addition to his visitation of the parishes is assisted in his office by the ministry of his chief town, which can be augmented by representatives of the other churches. Thirdly, final authority in a number of issues that might affect the Church and the country as a whole is in principle reserved for a supreme council or assembly 'of the Universal Kirk gathered within the Realm', that is, of that part of the Catholic Church which exists within the national boundaries.

THE 'REJECTION' OF THE BOOK OF DISCIPLINE

The extent to which the Book of Discipline was implemented has often been underestimated. By including it in his *History* 'to the end that the posterities to come may judge as well what the wordlings refused, as what Policy the godly Ministers required'[1] Knox may be regarded as having greatly contributed to this understanding of what happened. The fact that the Convention had failed to meet the wishes of the ministers by having the Book of Discipline accepted in the same way as the Confession of Faith had been accepted, did not mean, at least in the eyes of the ruling party who had approved it, that they did not intend in the spring of 1561 to carry out its proposals within the terms of their subscription. Indeed the evidence that is available points in the opposite direction.

[1] Dickinson, *Knox's History*, 1.373f; Laing, *Knox's Works*, 2.181f.

The authors of the Book had laid the responsibility of nominating the superintendents upon the civil power, and the evidence which we have about the nomination of the five superintendents, although not as complete as could be wished, shows that this was accomplished by the Privy Council at the end of February or early in March. The preamble to the 'mandate' from the Council for the election of John Spottiswoode as Superintendent of Lothian, dated 10th March 1560[61] refers to the fact that the Book of Discipline had been approved by the Lords of Secret Council and then goes on to charge Spottiswoode to fulfil his duties.[2] It will be seen on comparing the 'mandate' with the Book of Discipline that the Privy Council 'required' that the Church be organised in accordance with its programme. The Superintendent was to see that within every parish elders, deacons and 'utheris officars' were appointed and their offices discharged; that every minister was suitably qualified to fulfil his responsibilities; that every minister was 'sufficientlie provydit of thair levings'; that the manses and glebes were made available to the ministers; that the parish churches were repaired; and that the parishioners attended the worship of God. Further he was to try all faults committed within his diocese and to have them redressed; to seek out those who contravened the act of Parliament prohibiting the saying or hearing of Mass and the administration of the sacraments by men not 'admittit thairto', and report them to the Lords.

Spottiswoode, in his 'circular letter' dated 22nd March 1560[61] writes in similar fashion and, as was to be expected, commands the parishioners 'in the name of God, and of the secreit consale, oure present and lauchfull magistratis', to fulfil their responsibilities, to elect elders and deacons, to repair the Church, to exercise discipline over the members, and in general to comply with the Acts of Parliament and the Book of Discipline 'laitlie admittit'.[3]

The edict for the election of John Winram as Superintendent of St Andrews, dated 20th March 1560[61], which in all probability embodies the common style that was used in the other cases, also refers to the fact that 'ane gret part of the consail, nobilitie and estatis' had received, perused and approved the Book of Reformation and states that after giving their 'approbacion' the

[2] Donaldson, *Scottish Reformation*, 226f.
[3] Donaldson, *Scottish Reformation*, 227f.

Secreit Council had proceeded to carry out its requests by nominating the five superintendents.[4] Every indication is given in the edict that the procedure which the Church is to follow is that of the Book of Discipline. Further, an examination of 'The Form and Order of the Election of Superintendents', which was used at the election and admission of Spottiswoode and which was to serve in the election of the others (it should be noted, Knox planned to insert it in his *History* immediately after the account of the Convention of January–February), is likewise in complete conformity with the reformers' proposals.[5]

All these related documents demonstrates that those who were in charge of the civil government of the country and who had approved the Book of Discipline regarded themselves as bound by their subscription to discharge its provisions and took certain measures toward that end. That the Book of Discipline was binding and that it was placed on a par with the acts of the previous Parliament is implicit in all the documents mentioned, but perhaps is most clearly evident in Spottiswoode's 'circular letter'.

As will be seen from the notes supplied to the text the Book of Discipline became the pattern for local church organisation. Although it took some considerable time before every parish was provided with elders and deacons, there was no attempt throughout the rest of the century to provide any other form of local government. At the local level the only really significant departure in the years immediately following was the recognition of the patron's rights and it may be doubted if many elections of parish ministers took place exactly as the reformers planned.[6]

As we have seen only five superintendents were appointed, but the Church did not abandon the proposal. Repeatedly it requested that the vacant offices be filled and did not automatically recognise conforming bishops such as Alexander Gordon of Galloway or Adam Bothwell of Orkney as superintendents. For most of those areas that remained unprovided by the Privy Council the Church through the General Assembly appointed 'Commissioners' empowered to exercise superintendent's responsibilities, and although these officials were appointed for one year and were required to report to each general assembly they tended to be re-elected and seem to have been superintendents in all but

4 *StAKSR*, 1.72ff.
5 Dickinson, *Knox's History*, 1.355 n. 2, 2.273ff; Laing, *Knox's Works*, 2.143ff.
6 Donaldson, *Scottish Reformation*, 117.

name.[7] Despite the failure of the civil power to carry out these particular proposals in the precise terms of the Book of Discipline, – and that failure was due very largely to the unsettled political situation and the need to devise a more practical financial programme than that put forward by the reformers – the basic pattern of ecclesiastical organisation envisaged by those who drew up the Book of Discipline continued to be followed, until modified by the Convention of Leith in 1572.

In the matter of educational reform although considerable time was required before the authors' ideal of a school in every parish was fulfilled, the proposal was never abandoned. From what evidence is available it is clear that in many places within a short space of time not only were parish schools established or re-established in which instruction was given in 'grammar and the Latin tongue', but some important towns went further and provided at least the beginnings of a college for the study of the arts and the tongues including Greek and Hebrew. Although the development of the 'arts college', which was one of the most notable features of the contemporary French Protestant Church,[8] did not fully materialise in Scotland, it should not be forgotten that the University of Edinburgh in part owes its development to the Reformation ideal[9] as does more directly the foundation of Marischal College in New Aberdeen.[10]

The plans for the reformation of the ancient universities were, as has been seen, drawn up in great detail. Repeated attempts were made to have them carried out, or at least to have something done about the universities, and to this end several commissions were appointed. It was not, however, until the late seventies that anything of significance was accomplished. Nevertheless it is not difficult to discern in the proposals that were made and eventually carried out the basic principles contained in the Book of Discipline.[11]

In presenting their 'judgments' to the Lords the reformers wished to have the laws of the land brought into line with the law of God. In particular they desired not merely the abolition of religious practices which they regarded as incompatible with

[7] *Infra*, pp. 117ff; Donaldson, *Scottish Reformation*, 128f.

[8] Bourchenin, *Les Académies Protestantes*.

[9] Horn, *University of Edinburgh*, 3ff.   [10] Henderson, *Marischal College*, 44ff.

[11] Cant, *University of St Andrews*, 44ff; Mackie, *University of Glasgow*, 66ff; Rait, *Universities of Aberdeen*, 105ff.

F

the reformed faith, but the legal enforcement of the new requirements of moral and religious observance. Although little was done
at the national level that was regarded by Knox as sufficient, the
Kirk session records testify that there was considerable support
from the civil magistrate at the local level in the enforcement of a
rigorous discipline.

In their approval of the Book of Discipline, as has been noted,
the Lords had specifically stated that they wished those who
presently were benefice holders and who were prepared to accept
the Reformed faith to be allowed to retain the bulk of their
ecclesiastical revenues provided they made available sufficient
funds for the support of the reformed ministry. It seems that they
did not reject in principle at any rate the reformers' claim to
the patrimony of the Church, and consequently that where the
teinds were held by someone not capable of exercising the reformed ministry provision would be made by the benefice holder
during his lifetime, and in time the Church would acquire
possession.

The full implications of such an arrangement must, however,
have become obvious fairly soon. In claiming the entire teinds
the reformers were demanding too much, and although some
staunch supporters of the Reformation among the benefice
holders did make some sort of provision for ministers, the Church
experienced acute financial distress, and it became obvious that
other measures would have to be adopted. For some time the
Church had to be satisfied with payment made out of the thirds of
Benefices, and it was not until the reign of Charles I that the
Church was brought into possession of the teinds, and an adequate endowment provided.[12]

From the outset the reformers were aware of the significance of
their financial proposals.[13] In many ways they seem almost to
have foreseen that they would be set aside; nevertheless, for a
time they persisted. In the end they failed to gain the support they
sought, but this was virtually the only part of the Book of Discipline that was rejected. In the years that followed January 1561
modifications were made in the application of some details proposed in other parts and of the most important of these developments an attempt has been made to give some indication in the
notes; they are generally of a minor nature. That the 'judgments'

[12] Donaldson, *Thirds*, viii ff; Donaldson, *Scottish Reformation*, 68ff.
[13] *Infra*, p. 209.

of those commissioned to report on the 'Reformation of Religion' in Scotland profoundly affected the life of Scotland and the polity of its Church from the sixteenth century onwards must be obvious to all acquainted with its history.

THE TEXTS AND THE METHOD OF EDITING

The only extant manuscript version, as far as is known, of the Book of Discipline is contained in the manuscript of John Knox's History of the Reformation in Scotland (MS 1566) now preserved in the Laing collection in Edinburgh University Library.[1] This manuscript was carefully studied by the late Professor W. Croft Dickinson and is fully described by him in the Introduction to his edition of the History.[2] Dickinson's conclusions about that part of the manuscript which contains the Book of Discipline may be summarised in the following way.

A recension of the Book of Discipline originally occupied part of two quires of the History and all of one other (quires XII, XIV, and XIII). In the course of the completion of the main work a manuscript of the Book of Discipline containing the comments and observations of 'the Lords' came into Knox's hands and he decided to insert it in the History in place of the earlier version. In order to do so that quire which contained the central portion of the Book of Discipline and nothing else, and of which it was the major part, was simply replaced by the corresponding quire of the newly acquired manuscripts, but the other two quires which contained additional material had to be rewritten. Dickinson adduced evidence for dating this central quire to 1560–61, but did not go as far as Laing in regarding it as 'probably a portion of the copy which was laid before the convention in January 1561'.[3] There is, however, every reason for accepting the text of the Book of Discipline contained in MS 1566 and printed by Laing in his edition of Knox's Works[4] and by Dickinson in his 'modern' edition of the History[5] as representing the earliest and best authenticated text.

---

[1] Laing, *Works*, 1.xxx ff; Dickinson, *History*, 1.xcv ff.

[2] *History*, 1.xcv–cix.

[3] *History*, 1.cii f; Laing, *Works*, 2.201 n.2.

[4] *Works*, 2.183–260.

[5] *History*, 2.280–325.

The first printed edition of the full text of the Book of Discipline appeared in 1621 and although it carried no imprint it has been attributed to Leiden[6] and to Amsterdam.[7] There seem to be good bibliographical grounds for believing that it may have been printed by the press of the exiled English Church to which has also been attributed David Calderwood's *Altare Damascenum*[8] and which may during the years 1616 to 1620 have been responsible for printing some of the works of Henry Ainsworth.[9] The preparing of this edition of the Book of Discipline for the press has been attributed to David Calderwood.[10]

The edition of 1621 was reprinted down to the nineteenth century[11] and was used by Laing in his notes to the relevant portion of Knox's *History*. It is this text which is reproduced in this work; it has been taken from the copy preserved in the University Library, St Andrews.[12]

Every attempt has been made to see that the text has been accurately followed. The original spelling has been retained except in the case of the letter 'j' which is given the consonantal form throughout although no uniform practice was followed in the text. In the textual footnotes all instances where the text is at variance with that of Laing's manuscript have been noted and the manuscript reading given. It will be seen that in many instances the variant reading of the text has been due to an attempt to provide a more readily understood reading and that the 'alterations' are often of little or no consequence. In a few cases it will be clear that the editor of the 1621 text has erred or has had a faulty text in front of him, and in a very small number of instances the printed text although it has been retained must for a correct

[6] *British Museum Cat.* (1955), vol. 217, col. 194.

[7] St Andrews University Library, MS catalogue of Printed Books.

[8] *British Museum Cat.* (1955), vol. 52, col. 555. See further Harris, R. and S. K. Jones, *The Pilgrim Press*, Cambridge, 1922.

[9] *British Museum Cat.* (1955), vol. 2. col. 956. and vol. 17, col. 512.

[10] Laing, *Works*, 2.183 n. 1; *British Museum Cat.* (1955), vol. 217, col. 194. It should be noted that Calderwood, in his *History* (2.51), seems to have intended to have included the Book of Discipline but in fact only gives the first line of the Preface and the title and first line of the first head and then goes on to include extracts from the *Forme of Prayers* (cf. Laing, *Works*, 4.174ff, and 6.293ff).

[11] The 1621 edition was reprinted in 1641 in London by J. Sweeting and again in 1647. In the eighteenth century it was edited and printed in *A Collection of Confessions of Faith . . . of the Church of Scotland*, vol. 2, pp. 515–608. This edition is attributed to W. Dunlop and has a title page dated Edinburgh 1721. It was reproduced and published at Edinburgh in 1836.

[12] Typ. (NA.C21.JC).

understanding of the document be rejected in favour of that found in the Laing manuscript. These instances have all been specially noted. Any word added for the sake of clarity is placed within square brackets.

In the historical and exegetical notes an attempt has been made not only to comment on the text and to point to similar statements in contemporary writings but also to give some indication of the ways in which many of the practical suggestions of the reformers were implemented especially in the period 1560 to 1572.

This map published about 1568 is thought to be the first map of Scotland printed alone. It is based on a map by Sebastian Ré published in 1558 and which probably most nearly represents contemporary geographical knowledge. It is reproduced in *The Scottish Geographical Magazine*, vol. 35 (1919), p.41, and in *The Early Maps of Scotland*, edited for the Royal Scottish Geographical Society, second edition Edinburgh, 1936, plate 3.

TEXT AND COMMENTARY

✳✳✳✳

THE FIRST AND

SECOND BOOKE OF DISCIPLINE.

Together with some

ACTS OF THE GENERALL ASSEMBLIES,

Clearing and confirming the same : And

AN ACT OF PARLIAMENT.

Exod. 25. 9.
According to all that I shew thee, after the paterne of the Tabernacle, and the paterne of all the instruments therof, even so shall yee make it.

Printed Anno 1621.

CONTENTS

The Preface

To the Great Councell of Scotland now admitted to the Regiment,[1] by the providence of God, and by the common consent of the Estates thereof,[2] Your Honours humble servitors and ministers of Christ Jesus within the same, wish grace, mercy, and peace from God the Father of our Lord Jesus Christ, with the perpetuall increase of the holy Spirit.

From your Honours we received a charge[3] dated at Edinburgh the 29. of April, in the yeare of our Lord*a* 1560, requiring and commanding us in the name of the eternall God, as we will answer in his presence, to commit to writing, and in a book deliver*b* to your wisedomes our judgements touching the reformation of Religion which heretofore in this Realme (as in others) hath been utterly corrupted: upon the receit whereof (so many of us as were in this towne[4]) did convene, and in unitie of minde doe offer unto your wisedomes these subsequents*c* for common order and uniformitie to bee observed in this realme concerning doctrine, administration of Sacraments, election*d* of Ministers, provision for their sustentation,*e* Ecclesiasticall discipline and policie of the

a of God   *b* to deliver unto   *c* Headis subsequent
d-e These words are in fact in the Laing MS. despite the statement made to the contrary by Laing (*Knox's Works*, 2.184), and followed by Dickinson (*Knox's History*, 2.280).

[1] A 'Great Council of the Realm' was set up by the Lords of the Congregation – 'the Nobilitie, Barones and Provost of Burrowes' – on 21st October 1559 to undertake the government of the country in place of the Queen Regent, whom they professed by solemn proclamation to have 'suspended' until the next Parliament. (Laing, *Knox's Works*, 1.444ff; Dickinson, *Knox's History*, 1.251ff, 2.280 n.; Donaldson, *James V to James VII*, 97.)

[2] The bishops were not party to the transference of the regent's power. The Act of Suspension was signed by the 'Nobolity and Commons of the Protestants of the Churche of Scotland'. See further Laing, *Knox's Works*, 1.449 n., and Dickinson, *Knox's History*, 1.255 n.

[3] *i.e.*, from the Great Council, but in particular from the Protestant Lords who had signed the band on 27th April in Edinburgh. (Laing, *Knox's Works*, 2.61ff; Dickinson, *Knox's History*, 1.314ff; see further Introduction, pp. 3f.)

[4] *i.e.*, Edinburgh, see *infra*, p. 209.

Church;[f] Most humbly requiring your Honours, that as you look for participation with Christ Jesus, that neither ye admit any thing which Gods plain word shalnot approve, neither yet that ye shall reject such ordinances as equitie, justice and Gods word do specifie. For as we will not bind your wisedomes to our judgements further than wee are able to prove[g] by Gods plaine Scriptures: so must we most humbly crave of you, even as ye will answer in Gods presence (before whom both ye and we must appeare to render accounts of all our facts) that ye repudiate nothing for pleasure and[h] affection of men, which ye be not able to improve by Gods written and revealed word.[5]

[f] Laing MS has throughout quire XII (see Introduction, p. 75, and *Knox's Works*, 2.201 n.2) *Kirk* or *Kirkis* where the 1621 text has *Church(e)* or *Churches*. See further *infra*, p. 113 note *d*. A few exceptions are noted as they occur.

[g] *prove the same*   [h] *nor*

[5] A similar statement is found in the Preface to the *Confession of Faith*. Knox had previously upheld this doctrine in *A Vindication of the Doctrine that the Sacrifice of the Mass is Idolatry*. An attempt to have this statement put into practice was made in a discussion held in Edinburgh in January 1561. (Laing, *Knox's Works*, 2.96, 138ff; 3.31ff; Dickinson, *Knox's History*, 2.258, 1.352ff; see also Ridley, *Knox*, 95f; and *infra*, pp. 208f.)

THE FIRST HEAD

Of Doctrine

Seeing that Christ Jesus is he whom God the Father hath commanded onely to bee heard and followed of his sheepe, wee judge[a] it necessary that his Gospell[b] be truely and openly preached in every Church and Assembly of this realme, and that all doctrine repugnant[c] to the same, be utterly repressed[d] as damnable to mans salvation.[1]

The Explication of the First Head

Lest that upon this[e] generalitie ungodly men take occasion to cavill, this we adde for explication. By preaching of the Gospell we understand not onely the Scriptures of the new Testament, but also of the old, to wit, the Law, Prophets, and Histories, in which Christ Jesus is no lesse contained in figure, then we have him now expressed in veritie.[2] And therefore with the Apostle we affirme that 'all Scripture inspired of God is profitable to instruct,' to reprove, and to exhort.[3] In which bookes of old and new Testaments, we affirme that all thing[f] necessary for the instruction of the Church, and to make the man of God perfect, is contained and sufficiently expressed.[4]

[a] *urge*   [b] *Evangell* and throughout unless noted to the contrary
[c] *repugnyng*   [d] *suppressed*   [e] *Least upone this our*   [f] *thingis*

[1] The preaching of the Gospel was, in Protestant theology the first 'note' or 'mark' of the Church. The necessity of two marks, the preaching of the Gospel and the administration of the Sacraments, had been set out by Luther in a tract against Papal supremacy written during his period at the Wartburg. This doctrine was later embodied in the Augsburg Confession and subsequently followed by Calvin. Later reformed theologians sometimes added as a third mark the exercise of ecclesiastical discipline. (Rupp, *The Righteousness of God*, 310ff; Calvin, *Institutes*, 4.1.9, with notes in *LCC* and Benoit editions; cf. *The XXXIX Articles of the Church of England*, Article XIX; *Forme of Prayers* 1556; Laing, *Knox's Works*, 4.172; *Confession of Faith*, cap. XVIII.)

[2] This point was strongly emphasised by both Luther and Calvin. (See for example Kramm, *The Theology of Martin Luther*, 106; Wallace, *Calvin's Doctrine of the Word and Sacrament*, 8ff, 27ff.)

[3] Cf. 2 Timothy 3.16.

[4] The doctrine of the 'sufficiency of Scripture' is similarly expressed in the *Confession of Faith*, cap. XVIII. See also Wallace, *Calvin's Doctrine of the Word and Sacrament*, 99 n.2.

By the contrary doctrine we understand whatsoever men by lawes, counsells, or constitutions[5] have imposed upon the consciences of men, without the expressed commandment of Gods word, such as be the vowes of chastitie, forswearing of marriage,[6] binding of men and women to several and disguised apparrells,[7] to the superstitious observation of fasting dayes, difference of meat for conscience sake,[8] prayer for the dead,[9] and keeping of holy dayes of certaine Saints commanded by man, such as be all those that the Papists have invented, as the feasts (as they terme them) of the Apostles, Martyres, Virgines, of Christmasse, Circumcision, Epiphanie, Purification, and other fond feastes of our Ladie:[10] which things because in Gods Scriptures they neither

[5] A general reference to the main components of canon law.

[6] The vow of chastity, which forbids all voluntary sexual pleasure, strictly speaking differs (though in ordinary language the expressions may be synonymous) from the vow of celibacy or abstinence from marriage. See further *Cath. Ency.*, 12.752ff, 15.514f. For the teaching of the reformers on both topics see Calvin, *Institutes*, 4.12.23–28, 4.13.8–19 with notes in *LCC* edition.

[7] Distinctive religious dress was worn by all members of the old orders, monks, friars and nuns, and by all clergy in the Middle Ages.

[8] The reformers were not opposed to the celebration of fast days or to fasting but to the 'superstitious' observance of them as 'works of merit'. See further Calvin, *Institutes*, 4.12.19–21.

[9] Belief in purgatory and in prayer for the dead were rejected by reformers and formed popular topics of controversy. See for example Calvin, *Institutes*, 3.5.10 with notes in *LCC* edition.

[10] This rigorous attitude to the celebration of the festivals associated with the events of Christ's life was not that of Lutherans or of all reformed Churches, although the citizens of Geneva in 1550 in General Council pronounced 'un edict de l'abrogation de toutes les festes, reservant le jour du dimenche, comme il est ordoné de Dieu'. The attitude of the Scottish reformers was made perfectly clear in 1566 in a well-known reply to the Swiss Churches in which approval was given to the *Second Helvetic Confession* with the exception of the passage 'concerning the "festival of our Lord's nativity, circumcision, passion, resurrection, ascension and sending the Holy Ghost upon his disciples" '. 'These festivals', the letter continued, 'at the present time obtain no place among us, for we dare not religiously celebrate any other feast-day among us than what the divine oracles have prescribed.' The abolition of the observance of the Christian festivals was not, however, easily accomplished. It would appear from the *Register of the Privy Council* in 1566 that in Glasgow the Communion was normally celebrated at Easter. In 1574 so anxious were the citizens of Dumfries for the observance of Christmas that, when the minister and reader refused to conduct a service that day, they themselves procured a reader for the occasion. In the same year John Douglas, Archbishop of St Andrews, along with the kirk session denounced those who had been observing 'superstitious dayis and spetialie of Zwil-day' and ordained that Sunday only should be kept 'haly day'. The General Assembly in the following year petitioned the Privy Council that the celebration of Christmas and other festivals be abolished and a civil penalty meted out against those who observed them in any way. (Bergier, *Registres*, 1.74; *Zürich Letters*, 362ff; *RPC Scot.*, 1.492; Laing, *Knox's*

have commandement nor assurance,[11] we judge them utterly to be abolished from this Realme: affirming farther that the obstinate maintainers and teachers of such abhominations ought not to escape the punishment of the civill Magistrate.[12]

Works, 6.547f; *BUK*, 1.90, 334, 387; *StAKSR*, 1.387ff; and index *sub* Yule. See also Cowan, 'The Five Articles of Perth' in Shaw, *Reformation and Revolution*, 163f, and McMillan, *Worship*, 299ff; and *infra*, p. 183, note 15.)

[11] The limitation of the power of the Church by the Word of God with reference to the topics mentioned in this paragraph had been discussed at length by Calvin in *Institutes*, 4.8 and 9.

[12] On the relation of the civil magistrate to the Church as expressed in the Book of Discipline see Introduction, pp. 62ff. This first head is reminiscent of much that is contained in Martin Bucer, *De Regno Christi*, 1.5; see further, *Martini Buceri*, 15.54ff.

G

THE SECOND HEAD

Of Sacraments

To Christ Jesus his holy Gospell truely preached, of necessity it is, that his holy Sacraments be annexed and truely ministered, as seales and visible confirmations of the spirituall promises contained in the word,[1] and they be two,[2] to wit, Baptism and the holy Supper of the Lord Jesus, which are then rightly ministered, when by a lawfull Minister[3] the people, before the administration of the same, are plainely instructed, and put in mind of Gods free grace and mercie, offered unto the penitent in Christ Jesus; when Gods promises are rehearsed, the end and use of Sacraments preached and[a] declared, and that in such a tongue as the people doe understand: when farther to them is nothing added, from them nothing diminished, and in their practise nothing changed besides the Institution of the Lord Jesus and practise of his holy Apostles.[4]

And albeit the order of Geneva,[5] which now is used in some

---

[a] *preached and* not in Laing MS

[1] See *supra*, p. 87 n.4; *Confession of Faith*, cap. XXI; Calvin, *Institutes*, 4.14.3 'a sacrament is never without a preceding promise but it is joined to it as a sort of appendix, with the purpose of confirming and sealing the promise itself, and of making it more evident to us and in a sense ratifying it'. Cf. Wallace, *Calvin's Doctrine of the Word and Sacrament*, 133ff.

[2] Reformed theologians reduced the number of Sacraments accepted by mediaeval theologians from seven to two. Luther, unlike Calvin, was prepared to give a subordinate place to the Sacrament of Penance. (See further Calvin, *Institutes*, 4.19.1; and *Confession of Faith*, cap. XXI.

[3] The *Confession of Faith*, cap. XXII, defines lawful ministers as those 'Whome we affirmed to be onlie thei that ar appointed to the preaching of the Worde, or into whose mouthis God hes putt some sermoun of exhortatioun, thei being men lauchfullie chosin thairto by some Kirk'. Cf. Article XXIII of *The XXXIX Articles of the Church of England*; see also Sykes, *Old Priest and New Presbyter*, 10f.

[4] Matthew 26.26–29, Mark 14.22–25, Luke 22.17–20; 1 Corinthians 11.23–26; cf. Calvin, *Institutes*, 4.17.39, and Wallace, *Calvin's Doctrine of the Word and Sacrament*, 242f.

[5] *The Forme of Prayers and Ministration of the Sacraments etc. used in the English Churche at Geneva; and approved by the famous and godly learned man, John Calvyn*, 1556 and 1558. (This work is reprinted in Laing, *Knox's Works*, 4,149–214. Maxwell, *The Liturgical Portions of the Genevan Service Book*, prints the Orders for the administration of Baptism and the Lord's Supper on pp. 105–111 and 121– 128.) In 1562 the General Assembly enjoined its use in the administration of the Sacraments, the solemnisation of marriages and the burial of the dead. It was

of our Churches, is sufficient to instruct the diligent Reader how that both these sacraments may be rightly ministered, yet for an uniformitie to be kept, we have thought good to adde this as superaboundant.

In Baptisme we acknowledge nothing to be used except the element of water onely (that the word and declaration of the promises ought to preceed we have said before)[6] wherefore whosoever presumeth in Baptisme to use oyle, salt, waxe, spittle, conjuration[7] and[b] crossing accuseth the perfect institution of Christ Jesus of imperfection. For it was voyd of all such inventions devised by men, and such as would presume to alter Christs perfect ordinance you ought severely to punish.[8]

The Table of the Lord is then most rightly ministered when it approacheth most neare to Christs own action. But plaine it is, that at Supper[c] Christ Jesus sate with his Disciples; and therefore doe we judge that sitting at a table is most convenient to that holy action;[9] that bread and wine ought to be there; that thankes

[b] or   [c] that Supper

---

reprinted in Edinburgh in that year and again two years later when the General Assembly 'ordained that everie Minister, Exhorter and Reader, sall have one of the Psalme Bookes latelie printed in Edinburgh and use the order contained therein in Prayers, Marriage, and ministration of the Sacraments'. (*BUK*, 1.30, 54; Laing, *Knox's Works*, 210 n.2, Dickinson, *Knox's History*, 282 n.2; McMillan, *Worship*, 48 ff; Donaldson, *Scottish Prayer Book of 1637*, 13ff.)

[6] See *supra*, p. 90 n.1.

[7] For an account of these rites accompanying Baptism see *Cath. Ency.*, 2.273, §XVI. They were condemned by Calvin, *Institutes*, 4.15.9. Knox opposed their use in St Andrews in 1547 at a meeting of Friars in 'Sanct Leonardis yardis' which John Winram, Sub-prior and Vicar General, had summoned. The rites are also rejected in the *Confession of Faith*, cap. XXII. They are not mentioned in the brief section on Baptism in *Forme of Prayers*. (Laing, *Knox's Works*, 1.197; Dickinson, *Knox's History*, 1.90; see also Winzet, *Works*, 1.83; Law, *The Catechism of John Hamilton*, 189ff.)

[8] On the relation of the State to the Church as expressed in the Book of Discipline see Introduction pp. 62ff.

[9] The rubric in *Forme of Prayers* states that the minister 'commeth doune from the pulpet, and sitteth at the Table, every man and woman in likewise takinge their place as occasion best serveth'. Sitting for Communion was introduced by Zwingli in Zürich in 1525, but not followed in Geneva, or in other reformed cities of Switzerland. Zwinglian influence on English exiles no doubt accounts for this practice in Frankfurt and in Knox's congregation in Geneva. But as early as 1550 in his sermon *A Vindication of the Doctrine that the Mass is idolatry*, Knox, in describing the reformed service, wrote 'In the Lordis Supper, all sit at ane tabill; na difference in habit nor vestament betwene the Minister and the Congregatioun.' (Laing, *Knox's Works*, 3.68, 4.195; Vuilleumier, *Histoire*, 1.344f; Maxwell, *Christian Worship*, 84, 118f, 126f; McMillan, *Worship*, 163f; Winzet informs us that the table was covered with a white cloth, *Works*, 1.84.)

ought to be given; distribution of the same made; and commandement given that the bread should be taken and eaten; and that all should likewise drinke of the cup of wine, with declaration what both the one and the other is; we suppose no godly man will doubt.[10] For as touching the damnable errour of the Papists who dare[d] defraud the common people of the one part of that holy Sacrament, to wit, of the cup of the Lords bloud, we suppose their errour to be so manifest, that it needeth no confutation:[11] neither yet intend we to confute any thing in this our simple Confession. But to offer publick disputation to all that list oppugne any thing affirmed by us.[12]

That the Minister breake the bread and distribute the same to those that be next unto him, commanding the rest, everie one with reverence and sobrietie to breake with other,[13] we thinke it neerest to Christs action, and to the perfect practise, as we read in Saint Paul;[14] during the which action we thinke it necessarie, that some comfortable places of the Scripture[e] be read, which may bring in minde the death of Christ Jesus, and the benefit of the same. For seeing that in that action we ought chiefly to remember the Lords death, we judge the Scriptures making mention of the same, most apt to stirre up our dull mindes then, and at al times.[15]

---

[d] can [e] Scripturis

[10] Maxwell, The Liturgical Portions of the Genevan Service Book, 138 n.9, pointed out that 'no words of delivery are included' in the rubric in Forme of Prayers and brought together evidence in support of the view that in Scottish custom such words had been employed. He does not, however, mention this section which illustrates the way in which the Book of Discipline was intended to supplement the Service Book. This section should be compared with Calvin's brief narrative of the order of celebration in Institutes, 4.17.43. See also CR, 6.200; McMillan, Worship, 173f.

[11] The withdrawal of the cup from the laity came about gradually but was widespread by the end of the twelfth century. This practice was attacked by Wyclif, the Hussites, the sixteenth century reformers, and Knox in his sermon A Vindication of the Doctrine that the Sacrifice of the Mass is Idolatry. (Laing, Knox's Works, 3.50; Cath. Ency., 4.178f; Calvin, Institutes, 4.17, 47–50.)

[12] See p. 86.

[13] For a discussion of the Continental and Scottish practice in distributing the elements see Henderson, Scottish Ruling Elder, 59ff. For Winzet's contemporary description see Works, 1.84.

[14] Matthew 26.26ff, Mark 14.22ff, Luke 22.19ff, 1 Corinthians 11.23ff.

[15] This is a restatement in slightly different words of the rubric in Forme o, Prayers. (Laing, Knox's Works, 4.196 and 6.325. Cf. Calvin, Institutes, 4.17.43.) For details of the development of this practice see Maxwell, The Liturgical Portions of the Genevan Service Book, 138, n.10.

Let the discretion of the Ministers appoint the places to be read
as they think good. What times we thinke most convenient for
the administration of the one and of the other of these Sacraments,
shall be declared in the policie of the Church.[16]

[16] See *infra*, pp. 182ff.

Touching the Abolishing of Idolatrie[1]

As we require Christ Jesus to be truely preached and his holy sacraments rightly ministered, so [we] cannot[a] cease to require Idolatry, with all monuments and places of the same, as Abbeyes, Monkeries,[2] Frieries, Nonries, Chappels, Chanteries,[3] Cathedrall Churches, Chanonries,[4] Colledges,[5] others then presently are Parish Churches[6] or Schooles,[7] to be utterly suppressed in all bounds and places of this Realme (except onely[b] Palaces, Mansions, and dwelling places adjacent thereto with Orchards and Yards of the same), as also that idolatrie may be removed from the presence of all persons of what estate or condition that ever they be within this Realme.

For let your Honours assuredly be perswaded, that where idolatry is maintained, or permitted, where it may be suppressed, that there shall Gods wrath raigne, not onely upon the blind and

[a] *can we not*   [b] *the*

[1] By 'idolatrie' Knox and his associates understood primarily the Mass. See Laing, *Knox's Works*, 3.33–70.

[2] Monasteries.

[3] A chantry was a chapel, altar or part of a church endowed for the maintenance of a priest to say Mass for the souls of the founders or others named by them.

[4] Churches staffed by Secular Canons, as, for example, at Aberdeen, Elgin, Brechin or Fortrose.

[5] Collegiate Churches. For details of all the religious establishments mentioned in this paragraph see Easson, *Medieval Religious Houses Scotland*.

[6] On the use made by the Reformed Church of mediaeval buildings see Fleming, *Reformation in Scotland*, 381ff, 388f, and 417 n., and Easson, *Medieval Religious Houses Scotland*. Easson (p. 173) stated that with the exception of five 'the Scottish collegiate churches (*i.e.*, their buildings) survived the Reformation and more than half their number in whole or in part, are still extant. . . . Many of these churches continued as parish churches; some which had not been parochial became so.' See also *infra*, pp. 202ff.

[7] Probably 'academic Secular colleges' and grammar schools maintained by religious orders are intended. In 1562 the Privy Council ordained that the magistrates of Aberdeen, Elgin, Inverness, Glasgow and other burghs 'where the friaries were yet standing undemolissit' should maintain them for use as hospitals and schools. (Easson, *Medieval Religious Houses Scotland*, 189; *RPC*, 1.116f, 202; Fleming, *Reformation in Scotland*, 417, 516; Keith, *History*, 3.366f.)

obstinate idolater, but also the° negligent sufferers, especially if God have armed their hands with power to suppresse such abhomination.[8]

By idolatry we understand, the Masse, invocation of Saints, adoration of images and the keeping and retaining of the same. And finally all honouring of God, not conteined in his holy word.

° *upon the*

[8] Parliament on 24th August 1560 revoked all Acts made since the beginning of the reign of James I 'not agreeing with Goddis holie word' by which 'idolatrie and superstitioun' were maintained in the Church and then went on to pass a new Act against those who 'stubburnlie perseveris in their wickit idolatrie, sayand mess and baptizand conforme to the papis kirk'. The General Assembly repeatedly petitioned the Queen for the punishment of sayers and hearers of the Mass. The Privy Council in June 1561 passed an act for the destruction of all places and monuments of idolatry which according to Knox resulted in the burning of Paisley Abbey, and the 'casting down' of the abbeys at Kilwinning and Cross-raguel in the west by the Earls of Arran, Argyll and Glencairn, and of some unnamed places by Lord James in the north. (Laing, *Knox's Works*, 2.161, 164, 167; Dickinson, *Knox's History*, 1.360, 362, 364 and 2, Index *sub* Mass; *APS*, 2.535; *BUK*, 1.6, 8, 10, 19ff, 47, 53, 109; Fleming, *Reformation in Scotland*, 410ff; McRoberts, 'Material destruction caused by the Scottish Reformation' in McRoberts, *Essays on the Scottish Reformation*, 415ff.) It should be pointed out that the burghs of Edinburgh and Dundee even before August 1560 had passed acts against idolaters and blasphemers. See further *Edin. Rec.*, 1557–1571, 65f, and Maxwell, *Old Dundee*, 72, 81ff.

Concerning Ministers and their Lawfull Election

In a Church reformed, or tending to reformation, none ought to presume either to preach, either yet to minister the sacraments till that orderly they be called to the same.[1] Ordinarie Vocation consisteth in Election, Examination and Admission.[2] And because that election of Ministers in this cursed Papistrie hath altogether bene abused, we thinke expedient to intreate it more largely. It appertaineth to the people and to every severall Congregation to elect their Minister.[3] And in case that they be found negligent therein the space of fourty dayes: The best reformed Church, to wit, the Church of the Superintendent with his councell,[4] may present unto them a man, whom they judge apt, to feed the flock of Christ Jesus,[5] who must be examined aswell in life and manners, as in doctrine and knowledge.[6]

[1] Cf. The Augsburg Confession Art. XIV *De ordine ecclesiastico docent, quod nemo debeat in ecclesia publice docere aut sacramenta administrare, nisi rite vocatus.* And Calvin, *Institutes*, 4.3.10.

[2] Cf. the Ecclesiastical Ordinances of Geneva: 'Or affin que rein ne se face confusement en l'Esglise, nu, ne se doibt ingerer en cest office sans vocation en laquelle il fault considerer trois choses. Asscavoir l'examen, qui est le principal. Apres à qui il appertient de instituer les ministres. Tiercement quelle ceremonie ou facon de faire il est bon de garder à les introduire en l'office.' Bergier, *Registres*, 1.2.

[3] This is in accordance with both Luther's and Calvin's teaching. (Kramm, *Theology of Martin Luther*, 77ff; Calvin, *Institutes*, 4.3.15, with notes in *LCC* and Benoit editions.) The procedure for the election of ministers by the congregation was given in *Forme of Prayers*, 1556. (Laing, *Knox's Works*, 4.175f, and *infra*, p. 99 n.16.)

[4] The constitution of this council is not defined in the Book of Discipline, but we learn from the St Andrews Kirk Session Register that in the case of Fife it was composed of the Superintendent and the Kirk Session of St Andrews 'as principall town' of his residence. (*StAKSR*, 1.xxvii ff. See also Donaldson, *Scottish Reformation*, 115, 123, 204f.)

[5] Part of this sentence, which breaks the continuity of thought, is probably an interpolation made at an early stage in the compilation of the Book of Discipline and should therefore by placed in parentheses, and the relative clause that follows regarded as qualifying the word 'minister' at the end of the previous sentence. See further Introduction, p. 21.

[6] Cf. the Ecclesiastical Ordinances of Geneva: 'L'examen contient deux parties dont la premiere est touchant la doctrine. . . . La seconde partie est de la vie.' Bergier, *Registres*, 1.2.

And that this may be done with more exact diligence, the persons that are to be examinated, must be commanded to appeare^a before men of soundest judgement remaining in some principall towne next adjacent unto them, as they that be in Fife, Angus, Mearnes, or Straitharne, to present themselves in Saint Andrewes; These that be in Lowthian, Merse, or Tevidaill to Edinburgh,[7] and likewise those that be in other Countries must resort to the best reformed Citie and Towne,^b that is to the Town^c of the Superintendent;[8] where first in the Schooles or failing thereof in open assembly and before the Congregation, they must give declaration of their giftes, utterance and knowledge by interpreting some place of Scripture to be appointed by the Ministrie;[9] which being ended, the person that is presented or that offereth^d himselfe to the administration of the Church, must be examined by the Ministers and Elders of the Church, and that openly,[10] and before all that list to heare, in all the chiefe points

^a *compeir*   ^b *cities or townis*   ^c *citie*   ^d *offered*

[7] The areas described here do not correspond to those given in the subsequent section entitled 'The names and Places of Residence and Several Dioceses of the Superintendents'. This fact may be regarded as evidence for the position argued in the Introduction with regard to the compilation of the Book. See p. 20. In July 1562 the General Assembly sought to regulate the conduct of these examinations and to clarify the position of the superintendent, by enacting (*a*) that 'the examination of all these who have not been examined already shall be in the presence of the superintendent, and of the best reformed kirk within his bounds nearest the place where the minister is to be established; providing always that the judgement of the best learned being present be sought in the examination and admission, and that he who shall be so admitted shall not be removed, according to the order of the Book of Discipline'; and (*b*) 'Touching persons to be nominat to Kirks, that nane be admitted without the nomination of the people, and due examination and admission of the superintendent; and who have been otherwayes intrused since the yeir 1558, to make supplication for their provision according to the foresaid act'. (*BUK*, 1.15f; Donaldson, *Scottish Reformation*, 120.)

[8] This gloss may have been added at a later stage. See Introduction, p. 21.

[9] On the meaning of this word see Introduction, p. 68.

[10] In the *Ecclesiastical Ordinances* and in 'The Manner of Electinge the Pastors and Ministers' given in *Forme of Prayers* the examination was to take place in private. (*CR*, 10.1.17, cf. 94; Laing, *Knox's Works*, 4.175; see also Doumergue, *Calvin*, 5.99ff.) The interpretation of 'some place of Scripture' may have been intended to take place at the weekly Exercise and the examination in doctrine to follow thereafter. (See *infra*, pp. 187ff.) For accounts of the election of a minister for Geneva in 1549 and 1557 in which a similar procedure was followed see Bergier, *Registres*, 1.61ff, 2.77ff. On 25th April 1561 John Winram, as Superintendent of Fife, and the 'holl ministerie wyth consayll of the Provest of Sanctandrois, Rector and chiefe membris of the Universite' ordained 'that in tym cuming al sic as pretendis to be admitted to minister in ony kyrk wythin the

that now be[e] in controversie betwixt us and the Papists, Ana-baptists, Arrians, or other such enemies to the Christian religion.[11] In which, if he be found sound, able to perswade by wholesome doctrine, and to convince the gaine-sayer,[f] then must he be directed to the Church and Congregation where he should serve, that there in open audience of his Flock in diverse publick Sermons, he may give confession of his faith in the article[g] of Justification,[12] in[h] the Office of Christ Jesus, of the number, effect and use of the sacraments, and finally of the whole religion which heretofore hath bene corrupted by the Papists. If his doctrine be found wholesome and able to instruct the simple, and if the Church[13] justly can reprehend nothing in his life, doctrine, nor utterance, then we judge the church which before was destitute, unreasonable, if they refuse him whom the church did offer; and[i] they should be compelled by the censure of the Councell and Church,[14] to receive the person appointed and approved by the judgement of the godly and learned; unless that the same Church have presented a man better, or as well qualified to the examina-tion, before that this foresaid tryall was taken of the person presented by the counsell of the whole Church. As, for example, the counsell of the church presents to any church a man to be their

[e] lie   [f] gaynsayaris   [g] articles   [h] of   [i] and that

---

bowndis of Fyff, Fotheryk or Strathern, sall compeir wythin this citie, at sic daye and places as sal be assignit to tham be the Superintendent, to be examinated, fyrst privatle upon the cheaf puntis and headis in controversy, and tharefter ane porcion of text assignit to the minister to declar in the pulpiat in the essemble to reid or exhort in the public assemble'. (StAKSR, 1.75f.)

[11] On more than one occasion Calvin had to defend his teaching in Geneva against attacks from Anabaptists, Arians and Anti-Trinitarians. (McNeill, Calvin-ism, 119, 155, 182f, 207ff.)

[12] The Confession of Faith does not contain, as does the Augsburg Confession and many other Protestant confessions, a separate article on the doctrine of Justifica-tion by Faith.

[13] It is important to distinguish the use of the word 'church' in this section. Here it is the superintendent's church that is referred to and on line 16 infra; on line 13, it is clear that the local congregation is intended, and this congregation (which is without a minister) is referred to on line 17, as 'the same Church', 21 'any church', p. 99 line 2 'the church', line 7 'inferior church', line 11 'every several Church'.

[14] By the words 'the Councell and Church' is meant the Superintendent's Council meeting at the church of the principal town, which has the right of examination of all candidates. This Council is referred to under a number of different names: in line 20, 'the counsell of the whole Church', line 21 'the counsell of the church', on p. 99 'next reformed church', 'the counsell or greater Church', and 'the counsell of the Church'.

Minister, not knowing that they are otherwise provided: in the meantime the church is provided of another, sufficient in their judgement for that charge, whom they present to the learned Ministers and next reformed church to be examined. In this case the presentation of the people to whom he should be appointed Pastor must be preferred to the presentation of the counsell, or greater church, unlesse the person presented by the inferiour Church be judged unable of[j] the Regiment by the Learned. For altogether this is to be avoided, that any man be violently intruded[k] or thrust in upon any congregation. But this libertie with all care must be reserved to every severall Church, to have their Votes and Suffrages in election of their Ministers. But violent intrusion we call not when the counsell of the Church in the feare of God and for the salvation of the people offereth unto them a sufficient man to instruct them whom they shall not be forced to admit before just examination,[15] as before is said.[16]

[j] *for*   [k] *intrused*

[15] *i.e.*, by hearing his preaching and his confession of faith, as is mentioned on p. 98.

[16] In this complicated section two lines of procedure are envisaged.

(*a*) The local congregation, or 'inferior Church', has the right when without a minister to present to the Council of the Church in the principal town 'next adjacent' – 'next reformed Church' – a person of their own choice for examination by the learned in open audience. If this person is found qualified in public exercises, he then can appear before the local congregation for examination and election by them by preaching and giving a confession of his doctrine. Thereafter he would be admitted to the pastoral charge, for which see *infra*.

(*b*) The church of the principal town, 'the Counsell or greater Church', may examine someone, find him qualified for the ministry, and present him to the local congregation for their 'just examination' and election. They are not to be compelled to accept him, if they have a candidate of their own awaiting examination by the 'greater Church', and there must be no attempt at a violent intrusion; nevertheless the local church and congregation must not be allowed the exercise of an 'unreasonable' refusal.

In this section an attempt is made to exercise a balance between the rights of the people and the rights of ministers and councils of the Church. Calvin experienced in Geneva the reduction of the rights of the people and sought in his later years to gain more control for them in the election of their ministers, and in the *Institutes*, 4.4.12, he argued in favour of maintaining a balance between the people and the ministers. This position is upheld in *La Discipline ecclésiastique* of the French Church in 1559, by which this section of the Book of Discipline appears to have been greatly influenced. (See further *CR*, 10.1.94; *La Discipline ecclésiastique*, Arts. 6 and 11; *Institutes*, 4.3.13–15, 4.4.10–13, with notes in *LCC* and Benoit editions; Doumergue, *Calvin*, 5.101ff; and Heyer, *L'Eglise de Genève*, 9 n. 2.)

In 1564 Beza, replying to questions about the exercise of patronage raised by the pastors of Normandy, stated that the election 'doit estre libre et appartient aux gouverneurs de l'eglise avec le consentement de troupeaux'. (Bergier,

What may unable any person that he may not be admitted to the Minsterie of the Church

It is to be observed, that no person, noted with publique infamie or being unable to edifie the Church by wholesome doctrine or being known of corrupt judgement, be either promoted to the regiment of the Church or yet retained[1] in Ecclesiasticall administration.

Explication

By publick infamy wee understand not the common sinnes and offences which any hath committed in time of blindness[17] by fragilitie (if of the same by a better and more sober conversation he hath declared himselfe verily penitent) but such capitall crimes as the Civill sword ought and may punish with death by the word of God.[18] For besides that the Apostle requireth the life of Ministers to be so irreprehensible, that they have a good testimonie from those that be without,[19] wee judge it a thing unseemly and dangerous, that he shall have publick authoritie to preach to others life[m] everlasting from whom the Civil Magistrate may take the life temporall for a crime publickly committed. And if any object that the Prince hath pardoned his offence, and that he hath publickly repented, and so not onely his life is in assurance, but also that he may be received to the Ministrie of the Church, We answer that repentance doth not take away the temporall punishment of the Law, neither doth the pardon of the Prince remove his infamie before man.[20]

That the life and conversation of the person presented or to be elected may be the more clearly knowne, publick edicts should[n] be directed to all parts of this Realme, or at the least to those

---

[1] *receaved*   [m] *the lyiff*   [n] *must*

Registres, 2.140.) The way in which this head of the Book of Discipline was interpreted or rather re-interpreted by the Church is clearly but briefly stated by the General Assembly in December 1562 when it inhibited all from exercising a ministry who had not been presented by the people or any part thereof to the superintendent, and he after examination and trial had not appointed them to their charges. (*BUK*, 1.27; cf. Calderwood, *History*, 2.206; and Donaldson, *Scottish Reformation*, 150f.)

[17] i.e., prior to the establishment of the Reformation, cf. page 198.

[18] See *infra* and pp. 165ff.

[19] Cf. 1 Thessalonians 4.12.

[20] See Introduction, pp. 65f.

parts where the person had been most conversant; as where he was nourished in letters, or where he continued since*o* the yeares of infancie and childhood were passed. Straight command-ment would be given that if any capitall crimes were committed by him that they should be notified; as if he had committed wilfull murder, Adulterie,[21] *p*if he were*p* a common fornicator; a thiefe, a drunkard, a fighter, brawler or contentious person. These Edicts ought to be notified in the chiefe Cities, with the like charge and commandement, with declaration that such as con-cealed his sinnes known*q* did deceive and betray (so far as in them lay) the Church which is the Spouse of Christ Jesus, and did com-municate with the sinnes of that wicked man.

Admission

The Admission of Ministers to their offices must consist in consent of the people, and Church whereto they shall be appointed, and*r* approbation of the learned Ministers appointed for their examina-tion.[22]

We judge it expedient that the admission of Ministers be in open audience, that some speciall Minister make a Sermon touch-ing the duety and office of Ministers, touching their manners, conversation and life; as also touching the obedience which the Church oweth*s* to their ministers. Commandment should bee given as well to the Minister as to the people, both being present: To wit, that he with all carefull dilligence attend upon the flock of Christ Jesus over the which he is appointed Preacher.*t* That hee will*u* walke in the presence of God so sincerely that the graces of

o from   *p* Laing MS places these words after 'fornicator'.
q knawin   *r and in*   *s aw*
t Laing noted that the 1621 edition reads *pastor*; the St Andrews copy has *preacher*.
u Not in Laing MS

21 On adultery as a capital offence see *infra*, p. 165 n.4.

22 This paragraph summarises much of what has been stated previously but omits any reference to election by the people. By 'learned Ministers' is meant the 'men of soundest judgement remaining in some principal town next adjacent' (p. 97), 'the godly and learned' (p. 98), and 'the learned' (p. 99); *i.e.*, the min-isters of the 'superior Church' .This interpretation is in line with what precedes and with *La Discipline ecclésiastique* 1559, Art. 11. 'Celuy qui se seriot ingeré, encores qu'il fust approve de son peuple, ne pourra estre approuvé des ministres prochains ou autres.' The French *Discipline* goes on to state that if agreement is not reached, appeal has to be made to the provincial synod. Donaldson, *Scottish Reformation*, 119, understands by 'learned ministers appointed for ex-amination' those 'deputed . . . by the superintendent, for no one else can have authority to appoint examiners'.

the holy spirit may be multiplied into him, and in the presence of men so soberly and uprightly, that his life may confirme in the eyes of men, that which by tongue and word he perswaded unto others. The people would be exhorted to reverence and honor their ministers, chosen as servants[v] and Embassadors of the Lord Jesus, obeying the commandments which they pronounce from God's mouth and book,[w] even as they would obey God himselfe. For whosoever heareth Christs ministers, heareth himself, and whosoever rejecteth and[x] despiseth their ministerie and exhortation, rejecteth and despiseth Christ Jesus.[23] Other ceremonie than the publick approbation of the people, and declaration of the chiefe minister,[24] that the person there presented is appointed to serve the[y] Church, wee cannot approve, for albeit the Apostles used imposition of hands, yet seeing the miracle is ceased, the using of the ceremonie we judge not[z] necessarie.[25]

[v] *the servandis*
[w] Laing noted that the 1621 edition read *from God's word*. The St Andrews copy follows the Laing MS.
[x] *rejecteth thame*   [y] *that*   [z] *is nott*

[23] Cf. Luke 10.16. The teaching of this paragraph closely follows that of Calvin; see for example *Institutes*, 4.3.2., and Wallace, *Calvin's Doctrine of the Word and Sacrament*, 115ff, Niesel, *Theology of Calvin*, 203ff.

[24] Perhaps the presiding minister at the examination held in the principal town, or the minister presiding at the service of admission, who could, of course, be the same person. Keith, *History*, 3.16, thought that the superintendent was here intended.

[25] This paragraph resembles one in the *Ordonnances Ecclésiastiques* of 1541 in its revised form. In the Draft Calvin had written 'Quant a la maniere de lintroduyre, jl seroit bon de user de limposition des mains, laquelle ceremonye a este gardee des apostres et puys en leglise ancienne, moyennant que cela se face sans superstition et sans offence. Mais pource quil y a eu beaucoup de superstition au temps passe et quil sen pourroit en suivre de scandale on sen abstient pour linfirmite du temps.' But the civil authorities erased this section and replaced it in the definitive text with the following: 'Quant a la maniere de l'introduire, pource que les ceremonies du temps passe ont este tournees en beaucoup de superstitions a cause de l'infirmite du temps il suffira quil se fasse par un des ministres une declaration en remonstrance de loffice auquel on lordonne puis quon fasse prieresset praisons affin que le seigneur luy fasse la grace de sen acquiter.' This latter form was incorporated also in the revision of 1561. In *Institutes*, 4.3.16, Calvin stated that there was no express precept (*Certum praeceptum – nul commandment exprès*) for the laying on of hands, yet he strongly commended the practice 'provided it be not turned to superstitious abuse'. In the previous section he wrote 'the call of a minister is lawful according to the word of God, when those who seem fit are created by consent and approval (*approbation*) of the people'. It is interesting to note that the *Discipline ecclésiastique* of 1559, §8, reads: 'Et sera l'Election confirmée par prieres et par imposition des mains des Ministres, sans toutefois aucune superstition.' Erskine of Dun in 1571 stated that 'the admissioun be publict, be the impositione of handis be the pastouris, with admonitionis, fasting, and prayers passing befoir'.

The minister elected, or presented, examined and as sayd is, publickly admitted, may[a] neither leave the flocke at his pleasure to which he had[b] promised his fidelitie and labours neither yet may the flock reject nor change him at their appetite,[26] unlesse they be able to convict him of such crimes as deserve deposition, whereof we shall after speak.[27] We mean not but that the whole Church, or the most part thereof, for just considerations, may transferre a minister from one Church to another:[28] neither yet mean we, that men who now serve[c] as it were of benevolence,

[a] man   [b] hes   [c] do serve

With regard to the statement that the 'miracle is now ceased' Calvin is once again followed for in *Institutes* 4.19.6. he wrote 'If this ministry which the apostles then carried out still remained in the Church, the laying on of hands would also have to be kept. But since the grace has ceased to be given, what purpose does the laying on of hands serve?... But those miraculous powers and manifest workings, which were dispensed by the laying on of hands, have ceased; and they have rightly lasted only for a time.' (*CR*, 10.1.18, 95; Bergier, *Registres*, 1, 3; and the relevant notes and references in the sections of the *Institutes* mentioned above.) See also, Shaw, 'The Inauguration of Ministers in Scotland, 1560–1620' in *RSCHS*, 16 (1966), 35ff; *Miscellany of the Spalding Club*, 4.100; Donaldson, *Scottish Reformation*, 116; Sykes, *Old Priest New Presbyter*, 101, n.1, and *infra*, p. 206. Donaldson, *Scottish Reformation*, p. 104, writes that the reformers 'unable to discern in the existing bishops the characteristics they looked for in an apostolic ministry . . . considered it to be demonstrable that the succession had failed'.

[26] This sentence and indeed much of the following paragraph sets forth Calvin's teaching in *Institutes*, 4.3.7, cf. 4.3.16; and that of *La Discipline ecclésiastique* 1559, §§8–12. In June 1562 the General Assembly passed acts against ministers who left their charges and entered other vocations 'more profitable for the belly', and again in June 1564 and in July 1570 when it was decreed that ministers at their public inauguration should protest solemnly that they would not leave their vocation any time thereafter under pain of infamy and perjury. This promise was to be given in the presence of the superintendent or Commissioner for planting Kirks. Further all ministers already in charges were to make a similar promise at the Synod meetings and have it recorded. In 1564 it was enacted that a minister 'lawfullie may leave ane unthankfull peiple, and seik wher Jesus Christ his holy evangell may bring foorth great fruit; but lawfullie they may never change their vocatioun'. (*BUK*, 1.20, 50, 61, 73f, 172, 176, 2.421.)

[27] See *infra*, p. 177.

[28] In *Institutes*, 4.3.7, Calvin wrote, 'If it be expedient for any one to be transferred to another place, still he ought not to attempt this on his own private resolve, but to await public authority.' Cf. *La Discipline ecclésiastique*, §§9–14. In December 1562 the General Assembly agreed to translate a minister to 'sick a place as where his stipend should be more aboundantlie givin him' provided he change not at his 'awin privat opinioun' but at the direction of the Assembly. The Assembly, however, went on to give power to the superintendents within their bounds in their synods to translate ministers from one church to another, whenever necessary. Succeeding General Assemblies continued to stress this power of the superintendent. On the interpretation of the words 'the whole Church' see further Introduction, p. 68. (*BUK*, 1.17, 28, 61, cf. 2.468; Keith, *History*, 3.65.)

may not be appointed and elected to serve in other places, but once being solemnly elected and admitted, we cannot approve that they should change at their owne pleasure.

We are not ignorant that the raritie of godly and learned men shall seem to some a just reason why that so strait and sharpe examination should not be taken universally, for so it shall appeare that the most part of the[d] Kirks shal have no minister at all. But let these men understand, that the lack of able men shall not excuse us before God, if by our consent unable men be placed over the flock of Christ Jesus. As also that amongst the Gentiles godly and learned men were also[e] rare, as they be now among us, when the Apostle gave the same rule to trie and examine ministers, which we now follow.[29] And last, let them understand that it is alike to have no minister at all, and to have an Idoll in the place of a true minister:[30] Yea and in some case it is worse, for those that be utterly destitute of ministers, will be diligent to search for them; but those that have a vain shadow, do commonly without further care content themselves with the same, and so remain they continualy deceived, thinking that they have a minister when in verie deed they have none. For we cannot judge him a dispensator of Gods mysteries, that in no wise can breake the bread of life to the fainting and hungrie soules. Neither judge we that the sacraments can be rightlie ministred by him in whose mouth God has put no Sermon of exhortation.[31] The chiefest remedie left to your Honours, and to us, in all this rarietie of true ministers is fervent praier unto God, that it will please his mercie to thrust out[f] faithfull workmen in this his harvest.[32] And next, that your Ho[nours] with consent of the Church, are bound by your authoritie to compel such men as have gifts and graces able to edifie the Church of God, that they bestow them where greatest

[d] Not in Laing MS   [e] als
[f] Laing noted that the 1621 edition read 'forth' but this is not the reading in the copy in the St Andrews University Library.

[29] 1 Timothy 3.1–8.

[30] Bucer made a similar reply to objections of this nature. Cf. De Regno Christi, 2.12, Opera Latina, 15.128.

[31] On the inseparability of Word and Sacrament in reformed teaching see supra, p. 90, Calvin, Institutes, 4.14.3ff and 4.17.39; also Wallace, Calvin's Doctrine of Word and Sacrament, 135ff, 242f; Niesel, Theology of Calvin, 212ff. On the recruitment of the ministers of the Church in the period immediately following 1560 see Donaldson, Scottish Reformation, 85ff.

[32] Matthew 9.38. This paragraph is a particular application of a principle expressed in similar terms by Bucer, De Regno Christi, 1.5, Opera Latina, 15.56.

necessitie shall be known. For no man may be permitted to live idle, or as themselves list. But must be appointed to travell where your wisdoms and the Church shal think expedient: Wee cannot prescribe unto your Honors certain rules[g] how that ye shall distribute the ministers and learned men, whom God hath alreadie sent unto you. But herof we are assured, that it greatlie hindereth the progresse of Christs Gospell within this poore realm, that some altogether abstract their labours from the Church, and others remain altogether[h] in one place, the most part of them being idle. And therefore of your Honors we require in Gods name, that by your authoritie, which ye have of God, ye compel all men to whom God hath given any Talent to perswade by wholsome doctrine, to bestow the same, if they be called by the church to the advancement of Christs glorie, and the[i] comfort of his troubled flock. And that ye with the consent of the church, assigne unto your chiefest workmen, not onelie townes to remaine in, but also provinces that by their faithfull labours churches may be erected and order established where none is now.[33] And if on this manner ye shall use your power and authoritie, chieflie seeking Gods glorie, and the comfort of your brethren, we doubt not but God shall blesse you and your enterprises.[34]

For Readers[35]

To the Churches where no ministers can be had presentlie, must be appointed the most apt men that distinctlie can read the

[g] reull   [h] togither   [i] to the

[33] For a discussion of this proposal in relation to the appointment of superintendents see Introduction, pp. 5, 21, where it is argued that it was in response to this exhortation that between 20th [10th] July and the reassembly of Parliament in August 1560 'the Commissioners of Burghs, with some of the Nobility and Barons' were appointed to see the equal distribution of ministers and 'to change and transport as the most should think expedient'.

[34] On the relation of the state to the Church set forth in the Book of Discipline see Introduction, pp. 5, 21f, 62ff.

[35] 'Helfer' or 'auxiliaires des pasteurs de ville ou de très grand paroisses' were, on account of the shortage of protestant ministers, introduced first in German-speaking Swiss reformed churches, such as at Zürich, Basel and Bern, and were subsequently employed in the Pays de Vaud where they were termed 'diacres'. The use of this word, with its mediaeval connotation, was, however, repudiated by the Calvinists, but not the office. (See further Richter, *Evangelische Kirchenordnungen des XVI. Jahrhunderts*, 122, 125, 172, Vuilleumier, *Histoire*, 1.268f; MacGregor, *Scottish Presbyterian Polity*, 47f. The first General Assembly approved the names of a number of persons whom they considered qualified to be readers. *BUK*, 1.4.)

H

common praiers[36] and the Scriptures,[37] to exercise both themselves and the Church, till they grow to greater perfection and in
processe of time, he that is but a reader, may attain to a farther
degree,[j] [38] and by consent of the Church, and discreet ministers,[39]
may be permitted to minister the Sacraments, but not before that
he be able somewhat to perswade by wholesome doctrine, beside
his reading, and be admitted to the Ministerie, as before is said.
Some we know that of long time have professed Christ Jesus,
whose honest conversation deserveth praise of all godly men, and
whose knowledge also might greatly helpe the simple, and yet
they onely content themselves with reading, these must be
animated, and by gentle admonition encouraged by some exhortation to comfort their brethren,[40] and so they may be admitted to administration of the sacraments; but such readers as
neither have had exercise, nor continuance in Christs true
religion must abstaine from ministration of the sacraments till
they give declaration and witnessing of their honestie and
further knowledge.[41]

[j] *the further gree*

[36] See *supra*, p. 90 and Laing, *Knox's Works*, 4.179ff; McMillan, *Worship*,
111ff; Donaldson, *Scottish Reformation*, 82ff. McMillan, *op. cit.*, 42ff, argues that
the reference may be to the Anglican Book of Common Prayer, which had been
in use in Scotland prior to 1560. See also Donaldson, *Scottish Prayer Book of 1637*,
7ff, 18ff.

[37] For the order in the reading of the Scriptures see *infra*, pp. 185f. Donaldson,
Scottish Prayer Book of 1637, 22, adduces evidence in support of the view that
readers were also permitted to read the English Book of Homilies.

[38] *i.e.*, to the status of a minister with authorisation to preach and administer
the Sacraments. In the following Head, p. 111, it is stated that the reader was not
considered a 'true' minister. Donaldson, *Thirds*, provides considerable evidence
that some readers did in time become exhorters and some exhorters ministers.

[39] *i.e.*, the ministers of the principal town who examined those presented for
election and admission to pastoral charges (see *supra*, pp. 96ff) as is made clear by
the concluding part of this sentence which is in the nature of a gloss.

[40] This part of the sentence provides for the recognition of an intermediate
office of exhorter, for some of those who had previous to 1560 been active in
support of the Reformation, as is clearly indicated *infra*, p. 111 n.19.

[41] In 1562 the Superintendent of Fife took action against two readers for
administering baptism 'wythawt admission being onlye ane readar' (*StAKSR*,
1.176f, 179). From *BUK*, 1.63, however, it would appear that by 1565 exhorters
could be empowered to baptise and solemnise marriages. The General Assembly
in 1566, nevertheless, censured a reader for baptising of bairns and solemnising of
marriage, he being but a simple reader and two years later 'ordained that superintendents should command readers to abstain from all ministration of the sacraments, under the pain to be accused as abusers, and criminall according to the act
of Parliament', but in 1572 it was agreed at Leith 'that thair be redaires specialie

[For the Lords think]^k that none be admitted to preach but they that are qualified therefore, but rather be retained readers, and such as are preachers already not found qualified therefore, by the superintendent, be placed to be readers.[42]

^{k} From Laing MS. See note 42.

---

appointed at every severall kirk, quhair convenientlie it may be, quhilkis being found qualifeit be the Bischop or Superintendent, and enterand be the lauchfull order of the true reformit Kirk, sall ministrat the sacrament of baptysme, and make mariages after proclamatioun of the bannes . . .'. The prohibition against the administration of the Lord's Supper continued. In 1576 it would appear that this prohibition was extended to include also baptism. (*BUK*, 1.82, 124, 211, 276, 372.)

[42] This sentence is the first *additio* in the Laing MS. (See Introduction, pp. 22, 64f.) In the edition of 1621 the words within the brackets were omitted and the *additio* regarded as a continuation of the previous sentence. In April 1561, following his appointment, the Superintendent of Fife 'and holl ministerie, wyth consyll of the Provest of Sanctandrois, Rector and chief membris of the Universite' ordained that every minister, exhorter and reader be tried by the superintendent in his visitation. (*StAKSR*, 1.75; and *infra*, pp. 111f.)

Concerning the Provision for the Ministers

and

for the Distribution of the rents and possessions justly appertaining to the Church

Seeing that of our maister Christ Jesus and his Apostle Paul we have 'that the workman is worthy of his reward', and that 'the mouth of the labouring oxe ought not to be musseled',[1] of necessitie it is that honest provision be made for the ministers which we require to be such, that they have neither occasion of sollicitude, neither yet of insolencie and wantonnesse. And this provision must be made not onely for their owne sustentation, during their lives; but also for their wives and children after them. For we judge it a thing most contrarious to reason, godliness and equitie, that the widow and the children of him who in his life, did faithfully serve in the[a] kirk of God, and for that cause did not carefully make provision for his family, should after his death be left comfortlesse of all provision:[b] which provision for the wives of the ministers after their deceass is to be remited to the discretion of the Kirk.[2]

Difficle it is to appoint a severall stipend to every minister, by reason that the charge[c] and necessitie of all, will not be alike.[d] For some will be continuers in one place, some will be compelled to

---

[a] *serve the*

[b] Marginal *additio. Provisioun for the Wyffis of Ministeris efter thair deceise, to be remittit to the discretioun of the Kirk.* In the 1621 edition this was taken into the text and added to the previous sentence by supplying the relative *which* and the verb *is.*

[c] *chargis*   [d] *licke*

[1] Luke 10.7; 1 Timothy 5.18.

[2] Occasional payments to widows are recorded in Donaldson, *Thirds*; *e.g.*, in 1569 £100 was given to a minister's widow, and provision made for an exhorter's widow in 1568 and for a reader's widow in 1571. The provision made on Morton's request by the General Assembly for Knox's widow by the payment of his stipend for the year following his death appears to have been exceptional. (Donaldson, *Thirds*, 254, 266, 296; Brown, *John Knox*, 2.289f.)

travel, and oft to change their[e] dwelling place (if they shall have charge of divers kirkes),[3] among these some will be burdened with wife and children, and one with moe then others,[f] and some perhaps will be single men. If equall stipends should be appointed to [g]these that in charge should be so[g] unequall, either should the one suffer penurie, or else should the other have superfluitie and too much.

We[4] judge therefore that every minister have sufficient whereupon to keep an house, and be sustained honestly in all things necessarie as well for keeping of his house and[h] cloathes, flesh, fish, bookes, fewell,[i] and other things necessarie, of[j] the rents and treasurie[5] of the Kirke[k] at the discretion of the Congregation conforme to the qualitie of the person and necessity of the time: Wherein it is thought good[l] that every Minister shall have at least fourtie bolls[6] meal,[m] twenty six bolls malt, to finde his house bread and drinke, and more so much[n] as the discretion of the Church findes necessarie, besides money for buying of other provision to his house and other necessaries; the modification whereof is referred to the judgement of the Kirk, to be made every yeare at the choosing of the Elders and Deacons of the Kirk.[7] Providing alwaies that there bee advanced to every Minister sufficient provision for a quarter of a yeare before hand of all things.

But[o] to him that travels from place to place, whom we call Superin[ten]dent,[p] who remaines as it were a month or lesse in one place for establishing of the Kirk, and for the same purpose changing to another,[q] must[r] consideration be had. And therefore to such we think sixe chalders[8] beere, nine chalders meale, three

[e] Not in Laing MS   [f] ane other
[g] to all those that in charge ar so   [h] as   [i] Not in Laing MS
[j] furth of   [k] Laing in the printed text added where he serveth
[l] Not in Laing MS   [m] meill and   [n] mekill   [o] Not in Laing MS
[p] Superintendetis   [q] ane uther place   [r] must farther consideratioun

[3] i.e., the superintendents.

[4] This and the following paragraph form an additio in the Laing MS. See further Introduction, p. 23.

[5] The reference appears to be to local parochial revenues. According to this decision the autonomy of the local congregation in financial matters was to be assured. It was taken for granted that the local congregation would inherit the income of the previous incumbent and be able to collect the accustomed revenue, and that the 'modification', i.e., the determination of the exact amount of the stipend, be decided once a year. See infra, pp. 157ff.

[6] For details of the measuring of grain see Henderson, Scottish Reckonings, 7ff.

[7] See infra, p. 175.

[8] Sixteen bolls constituted a chalder. See further Henderson, op. cit., 7f.

chalders oats,[s] sixe hundreth merkes[t] money,[9] to be eiked and paired at the discretion of the Prince and councell of the Realme, to be payed to him[u] in manner foresaid.[10]

The children of the Ministers must have the liberties of the Cities next adjacent where there fathers laboured freely granted.[11] They must have the priviledges in Schooles and bursisses[v] in Colledges:[12] That is, that they shall be sustained at learning, if they be found apt thereto; And failing thereof, that they be put to some handie craft, or exercised in some vertuous industry whereby they may be profitable members of the[w] Commonwealth.[13] And the same we require of their daughters: To wit, that they be vertuously brought up and honestly doted when they come to maturity of yeares at the discretion of the kirk.[x] And this[14] in God's presence we witnesse we require not so much for our selves, or for any that appertaine to us, as that we do it for the increase of vertue and learning, and for the profite of the posterity to come. It is not to be supposed that any[y] man will dedicate himselfe and his[z] children so to God and to[a] his Kirk, that they look for no worldly commodity, but this cankered nature which we beare, is provoked to follow vertue when it seeth profite and honour thereto[b] annexed; and contrarily, then is vertue in[c] many despised, when vertuous and godly men are[d] without honour, and sory would we be that poverty should discourage men from studie and following of the way of vertue, by which they might edifie the Kirk and flock of Christ Jesus. Nothing have we spoken of the stipend of

[s] *aittis for his horse*   [t] *V[c] markis*   [u] *him yeirlie*   [v] *bursis*   [w] *in a*
[x] This sentence forms in the Laing MS an *additio.*   [y] *all*
[z] Not in Laing MS   [a] *to serve*   [b] *honour and profeit annexit to the same; as*
[c] *of*   [d] *leve*

[9] The mark was two thirds of the pound. On the stipends of the superintendents see Donaldson, *Scottish Reformation*, 127f, and *Thirds*, xxi, xxxv. It is significant that the determination of the amount of the stipend of the superintendent was to be at the discretion of the Prince and Council of the Realm, although it is not clear at this point how the actual payment was to be made or from what specific source the stipend was to be derived, but see *infra*, p. 161f.

[10] *Supra*, p. 109.

[11] i.e., the children of ministers who have died were freely to enjoy the immunities and privileges of those who lived in the nearest city.

[12] See *infra*, p. 132.

[13] This sentiment is repeated in the general section on education, see *infra*, p. 135.

[14] i.e., the adequate provision for ministers (those settled and those who 'travel'), their wives and children (if they are widowed or left fatherless).

Readers, because if they can doe nothing but reade, they neither can be called nor judged true Ministers and yet regard must be had to their labours; but so that they may be spurred forward to vertue and not by any[e] stipend appointed for their reading to be retained in[f] that estate.[15] To a Reader therefore that is newly entred,[g] fourty merkes, or more or less, as Parishioners and Readers can agree, is[h] sufficient; Provided that he teach the children of the Parish which he must doe,[16] beside the reading of the common prayers,[17] and bookes of the old and new[i] Testament.[18] If from reading he begin to exhort, and explain the Scriptures,[19] then ought his stipend to be augmented, till finally he come to the honour of a Minister. But if he be found unable after two yeres, then must he be removed from that office, and discharged of all stipend, that another may be proved as long.[20] For this alwaies is to be avoided, that none who is judged unable to come at any time to some reasonable knowledge whereby he may edifie the Kirk, shall be perpetually susteined[j] upon the charge of the Kirk. Farther it must be avoided that no child, nor person within age, that is, within twentie one yeares of age, be admitted to the office of a Reader.[21] But Readers ought to be endued with gravity[k] and discretion, lest by their lightnesse the prayers or Scriptures read be of lesse price or[l] estimation. It is to be noted that the Reader[m] be put in[n] the Kirk at[o] the admission

[e] a   [f] still in   [g] we think fourty   [h] Not in Laing MS
[i] New and Auld
[j] sall perpetuallie be nurisshed   [k] witt and   [l] and   [m] Readaris
[n] in by   [o] and admission

[15] See *supra*, p. 106 and n.38.

[16] This is the first indication in the Book of the teaching duties of the reader. See further *infra*, p. 130.

[17] See *supra*, pp. 90 and 106.

[18] See *supra*, p. 106 n.37, and *infra*, pp. 184f.

[19] See *supra*, p. 106 n.40, and Introduction, pp. 22f.

[20] No evidence has come to light that this injunction was ever put into effect, but rather the reverse. Many readers continued in office as such for a considerable number of years (probably their entire lives), although some did become in time exhorters and ministers. (See *supra*, p. 106 n.38.)

[21] Possibly to avoid any confusion with the minor order of lector or reader in the Mediaeval Church which could be conferred on young persons. See *Dictionnaire du Droit Canonique*, 6.370. It is, however, noteworthy that Winzet accused the reformers of admitting as preachers and ministers in 'sindry places, young children of na eruditioun, except the reiding of Inglis and small entresses in grammar'. (Winzet, *Works*, 1.101.)

of the Superintendent.[22] The[p] other sort of Readers,[23] who have long continued in godlines, and have some gift of exhortation, who are of[q] hope to attain to the degree of a Minister and teach the children: we think an hundred merkes, or more or lesse,[r] at the discretion of the Kirk, may be appointed; so that difference be made, as said is,[s] betwixt them and the Ministers, that openly preaches the word and ministers the Sacraments.

Rests yet two[t] sorts of people to be provided for, upon[u] that which is called the Patrimony of the Kirk,[24] to wit, the poore, and teachers of the youthead.[25] Every several Kirk must provide for the poore within itselfe:[v] For feareful and horrible it is, that the poore, whom not onely God the Father in his Law, but Christ Jesus in his Evangel,[w] and the holy Spirit speaking by S. Paul hath so earnestly commended to our care; are universally so contemned and despised.[26] We are not Patrones for stubborne and

[p] In margin: *Nota*　　[q] *in*　　[r] *or lesse* not in Laing MS
[s] *difference, as said is, be*　　[t] *other two*　　[u] *of*　　[v] *the self*
[w] Hitherto *Evangell* in the Laing MS has been rendered Gospell, but not here. (See *supra*, p.87 n.*b*.)

[22] No specific mention was made of this on p. 106, but may have been implied in the *additio*. In April 1561 the Superintendent of Fife and his council at the meeting referred to on p. 107 n.42 decreed that the superintendent was to take the leading part in the examination of readers in future, but nothing further was said about his admission. (*StAKSR*, 1.75f.)

[23] This section refers to the statement about those who are to be encouraged to exhort, see *supra*, p. 106.

[24] See *infra*, p. 156.

[25] The responsibility of the Church for the poor (Canon law, *Corpus Iuris Canonici*, II c. XII q., 2, c. 26, 27, 28, 30, 31, Friedberg, 1.696ff, required that a quarter of the income of a church be set aside for the poor.) and for the furtherance of education was universally accepted in the Middle Ages, and the Continental reformers advocated that ecclesiastical revenues be continued to serve these ends. See for example Bucer, *De Regno Christi*, 1.14, 2.13, *Opera Latina*, 15.87ff, 140 and n. 28, 143ff, and Durkan, J., 'Care of the Poor: Pre-Reformation Hospitals' and 'Education in the Century of the Reformation', in McRoberts, *Scottish Reformation*, 116ff, and 145ff.

[26] Cf. Deuteronomy 15.4, Matthew 6.3, 1 Corinthians 16.2. Interesting information about the procedure adopted by one parish church for collecting alms and distributing them to the poor is found in Calderwood, *Buik of the Canagait*, 7, 13, 26, 29, 39. See also *StAKSR*, 1.lii and 2.lxxxv and Index *sub* Poor. In July 1569 the General Assembly petitioned the Regent for a portion of the teinds for the poor and in 1572 the Convention at Leith ordained for the partial support of the poor that all admitted to 'spiritual promotion' be required to pay a tenth part of that part of their promotion that was derived from teinds. (*BUK*, 1.146, 216.) It would appear, however, that the poor had very largely to depend upon the alms of the faithful and the sums collected as penalties for offences, although it is recorded in the *Accounts of the Collectors of Thirds of Benefices* that 'Beadsmen', formerly supported from Common Kirks now annexed to

idle beggars, who running from place to place make a craft of their begging whom the Civill Magistrat ought to punish.[27] But for the widow and fatherlesse, the aged, impotent or lamed, who neither can nor may travell for their sustentation, we say that God commands his people to be carefull, and therefore for such as also for persons of honestie fallen into decay and poverty,[x] ought such provision to[y] bee made, that of our aboundance their indigence might[z] be relieved. How this most conveniently and most easily may be done in every Citie and other parts of this Realme, God will shew you wisdome, and the meanes, so that your mindes be godly inclined thereto. All must not be suffred to beg that gladly would so doe, nether yet must beggers remain where they would;[a] but the stout and strong beggers[b] must be compelled to worke; and every person that may not worke, must bee compelled to repaire to the place where he or she was borne, unlesse of long continuance they have remained in one place, and there reasonable provision must be made for[c] sustentation as the Kirk[d] shall appoint. The order nor summes in our judgements can not particularly be appointed unto such times as the poore of everie Citie, Town and[e] Parish bee compelled to repaire to the places where they were borne, or of their residence,[f] where their names and number must be taken and put in roll, and then may the wisedome of the Kirk appoint stipends accordingly.[28]

[x] *penuritie*   [y] Not in Laing MS   [z] *should*   [a] *chuse*   [b] *beggar*
[c] *for their sustentatioun*
[d] *Churche* From this point the Laing MS has *Churche or Churches* and the 1621 text *Kirk* or *Kirkes*. See *supra*, p. 86 n.*f*, and *infra*, p. 129 n. *a*.
[e] *or*   [f] *residences*

---

the Crown, received allowances; a quantity of beer was given to the poor of Arbroath in 1566; and charitable payments by the religious houses were generally allowed as deductions from the sums on which the thirds were assessed. (Donaldson, *Thirds*, xx f.) See also the extracts from Edinburgh Burghs Records relative to the poor of the city in the immediate post-reformation period in Lee, *Lectures on the History of the Church of Scotland*, 2.392f.

[27] The Protestant reformers were uniformly severe in their criticism of begging. See Holl, *Cultural Significance of the Reformation*, 91ff. It is significant that the *Corpus Iuris Civilis, Codex Iustinianus*, XI.xxvi, prohibited those able to work from begging and that it was appealed to by Bucer, *De Regno Christi*, 2.14, *Opera Latina*, 15.147.

[28] Laws against beggars and vagrants were on the statute book and had been repeatedly re-enacted. In March 1574 Parliament sought to re-enforce those laws by ordaining that the elders and deacons in the cities and burghs and the 'heidsmen' in rural parishes should compile a register of the aged poor and impotent who must of necessity depend upon alms, and should then stent all parishioners for their maintenance. The collection of the tax and its distribution was to be

carried out by the deacons on the instructions of the elders. A similar act passed in 1579 transferred these responsibilities to the civil magistrates. (*APS*, 3.87ff, 140ff; cf. *StAKSR*, 2.678 n.; see also Calderwood, *Kirk of the Canagait*, 17, 19, and Index.) This section echoes many of the proposals made by Bucer, *De Regno Christi*, 2.14, *Opera Latina*, 15.143ff.

THE HEAD[a]

Of the Superintendents

Because we have appointed a larger stipend[1] to them that shall be Superintendents then to the rest of the Ministers, we have thought good to signifie to your Honours such reasons as moved us to make difference betwixt Preachers at this time,[2] as also how many Superintendents we thinke necessarie, with their bounds, office, election and causes that may deserve deposition from that charge.

We consider that if the Ministers whom God hath endowed with his singular[b] graces amongst us should be appointed to severall places[c] there to make their continuall residence, that then the greatest part of the[d] Realme should be destitute of all doctrine: which should not onely be the[e] occasion of great murmur, but also be dangerous to the salvation of many. And therefore we have thought it a thing most expedient at[f] this time,[3] that from the whole number of godly and learned men,[g] now presently in this realm, be selected ten[4] or twelve[h] (for in so many Provinces we have divided the whole) to whom charge and commandment should be[i] given, to plant and erect Kirkes, to set, order, and appoint Ministers, as the former order prescribes,[5] to the Countries that shall be appointed to their care where none are now. And by their meanes, your[j] love and common care over all Inhabitants

---

[a] Not in Laing MS, see Introduction, p. 26.   [b] Not in Laing MS
[c] *severall and certane placis*   [d] *this*   [e] Not in Laing MS   [f] *for*
[g] Not in Laing MS   [h] *twelf or ten*   [i] *shalbe*   [j] Not in Laing MS

---

[1] See *supra*, pp. 109f.

[2] This phrase seems to imply that the 'difference' had not been made earlier, but that, when circumstances had changed and plans had to be made to meet the needs of the whole country in the face of a considerable dearth of preachers, necessity or rather expediency required such an arrangement. See further Introduction, pp. 20f, 49f.

[3] *i.e.*, in the present situation.

[4] Ten dioceses are delimited in the following section. In the Mediaeval Church there had been thirteen dioceses. The words 'province' and 'diocese' are used interchangeably throughout.

[5] *i.e.*, in accordance with the order prescribed in the fourth head, *supra*, pp. 91ff.

of this Realme, to whom you are equally*k* debtors,[6] shall evidently
appear, as also the simple and ignorant, who perchance have never
heard Jesus Christ truely preached, shall come to some knowledge:
By the which many that are*l* dead in superstition and ignorance
shall attaine to some feeling of godlinesse, by the which they may
be provoked to search and seek farther knowledge of God, and
his true Religion and worshipping; where by the contrary, if they
shall be neglected,*m* then shall they not onely grudge, but also
seek*n* the meanes whereby they may continue in their blindnes,
or returne to their accustomed Idolatry; and therefore nothing
we desire more earnestly then that Christ Jesus bee universally
once preached throughout this Realme, which shall not suddenly
be, unlesse that by you, men be appointed, and compelled, faithfully to travell in such Provinces as to them shall be assigned.

*The names of the places of residence and severall Diocesses
of the Superintendents*

In primis, the Superintendent of Orknay, whose Diocesse shall*o*
comprehend the Iles Orknay,*o* Zetland, and Cathness and Stran-
aver;[7] his residence to be in*p* Kirkwall.[8]

k equall   *l now be*   *m thei shall not*   *n thei shall seik*
o shalbe to the Ylis of   *p in the Toun of*

[6] On the responsibility of the civil power for the religious well-being of the
realm see Introduction, pp. 62ff.

[7] This area thus covered the whole of the mediaeval diocese of Orkney and
part of the diocese of Caithness. It represents the modern Orkney, Shetland,
Caithness, and the north-eastern part of Sutherland. The combining of these
areas in one diocese, for which Kirkwall formed a natural centre, was in all
probability dictated by contemporary geographical knowledge. (See accompanying map on p. 80, and Introduction, pp. 80f.

[8] Kirkwall, the chief town of Orkney, had been the principal residence of the
Bishop from the middle of the 12th century. In the summer of 1560 the bishopric
was held by Adam Bothwell (*c.* 1530–93), who remained in Orkney. He joined
the reformers and became actively engaged in the work of reforming his diocese.
In 1561 and 1562 he was acting 'in place of a superintendent' and in 1563 he was
given a commission 'to plant kirks etc.' within his own bounds for one year by
the General Assembly and this commission appears to have been renewed until
1567; by 1568 two of the ministers of the diocese had been appointed commissioners to 'visit and plant kirks' in Orkney and Shetland. Robert Stewart (*c.* 1523–
1586), who had been appointed Bishop of Caithness in 1542, supported the
Reformation in 1560 and 1561 and in June 1563 was given a commission by the
General Assembly to plant kirks within his diocese and appears to have been
engaged in this work until 1571. Donaldson suggests that he may have been
active as a reforming bishop from 1560 and that the decision of the General
Assembly in 1563 may have been an attempt to 'remove any uncertainty as to
the legality of his work'. It is certainly clear that the plan for one united diocese

[2] The Superintendent of Rosse, whose Diocesse shall comprehend Rosse, Sutherland, Murray, with the north Iles of ^q Skie and^r Lewes with the^s adjacents; his residence to be in the Channonrie of Rosse.[9]

[3] The Superintendent of Argyle, whose Diocesse shall comprehend Argyle, Kyntyre,^t Lorne, the south Isles, Arran and^u Buite with their adjacents, with Lochwhaber; his^v residence to be in Argyle.^v [10]

| ^q of the | ^r and the | ^s with thair | ^t Not in Laing MS |
| ^u Not in Laing MS | | ^v Not in Laing MS | |

did not materialise as both incumbents were active on the side of the reformed Church in their respective bounds in the years immediately following the Reformation Parliament. (Donaldson, 'Bishop Adam Bothwell and the Reformation in Orkney' in *RSCHS*, 13 (1959), 85–100; Donaldson, 'The Scottish Episcopate at the Reformation' in *EHR*, 60 (1945), 355f; *BUK*, 1.32, 38, 112, 134, 165ff; Calderwood, *History*, 2.224; Watt, *Fasti Eccl. Scot.*, 61.)

[9] The area proposed for the new diocese of Ross comprehended those parts of the diocese of Caithness that had not been combined with Orkney (*i.e.*, the most of Sutherland), the diocese of Ross and a considerable part of the diocese of Moray with Skye and the outer Hebrides from the diocese of the Isles. This proposed new area represents an attempt to bring together those parts of the country for which the Chanonry of Ross, according to contemporary geographical knowledge, formed a convenient geographical centre, and an area that would be comparable in size to the other areas, and which could be supervised by one superintendent. The Chanonry of Ross had been the site of the diocese of Ross from the thirteenth century. Henry Sinclair (1508–65) held the Bishopric and Patrick Hepburn (†1573) the bishopric of Moray; neither was active in furthering the cause of the Reformation. In 1562 the General Assembly commissioned John Hepburn of Brechin to go to Moray to preach and if he found anyone qualified for the ministry to send them to the superintendent to be appointed for Aberdeen for examination and admission. In June of the following year three ministers were appointed commissioners for the area, John Hepburn for Moray, Robert Pont for Inverness and Donald Munro for Ross. Munro continued to be reappointed and was active until 1574; Pont is described as Commissioner for Moray, Inverness and Banff in 1563, 1565, 1568 and 1570, and in 1572 he is described as 'Superintendent of Murray'; he continued as Commissioner in 1573 and 1574. Hepburn was not reappointed after 1564. John Lesley succeeded to the bishopric of Ross 'presumably by papal provision' in 1566. From the records of the General Assembly it may be concluded that while attempts were made to have the area superintended by commissioners no attempt was made to unite the various parts under one commissioner. (Donaldson, *Scottish Reformation*, 56f, 66; Donaldson, 'The Scottish Episcopate at the Reformation' in *EHR*, 60 (1945), 354; Donaldson, *Thirds*, 214, 217; *BUK*, 27, 34, 40, 51, 63, 129, 150, 175, 178, 183, 203, 214, 217, 257, 282, 297, 321; Watt, *Fasti Eccl. Scot.*, 217, 270.)

[10] The diocese of Argyll comprised almost all the area defined here with the exception of the South Isles, Arran and Bute which were taken from the diocese of the Isles. The bishop's residence had from the thirteenth century been on the island of Lismore. By fixing the superintendent's place of residence in Argyll, *i.e.*, the district which has Inveraray as its centre, the reformers were pursuing the same

[4] The Superintendent of Aberdene, whose Diocesse is betwixt Dee and Spay conteining the Shirefdom of Aberdene and Bamfe; whose residence shall be in old Aberdene.[11]

[5] The Superintendent of Brechen, whose Diocesse shall be

---

policy which we have already noted of selecting a site which was, according to contemporary geographical knowledge, central in the proposed new area and one from which one person might reasonably be expected to carry out the responsibilities of his office. It was also the part of the country over which the Earl of Argyll, an active reformer, had control. The bishopric of Argyll was held by James Hamilton (†1580), half-brother of the Duke of Châtelherault. He joined the reformers, was present at the Parliament in August 1560, but did not actively engage in the reformation of his diocese. John Carswell (c. 1525–72) was present as Superintendent of Argyll at the Assembly in June 1562. Two years later he excused his absence from assemblies on account of the travelling required in the Isles. In 1566 he was presented to the bishopric of the Isles. Three years later he was censured by the Assembly for accepting the presentation without informing the Assembly. He is best remembered for his translation and adaptation of the Book of Common Order into Gaelic, which was published in 1567. (Matheson, 'Bishop Carswell' in *Transactions of the Gaelic Society of Inverness*, 42 (1953–59), 182–205; Donaldson, 'The Scottish Episcopate at the Reformation' in *EHR*, 60 (1945), 351, 354; *BUK*, 1.13, 144; Donaldson, *Scottish Reformation*, 59, 66; Watt, *Fasti Eccl. Scot.*, 206.)

11 The area to be covered by the Superintendent of Aberdeen comprised the former diocese of Aberdeen and part of the diocese of Moray. From the accompanying contemporary map it will be seen that this proposed area formed a natural geographical unit. Old Aberdeen had been the residence of the bishop from the twelfth century. William Gordon (†1577), who held the bishopric from 1546, did not take an active part in the Reformation, but retained and exercised the temporal functions of his title until his death. According to Calderwood the General Assembly in December 1561 gave commission to the Superintendent of Angus to visit the sheriffdoms on Aberdeen and Banff and in the following year petitioned the Privy Council for 'assistance' for him, and at the same time joined to him as 'associates' Christopher Goodman and John Row. In December of the same year it was complained that 'the order of the election and admission of the Superintendent of Aberdeen was not put in execution'. The Assembly thereupon nominated three ministers for election, ordained that the necessary edicts be published, and entrusted the Superintendents of Fife and Angus with the responsibility for inaugurating the person elected. Before the Assembly had, however, concluded its business it was decided to remit 'further advisement and nomination of persons to the Lords of the Privy Council', provided that the time set for the election was not altered. Two years later the Assembly repeated its nominations, fixed new dates for the election and inauguration and again petitioned the Privy Council for its assistance. In June 1565 the Assembly commissioned George Hay to plant kirks in the area until a superintendent be appointed or until the next Assembly. Hay continued to act as a commissioner on a yearly basis until well into the seventies. Clearly the reformers were anxious to have their proposals for this area put into effect. The fact that Gordon continued to receive the income of his title probably largely accounts for the fact that they were repeatedly thwarted, but it would appear that from 1565 Hay, despite his recurrent requests to be relieved, did exercise the oversight of the area. (Donaldson, 'The Scottish Episcopate at the Reformation' in *EHR*, 60 (1945), 354; Donaldson, *Scottish Reformation*, 56; *BUK*, 1.19, 27, 30, 54, 63, 141, 186, 321ff; Watt, *Fasti Eccl. Scot.*, 4.)

the whole S[h]irefdomes of^w the Mernes, Angus,^{w} and the brae of Marre to Dee: his residence to be in Brechen.[12]

[6] The Superintendent of^x Fiffe and^x Fotheringhame to Stirling and the whole Shire[f]dome of Perth; his residence to be in Saint androes.[13]

$^{w-w}$ *of Mearnis and Anguss*
$^{x-x}$ *of Sanctandrois; whose Diocesye shall comprehend the hoill schirefdome of Fyffe and*

[12] In delimiting this area the reformers again completely disregarded the existing ecclesiastical division in which the diocese of Brechin was extremely small and broken up and sought to create from lands that formerly belong to the dioceses of Brechin and Dunkeld and the archdiocese of St Andrews a new area roughly comparable to the size of that proposed for Aberdeen and, as will be seen from the accompanying map, forming a unit with clear natural boundaries. Brechin had been the residence of the bishop of the diocese from the twelfth century. At the reformation the bishopric was vacant. The way was therefore comparatively clear for putting this newly defined area under John Erskine of Dun (1509–89) who had for some considerable time been active in furthering the cause of the Reformation. His name appears in the list of those recognised by the first General Assembly as one 'apt and able to minister'; he was probably nominated as Superintendent of Angus in 1561, elected in 1562; he appears to have been in office by July 1561, and is recorded as having been present at the General Assembly of June 1562 in that capacity. In the following years he was prominent in the affairs of the Church but repeatedly requested to be relieved of his office. In March 1575 Erskine was continued as superintendent until the next Assembly and the Bishop of Brechin, a young man in his early twenties, was required to be present with him at visitation 'that he may see the order and proceeding used by the Superintendent in his office'. (*BUK*, 1.4, 13, 65, 92, 190, 242, 318; Donaldson, *Scottish Reformation*, 65, 127; St*AKSR*, 1.113.)

[13] This area, taken from the extensive mediaeval archdiocese of St Andrews, and the diocese of Dunblane, will be seen from the accompanying map to have been regarded as clearly delimited by its physical geography, on the north by the Tay, on the south by the Forth and on the west by the Trossachs. It was also probably thought to have been roughly comparable in size to the provinces already outlined for the superintendents of Aberdeen and Brechin. St Andrews had been the residence of the bishop from the eleventh century. John Winram (c. 1492–1582), sub-prior of the Augustinian priory of St Andrews, had remained outwardly loyal to the mediaeval Church but in 1560 firmly took his stand with the reformers. He was elected 'Superintendent of Fyff, Fotheryk and Strathern' in St Andrews on 13th April 1561, by the 'common consent of lordis, barronis, ministeris, eldaris of the saidis bowndis, and otheris common pepill present for the tym, according to the ordor provydit in the Buk of Reformacion', *i.e.*, the Book of Discipline. The *Register of the Minister, Elders and Deacons of the Christian Congregation of St Andrews* (referred to as St*AKSR*) contains the record of the proceedings of the Superintendent's Court when it met in St Andrews. On the appointment of John Douglas as Archbishop of St Andrews in 1572 the General Assembly requested Winram to 'use his own jurisdiction as of before in the provinces not yet subject to the Archbishop of St Andrews and to concur with the Archbishop, when he requires in his visitation or otherwise within his bounds'. In the following two years he is referred to as Superintendent of Strathearn. In March 1574 he demitted his office at the General Assembly, but in the next

[7] The Superintendent of Edinburgh, whose Diocesse shall comprehend the whole Shirefdom^v of Lowthian and Stirling, and^z the South side of the water of Forth;^{a} his residence to be in Edinburgh.^{b} ^{14}

[8] The Superintendent of Jedburgh, whose Diocesse shall comprehend the whole^c Tivitdail, Tweeddaill, Liddisdail,^{d} and thereto is added by consent of the whole Kirk, the Merse, Lawderdaill and Weddaill,^{d} with the forrest of Ettrick; his residence to be in Jedburgh.^{e} ^{15}

^{v} *schirefdomes* ^{z} *on*
^{a} Adds '*and thairto is added by consent of the hoill Churche, Mersse, Lauderdaill and Weddell*' which appear in the 1621 edition in the following paragraph.
^{b} Not in Laing MS ^{c} Not in Laing MS $^{d-d}$ See *supra*, note *a*.
^{e} Not in Laing MS

---

year the General Assembly gave 'commission of a superintendentship to Mr John Winram, Prior of Portmook, in the bounds of Fife and Strathern, exeming the bounds appertaining to the Bishop of Dunkeld'. He is thereafter referred to as Superintendent of Fife. (*BUK*, 1.13, 65, 175, 223, 237, 242, 261, 271, 297, 318, 320ff; *Bannatyne Memorials*, 228; *StAKSR*, see Index.)

^{14} This area stretching from Stirling to the Lammermuir Hills formed much of that part of the mediaeval archdiocese of St Andrews that lay to the south of the Forth and which was administered as the archdeaconry of Lothian. As will be seen from the accompanying map it was probably thought of as comparatively small. It is not therefore surprising to note in the Laing MS that by consent of the whole Church (by which we are to understand the General Assembly of December 1560) was added 'the Merse, Lauderdale and Wedale' (Stow), which were also within the archdeaconry and which would appear to have been regarded by the maker of the map as fairly extensive. Thus when all parts assigned to this province were taken together they were probably thought to have formed an area roughly similar in size to those already proposed for the superintendents of Aberdeen, Angus and Fife, and to have been similarly delimited by natural boundaries of the Forth, the Pentland and Lammermuir Hills and the lower reaches of the Tweed. John Spottiswoode (1510–85) had received orders from Archbishop Cranmer in 1538 and had been presented to the vicarage of Calder in 1547. He joined the reformers and was nominated Superintendent of Lothian in March 1561, but continued at Calder. He appears to have actively engaged in the oversight of his province, of which interesting evidence is presented in Calderwood, *Kirk of the Canagait*. In 1572 Spottiswoode was requested by the General Assembly to continue in his jurisdiction without prejudice of the Archbishop of St Andrews except by virtue of his commission. (Donaldson, *Scottish Reformation*, 65, 123f, 226ff; *BUK*, 1.13, 41f, 223, 242, 280; Introduction, p. 69.)

^{15} The area of this proposed diocese (including the section *d–d*, see note 14) comprised those parts of the Border Country known as the Middle and East Marches. The East March (the Merse, Lauderdale and Wedale) as has been pointed out above formed part of the archdiocese of St Andrews, whereas the Middle March formed part of the archdiocese of Glasgow. The fact that the two texts assign the section *d–d* to different superintendent's areas may be due to a slip in manuscript transmission or to some disagreement in the drawing up of this section; some may have held that a more viable superintendent's diocese would be created by treating the Middle and East Marches as one unit for ecclesiastical

[9] The Superintendent of Glasgow, whose Diocesse shall comprehend Clidsdaill, Renfrew, Menteth, Lennox,[f] Kyle and Cunninghame; his residence to be in Glasgow.[16]

[10] The Superintendent of Dumfriess, whose Diocesse shall comprehend Galloway, Carrik, Nithisdal, Annandaile with the rest of the dailes in the west; his residence to be in Dumfriesse.[17]

[f] *Levinax*

---

purposes, others may have held that the Superintendent of Edinburgh's diocese ought to coincide with the mediaeval archdeaconry of Lothian. In any event the East March was taken into the area superintended by John Spottiswoode. The reformers considered the proposed new diocese important and had appointed one of their trusted ministers, Paul Methven, as minister at Jedburgh. In December 1562 the General Assembly nominated two ministers for election as Superintendent of Jedburgh and appointed Knox and Spottiswoode to inaugurate the person elected, but before the close of the Assembly the matter was remitted to the Privy Council 'provided the date was not altered'. But in December 1564 the General Assembly again is found petitioning the Privy Council for a superintendent for the area. Nothing further is recorded in the register of the General Assembly until August 1573 when commission was given to John Brand, minister of Holyroodhouse, to visit the area until the next General Assembly. A similar commission was given to Andrew Clayhill in March 1575. (Laing, *Knox's Works* 2.87; Dickinson, *Knox's History*, 1.334; *BUK*, 1.28, 30, 53, 283, 318.)

[16] The area of this proposed new diocese comprised parts of the former archdiocese of Glasgow and part of the diocese of Dunblane. As will be seen from the map Glasgow was thought to have formed a fairly central point from which to superintend an area roughly comparable in size to those proposed for the other superintendents. At the time of the Reformation the see was in the possession of James Beaton (1517–1603), who remained loyal to the Mediaeval Church and left for France in July 1560. John Willock (†1585) was assigned to Glasgow soon after the Reformation Parliament and was elected superintendent of Glasgow in March 1561 but was not admitted until 14th September. He attended the General Assembly in June 1562 and 'was almost certainly elected moderator' – an office which he occupied in 1563, 1564, and 1565, but during the following two years of uncertainty he was out of the country for much of the time. He was again moderator of the General Assembly in July 1568 but left for England immediately thereafter. In June 1563 he was commissioned to plant kirks in Nithsdale, and in December to visit Urr and Nith because the Kirks 'pertained to that diocie of old'. The General Assembly in 1563 had also commissioned two ministers to plant kirks in Menteith and in 1565 John Row of Perth was commissioned by the Assembly to visit Kyle, Carrick and Cunningham. It would therefore appear that, as Superintendent, Willock's area of responsibility did not always coincide with that proposed here for the Superintendent of Glasgow. In the years following Willock's departure the General Assembly repeatedly appointed Andrew Hay as commissioner for the diocese. (Watt, *Fasti Eccl. Scot.*, 150; Shaw, 'John Willock' in Shaw, *Reformation and Revolution*, 42–69; *BUK*, 1.13, 35, 38, 73, 121, 150, 158, 200, 203; and Introduction, p. 6.)

[17] The area proposed for this superintendent comprised the entire diocese of Galloway and a considerable part of the archdiocese of Glasgow; it was probably regarded as similar in size to those areas outlined for the other superintendents and for which Dumfries was the most important town. Alexander Gordon

Those men must not be suffered to live as your idle Bishops have done heretofore; neither must they remaine where gladly they would, but they must be preachers themselves, and such as may*g* not make long*g* residence in any*h* place till their Kirkes be planted and provided of Ministers, or at the least of Readers.[18] Charge must be given to them that they remain in no*i* place above twenty*j* daies in their visitation, till they have passed through their whole bounds. They must thrice everie week preach at the least; and when they returne to their principall Towne and Residence, they must be likewise exercised in preaching and*k* edification of the Kirk:*l* and yet they must not be suffered to continue there so long, that*m* they may seeme to neglect their other kirks: But after they have remained in their chiefe towne three or foure moneths

g-g may mak no long   *h* ony one   *i* no one   *j* twenty or threttye
k and in   *l* Churche thaire   *m* as

(†1575) had been nominated to the see of Galloway in 1559, and had been since September of that year closely associated with the leaders of the reformation movement. He attended the Reformation Parliament and in January 1561 signed the Book of Discipline and was active in his diocese in support of the reformation. The General Assembly of June 1562 in response to a request from Gordon for formal recognition considered that he was not Superintendent of Galloway as he had no nomination or presentation by the Privy Council or the province of Galloway, but, if he had such a nomination from the Lords he had not kept the 'order' for the election of superintendents. The Assembly was, however, prepared to further him, if the proper order was followed. In the meantime, Knox, Willock, George Hay and Robert Hamilton were commissioned to preach in the unplanted kirks. In the following December the Assembly nominated for the office Alexander Gordon and Robert Pont and appointed a committee to inaugurate the nominee elected, but as in the cases mentioned above the matter was remitted before the conclusion of the Assembly to the Privy Council, provided the date set for the admission was kept. At the same Assembly Gordon was given a commission to 'admit ministers, exhorters and readers, and to doe such other things as war before accustomed in planting kirks'. In June 1563 Gordon was 'tried' in the same way as the other superintendents present and had his commission to plant kirks in Wigton and Kirkcudbright renewed for a further year. Gordon was listed after the superintendents in the record of the General Assembly of December 1563 and is styled elsewhere in that record as commissioner and as superintendent. From 1565 he was accused of neglecting his responsibilities and in July 1568 discharged from exercising the office of a commissioner. In subsequent years John Row and David Lyndsay were appointed commissioners for various parts of the west, and later Patrick Adamson and Peter Watson. (Donaldson, 'Alexander Gordon, Bishop of Galloway (1559–75) and his Work in the Reformed Church' in *Trans. Dumfries and Galloway*, 24 (1945–46), 111–128; Donaldson, *Scottish Reformation*, 58f, 157f; *BUK*, 1.15, 17f, 28ff. 38f, 130f, 150, 186, 239, 256, 273, 316, 318ff; Watt, *Fasti Eccl. Scot.*, 132.)

18 The compilers of this section, anxious to make it absolutely clear that the superintendent is not to be confused with the bishops of the pre-Reformation Church, restate his responsibilities (cf. *supra*, p. 115) and in the following sentences lay down precise details for the conducting of his visitations.

at most, they shall bee compelled (unlesse by sicknesse they be retained) to re-enter in visitation, In which they shall not onely preach, but also examine the life, diligence and behaviour of the Ministers,[19] as also the order of the[n] kirkes, the[o] manners of the people. They must further consider how the poore be provided, how the youth be instructed; They must admonish where admonition needeth and dresse such things as by good counsell they be able to appease. And finally they must note such crimes as be heynous, that by the censure of the Kirk the same may be corrected.[20] If the Superintendent be found negligent in any of the[p] chiefe points of his office, and especially if he be noted negligent in preaching of the word, and[q] visitation of the[r] Kirkes, or if he be convict of such crimes, which in[s] common Ministers are damned, he must be deposed, without respect of his person, or office.[21]

The[t] Election of Superintendents

In this present necessity, the nomination, examination and admission of the Superintendent[u] cannot be so straight as we require and as afterwards it must be.[22]

For this present, therefore, we think it[v] expedient, that either your Honours by yourselves nominate so many as may serve the

[n] thaire   [o] Not in Laing MS   [p] these   [q] and in   [r] his
[s] of ony of those crymes which in the   [t] Off the   [u] Superintendentis
[v] sufficient

[19] In head VIII (*infra*, pp. 174ff) details are outlined for the procedure in the disciplining of ministers which are not in complete agreement with the contents of this paragraph. See further Introduction, pp. 36ff, 52.

[20] An informative picture of the oversight of a minister and congregation exercised by the Superintendent of Lothian is provided by the minutes of the Kirk Session of the Canongate. During the period August 1564 to August 1567 the Superintendent is recorded as having been present on four occasions at a general assembly of all the members of the congregation prior to the Communion and to have inquired into the life and doctrine of the ministers, elders and deacons and into the general affairs of the church. On one occasion he was present when the Kirk Session was discussing the arrangements for the reception into the Church of a penitent woman who had committed murder. On one pre-communion visitation when he could not be present his place was supplied by John Craig, Knox's colleague at St Giles. (Calderwood, *Kirk of the Canagait*, 24, 32, 36, 42, 62, 70.)

[21] The records of the General Assemblies indicate that the trial and censure of the diligence of the superintendents in the fulfilling of their responsibilities was regularly the business of the first days and was of a most thorough and exacting nature. (*BUK*, 1.14, 25f, 31, 39, 52f, 57, 65, 77, 112.) See also *infra*, p. 127 n.29.

[22] See *infra*, p. 125.

forewritten Provinces, or that ye give commission to such men as[w] ye suppose the feare of God to be in,[x] to do the same. And[y] the same men being called in your presence shall be by you and such as your Hon[ours] please call unto you for consultation in that case appointed to their provinces. Wee thinke it expedient and necessary, that as well the Gentlemen as Burgess[z] of every diocie be made privy at the same[a] to the election of the superintendent, as well to bring the kirk in some practise of her liberty, as that[b] the Pastor may[c] be the[c] better favoured of the flock whom themselves have chosen.[23]

If your Honours cannot finde for this present so many able as[d]

[w] *as in whom*   [x] Not in Laing MS   [y] *And that*
[z] *burgesses*   [a] *same tyme*   [b] *to make*   [c-c] Not in Laing MS
[d] *able men as the*

[23] In the period immediately following the Convention in January–February 1561 and before the end of the first week of March five superintendents were nominated by the Privy Council. The edict for the election of the Superintendent of St Andrews, dated 20th March 1561, states that after the approval of the Book of Reformation the Privy Council directed and commanded the ministers, elders, and deacons of Lothian, Fife, Mearns, Glasgow and Argyll to issue election edicts in favour of John Spottiswoode for Edinburgh, John Winram for St Andrews, John Erskine of Dun for Brechin, John Willock for Glasgow and John Carswell for Argyll. The election of Winram was to take place in St Andrews on 13th April; the earls, lords, barons, burgesses, ministers, elders of kirks and all others 'to quhom vot apperteins in eleccion of sic cheef ministeris' were charged to be present and vote. John Spottiswoode was elected and admitted, according to 'The Form and Order of the Election of the Superintendents', on 9th March 1561, which states that 'The Lords of Secret Council had given charge and power to the Kirks of Lothian to chosse' him as 'Superintendent'. The mandate from the Privy Council to John Spottiswoode as superintendent, dated 10th March 1561, indicated that he had in conformity with the book 'of reformatioun and discipline' been previously elected to that office, and his own circular letter of 22nd March states that he was appointed 'by the consent of the kirks of Lautheane and by the commandement of the nobilitie'. No additional details of the nomination of Erskine of Dun have been discovered and it 'appears that he was not formally "elected" ' until the beginning of 1562. John Willock, as has been noted above, was immediately after the Reformation Parliament appointed to Glasgow, and was to be elected superintendent in the same way as Spottiswoode and Winram in March. He was not, however, admitted until 13th September and then in the company of many of the leading Protestants of the west including the Duke of Châtelherault, the Earls of Arran and Glencairn, and Lords Ruthven, Boyd and Ochiltree. It would appear that the election and admission took place at one service. No details of the election and admission of Carswell have survived. The presence of all five superintendents at the General Assembly of June 1562 is recorded, in the order given in the St Andrews edict, at the head of the sederunt. Despite repeated requests by the General Assemblies no further nominations were made by the Privy Council. (*StAKSR*, 72–75; *CSP Scot.*, 1, no. 967, p. 523, no. 1023, p. 555; *BUK*, 1.13. Laing, *Knox's Works*, 2.144; Dickinson, *Knox's History*, 2.273; Donaldson, *Scottish Reformation*, 65f, 226ff; Shaw, 'John Willock' in *Reformation and Revolution*, 62, and Introduction, pp. 5, 21f, 53ff, 64f.)

necessity requireth, then in our judgements, more profitable it is those provinces vaike till God provide better for[e] them,[e] then that men unable to edifie and governe the Kirk, so[f] suddenly be[f] placed in that charge; for experience hath teached[g] us what pestilence hath been ingendred in the Kirk by men unable to discharge their offices.[24]

When therefore after three yeares any Superintendent shall depart, or chance to be deposed, the cheefe Towne within the[h] Province, to wit, the Ministers, Elders and Deacons, with the Magistrate and Councell of the same Towne shall nominate and by publick Edicts proclaime, as well to the Superintendent, as to two or three Provinces next adjacent, two or three of the most learned and godly[i] Ministers within the whole Realme, that from amongst them one with publick consent may be elected and appointed to the office then vacant. And this the chiefe towne shall be bound to doe within the space[j] of twenty daies, which being expired, and no man presented, then shall three of the next adjacent Provinces with consent of their Superintendents, Ministers and Elders enter in[k] the right and priviledge of the Town[l] and shall present everyone of them, one or twa if they list, to the chiefe Town to be examined, as the order requires.[25] As also it shall be lawfull for all the kirkes of the Diocesse to nominate within the same time such persons as they thinke worthy to stand in Election, who[m] all must be put in an Edict.[m]

After[n] nomination to be made,[n] publick Edicts must be sent forth[o] warning all men that have any exception[p] against the

---

[e-e] Not in Laing MS   [f-f] be suddanlie   [g] taught   [h] that
[i] most godlie   [j] terme   [k] in into   [l] the cheaf town
[m-m] which man be put in edict   [n-n] After the nominationis be maid
[o] first   [p] objectioun

---

[24] A reference to the appointment of unqualified persons in the Mediaeval Church. That no more than five superintendents were appointed was not due to a lack of suitable ministers, but to the facts that some parts of the new diocese were being adequately cared for by conforming bishops, in particular Bothwell of Orkney and Gordon of Galloway, and that the Lords were unprepared to make available the sums required for the maintenance of the superintendents – the revenue of the temporality of the bishoprics. As has been noted above, the General Assembly repeatedly requested further appointments and even drew up leets in December 1562 for Aberdeen, Jedburgh and, Dumfries, but were prevented from having their plans executed. The General Assemblies also made provision for those parts of the new diocese of Orkney which were not being superintended by Bothwell and the new diocese of Ross. (BUK, 28, 30, and supra, notes 8, 11, 15, and 17, and infra, p. 162; Donaldson, Scottish Reformation, 128.)

[25] See infra, p. 126 n.28.

persons nominate or against any[q] of them to be present in the chiefe Town at the[r] day affixed and place[r] to object what they can against the election of any[s] of them. Thirty dayes we thinke sufficient to be assigned thereto. Thirty dayes, we meane, after the[t] nomination be made.[26]

Which day of the[u] election being come, the whole ministers of the[v] Province, with three or foure[w] Superintendents next adjacent or that shall be thereto nominated,[x] shall examine not onely the learning, but also the manners, prudence and habilitie to governe the Kirk of all those that be nominated; that he who shall be found most worthy may be burdened with the charge. If the ministers of the whole Provinces should bring with them the votes of them that were committed to their care, the election should be the more free. But alwayes the votes of them[y] that convene should be[z] required.[27]

The examinations must be publickly made. They that stand in election must publickly preach and men must be charged in the name of God, to vote according to conscience and not after affection.

If any thing be objected against him[a] that standeth in election, the Superintendents and Ministers must consider whether the objection be made of conscience or malice, and they must answer accordingly. Other ceremonies then sharp examination, approbation of the ministers and Superintendents with the publicke consent of the Elders and people[b] we cannot allow.[28]

The Superintendent being elected and appointed to his charge

[a] ony one   [r-r] day and place affixit   [s] any one   [t] that the
[u] Not in Laing MS   [v] that   [w] or mo of the   [x] named   [y] all those
[z] must be   [a] any   [b] people then present

[26] For the edict issued by the ministers, elders and deacons of St Andrews see StAKSR, 72 ff.It is dated 20th March; the election was fixed for the 13th April. As the five superintendents were probably nominated by the Privy Council at the same time, it would appear that this injunction was not followed, except perhaps in the case of Spottiswoode. (See supra, note 23.)

[27] The St Andrews edict charges all those who have a vote to be present 'to assist the said eleccion, and be ther votis to consent to the same, or else to oppone aganis the lyff and doctrine of the person nominated'. The edict, however, makes no mention of an examination of the nominee. (StAKSR, 74f; cf. Laing, Knox's Works, 2.144f; Dickinson, Knox's History, 2.273.)

[28] The procedure outlined is in essentials similar to that already presented for the admission of a minister. See supra, pp. 101ff. 'The Form and Order of the Election of Superintendents' dated 9th March 1561 and used in the election and admission of John Spottiswoode is printed in Laing, Knox's Works, 2.144ff; Dickinson, Knox's History, 2.273ff.

must be subject to the censure and correction of^c ministers and Elders, not of his chiefe towne onely, but also of the whole Province over the which he is appointed overseer.[29]

If his offence^d be knowne and the ministers and Elders of the^e towne and Province^e be negligent in correcting him, then the next one or two Superintendents with their ministers and Elders may convene him and the ministers and Elders of his chief town (provided that it be within his owne Province or chiefe towne) and may^f accuse or^g correct as well the Superintendent in these things that are worthy of correction as the ministers and Elders of^h their negligence and ungodly tolerance of his offence.^{i}

Whatever crime deserves deposition or correction of any other minister, deserveth the same in the Superintendent, without exception of persons.^{j} [30]

After that the Kirk is^k established and three yeares be passed, we require that no man be called to the office of a superintendent who hath not at the least two years given declaration of his faithful labours in the ministrie of the same^l Kirk.

No Superintendent may be transferred at the pleasure or request of any one province, no, not without the consent of the whole counsell of the Kirk and that for grave causes and considerations.[31]

Of one thing in the end we must admonish your Honours, to wit, that in the^m appoynting of the^n Superintendents for this present, ye disappoint not your chief townes and where learning is exercised, of such ministers as more may profit by residence in one place than by continuall travell from place to place. For if ye so doe, the youth in these places shall lack the profound interpretation of Scripture;^{o} and so shall it be long before Four^p garden^p send forth many plants; where by the contrary, if one or two

^{c} *of the*	^{d} *offencis*	$^{e-e}$ *of his Province*	^{f} *and may*	^{g} *and*	^{h} *for*
^{i} *offencis*	^{j} *persoun*	^{k} *be*	^{l} *of some*	^{m} Not in Laing MS
^{n} Not in Laing MS		^{o} *of the scriptuis*	$^{p-p}$ *that your gardenis*

[29] This paragraph and the one following are merely an adaptation of the procedure outlined on pp. 176ff for the disciplining of a minister. Although the trial and censure of superintendents took place at the beginning of every General Assembly, no evidence of censuring by the lower courts of the Church has been discovered. It would appear that in practice their complaints were brought directly to the Assemblies. (See reference to note 21 *supra*.)

[30] See *infra*, p. 177.

[31] This paragraph embodies the same principle which was to be applied to ministers. See *supra*, p. 103, where the decision is said to lie with 'the whole church or the most part thereof'. On the meaning of this phrase and the 'whole council of the Kirk' see Introduction, pp. 69f.

townes be continually exercised as they may, the Commonwealth shall shortly feast*q* of their fruit, to the comfort of the godly.[32]

q taist

[32] As has been pointed out *supra*, p. 105, and Introduction, p. 5, one of the earliest actions of the leaders of the Reformation in August 1560 was to assign certain of their leading preachers to towns and cities. We have here further evidence of the importance they attached to them and to the academic centres.

For the Schooles[1]

Seeing that the office and duty of the godly Magistrate is not onely to purge the Church[a] of God from all superstition and to set it at libertie from tyranny[b] and bondage,[b] but also to provide at[e] the utmost of his power, how it may abide in some[d] puritie in[e] the posteritie[e] following, we can but[f] freely communicate our judgments with your Honours in this behalfe.[2]

The Necessity of Schooles

Seeing that God hath determined that his Kirke here in earth shall be taught not by Angels, but by men;[3] and seeing that men are borne ignorant of[g] God and[g] of all godlinesse,[4] and seeing also he[h] ceases to illuminat men miraculously, suddenly changing them as he did the[i] Apostles and others in the primitive Kirk:[5] Of

[a] One of the few ocasions where the Laing MS and the 1621 text both have *Church*. See *supra*, p. 113 n.d.
[b-b] *bondage of tyrranis*   [c] *to*   [d] *in the same*   [e-e] *to the posteriteis*
[f] *can not but*   [g-g] Not in Laing MS   [h] *now God*   [i] *as that he did his*

[1] On the relation of this section to the rest of the Book see Introduction, pp. 25ff, 54ff.

[2] Knox had previously emphasised the necessity and importance of education in 'Forme of Prayers' and in 'A Brief Exhortation to England'. A similar emphasis had been made by both the Lutheran and reformed Churches. For example, Martin Luther, in 'The Address to the Christian Nobility of the German Nation' published in 1520, and in 'The Address to the Council men of all the Towns of Germany' published in 1524, emphasised the responsibility of the princes and magistrates to provide for the education of children; and Bucer, in *De Regno Christi*, 2.48, 49, *Opera Latina*, 15.236ff, advocated that in every village, town, and city, men should be appointed to take charge of education from childhood to manhood. (Laing, *Knox's Works*, 4.177, 5.520; Dunkley, *Reformation in Denmark*, 80ff; Herminjard, *Correspondance*, 4.299; *Ordonnances ecclésiastiques*, Bergier, *Registres*, 1.6, and *CR*, 10.1.21ff; Borgeaud, *L'Académie de Calvin*, 29ff.)

[3] Cf. Calvin, *Institutes*, 4.1.5: 'But as he [God] did not entrust the ancient folk to angels but raised up teachers from the earth truly to perform the angelic office, so also it is his will to teach us through human means.'

[4] Cf. *Confession of Faith*, cap. XII, and Calvin, *Institutes*, 2.2.19.

[5] Cf. Calvin, *Institutes*, 1.9.3. Cf. Bucer, *De Regno Christi*, 2.48, *Opera Latina*, 15.239: 'Quamobrem veteres sancti patres apud quamlibet Ecclesiam scholam esse voluerunt, in qua cuncti pueri Christo Domino per sacrum baptisma consecrati literas atque religionis nostrae catechismum edocerentur. Tales scholas necesse est ... apud nos frequentes restituti, si volumus Christum plene apud nos regnare.'

necessitie it is that your Honours be most careful for the vertuous education and godly upbringing of the youth of this realme; if either ye now thirst unfainedly [for] the advancement of Christ's glorie or yet desire the continuance of his benefits to the generation following. For as the youth must succeed to us so we ought to bee carefull that they have[j] knowledge and erudition to profit and comfort that which ought to be most deare to us, to wit, the kirk and spouse of our[k] Lord Jesus.

Of necessitie therefore we judge it, that every severall kirk have one[l] School-maister appointed,[6] such a one at least as is able to teach Grammar and the Latine tongue if the town be of any reputation.[7] If it be upaland where the people convene to doctrine but once in the week,[8] then must either the reader or the minister there appointed take care over the children and youth of the parish,[9] to instruct them in the[m] first rudiments and especially in the Catechisme[10] as we have it now translated in the booke of

---

[j] *the knowledge*   [k] *the*   [l] *a*   [m] *thair*

[6] For a discussion of the evidence for the existence of some parish schools in Scotland in the sixteenth century see Durkan, 'Education in the Century of the Reformation' in McRoberts, *Essays on the Scottish Reformation*, 146ff. For general accounts of education in Scotland prior to the Reformation see Grant, *Burgh Schools*, p. 1–75; Edgar, *History of Early Scottish Education*, 84–239, 252–254; and Kerr, *Scottish Education*, 1–30.

[7] By 'grammar and the Latine tongue' was understood, Latin syntax and spoken Latin, the language of all academic study. The second half of this sentence echoes Canon 201 of the Provincial Council of 1549; 'Item the archdeacon of St Andrews shall take care concerning the grammar school of the city of St Andrews that he be versed in grammatical subjects . . . amply competent in other respects to teach the boys and such as do not know the simplest elements of grammar.' The reformers clearly wished to bring within their educational scheme for the whole country the already existing grammar schools which had been founded in most burghs. As early as November 1559 the reformers had procured the appointment of a suitably qualified master for Ayr. At the school attended by James Melville at Logie-Montrose an educational programme comparable to that of a grammar school was followed and this was continued by him at the grammar school of Montrose from which he was at the age of fourteen prepared to enter the Arts course at St Andrews. (Patrick, *Statutes*, 109; Melvill, *Diary*, 16ff; Boyd, *Education in Ayrshire*, 12f; Pryde, *Ayr Burgh Accounts*, lxii ff; Grant, *Burgh Schools*, 44ff.)

[8] See *infra*, p. 180.

[9] The General Assembly of December 1565 enacted 'That everie superintendent within his owne bounds inquire diligentlie if ministers and exhorters having stipends, manses, and gleebes, teache the youth in countrie parishes; and if they doe not, that he compell them to doe the same, under paine of removall, and others to be placed in their rowme'. (Calderwood, *History*, 2.300.)

[10] In 1563 James Melville at the age of seven was sent to a school in the rural parish of Logie-Montrose which was conducted by the minister and where he

common[n] order called the order of Geneva.[11]

And furder we think it expedient that in every notable town, and specially in the town of the Superintendent,[12] there[o] be erected a Colledge, in which the arts, at least Logick and Rhetorick, together with the tongues, be read by sufficient masters, for whom honest stipends must be appointed.[13] As also provision for those that be poore and not able by themselves, nor by their friends to be sustained at letters, and[p] in speciall those that[p] come from Landward.[14]

The fruit and commoditee hereof shall suddenly appeare. For first, the youthhead and tender children shall bee nourished, and brought up in vertue in presence of their friends, by whose good attendance many inconveniences may bee avoyded in which the youth commonly fall either by overmuch[q] libertie which they have in strange and unknowne places, while they cannot rule themselves: or else for lack of good attendance and such[r]

[n] *of our Common*   [o] Not in Laing MS   [p-p] *especiallie such as*
[q] *too muche*   [r] *of suche*

---

was taught 'to reid the Catechisme, Prayers and Scripture . . . the Rudiments of the Latin Grammair, withe the vocables in Latin and Frenche . . .'. (Melvill, *Diary*, 16f.)

[11] Instruction of children by using a catechism became universal practice in the sixteenth century among Protestants. In the programme of education outlined for Lausanne in 1547 and for Geneva in 1559 the catechism was taught in the first year at school along with 'prima literarum elementa'. An English translation of the catechism composed by Calvin for Geneva was included in *Forme of Prayers* in 1556. (Vuilleumier, *Histoire*, 1.409; Borgeaud, *L'Académie de Calvin*, 628; Laing, *Knox's Works*, 4.143ff; Torrance, *School of Faith*, 3ff; and *infra*, p. 134.)

[12] See *supra*, pp. 116ff, where eight superintendents' towns are named.

[13] An arts college or *Schola publica* which provided an intermediate programme of education for those between the ages of fifteen (or sixteen) and twenty (or twenty-one) and preliminary to study in one of the higher faculties of medicine, law or theology formed an essential part of the programme of humanist education advocated by the educational reformers of the sixteenth century, especially by Gouvea, for the famous Collège de Guyenne at Bordeaux in 1534, by Sturm for Strasbourg in 1538, by Baduel for Nîmes in 1542. This was followed by Cordier in Lausanne in 1547 and by Calvin in Geneva in 1559. It was also followed at Basel in 1541 and at Heidelberg in 1546. For the arts college it was considered that the curriculum of the mediaeval university, which had been fixed by long tradition, should be redrawn and that the later poets and the languages, especially Greek, should be studied before rhetoric and dialectic which were in origin Greek studies. (Gaullieur, *Histoire du Collège de Guyenne*, 95ff; Schmidt, 'Mémoire de Jean Sturm sur le projet d'organisation du Gymnase de Strasbourg' in *Bulletin de l'Histoire du Protestantisme français*, 25 (1876), 499ff; Le Coultre, *Maturin Cordier*, 481ff; Gaufrès, *Claude Baduel*, 14ff, 39ff, 47f; Vuilleumier, *Histoire*, 1.411f; Borgeaud, *L'Académie de Calvin*, 25ff.

[14] See *infra*, p. 132.

necessitie as their tender age requires.[15] Secondly, the exercise of[s] children[16] in every kirke shall bee great instruction to the aged. Last, the great Schooles, called the[t] universities, shall bee replenished with these that shall[u] bee apt to learning.

For this must bee carefully provided that no father of what estate or condition that ever he be, use his children as his own fantasie, especially in their youthhead, but all must be compelled to bring up their children in learning and vertue.[17] The rich and potent[18] may not be permitted to suffer their children to spend their youth in vaine idlenesse as heretofore they have done, but they must be exhorted and by the censure of the Kirk compelled to dedicate their sonnes by good exercises[v] to the profite of the Kirk and[w] Commonwealth; and that they must doe of their own expences because they are able. The children of the poore must be supported and sustained of[x] the charge of the Kirk,[19] tryall[y] being taken[y] whether the spirit of docility be[z] in them found[z] or not. If they be found apt to learning and letters, then may they not (we meane niether the sonnes of the rich nor yet of[a] the poore) be permitted to reject learning but must be charged to continue their studie, so that the Commonwealth may have some comfort by them. And for this purpose must discreet, grave and learned

---

[s] *of the*   [t] Not in Laing MS   [u] Not in Laing MS   [v] *escercise*
[w] *and to the*   [x] *on*   [y–y] *till tryell be tackin*   [z–z] *be fund in them*
[a] *yit the sonis of*

[15] An allusion to the well-known behaviour of mediaeval students. The French Swiss reformers were strongly opposed to the education of children away from home, but not Baduel. 'Lorsque Calvin réalisa son plan d'établir une Académie à Genève il renonça entièrement à organiser un internat.' (Le Coultre, *Maturin Cordier*, 188f; Gaufrès, *Claude Baduel*, 76f.)

[16] A reference to the public interrogation of the children at the afternoon service. See *infra*, p. 182.

[17] By the 'Education' Act of 1496 of the Scottish Parliament all barons and freeholders of substance were ordained to put their eldest sons and heirs to the grammar schools at eight or nine and to have them remain there until they were 'competentlie foundit' and had 'perfite Latyne', and then to remain three years at the 'sculis of art and Jure' in order thereafter to be able to execute justice. The authors of the Book of Discipline seek to make it incumbent upon all fathers to arrange for the education of their children. (*APS*, 2.238; Grant, *Burgh Schools*, 25ff; Edgar, *History of Early Scottish Education*, 187ff, 262ff; Dunlop, *Acta Facultatis Artium*, xxxix ff; and *infra*, note 20.)

[18] *i.e.*, those able to pay. Students whose parents were able to meet the fees and charges were sometimes described as such in the matriculation registers or as *dives*, but more often only those unable to pay were noted – as *pauperes*.

[19] See *infra*, p. 160. Payment of small sums of money to a parent to assist in the education of a child are sometimes recorded in kirk session registers. For example see *StAKSR*, 2.845.

men be appointed to visit Schooles[b] for the tryall of their exercise, profite and continuance: To wit, the Minister[c] and Elders and[d] the rest of learned men[d] in every town shall in[e] every quarter make[f] examination how the youth have profited.[20]

And certain times[g] [21] must be appointed to reading and learning of the Catechisme, and[h] certain[h] to the Grammer and to the Latine tongues,[i] and a[j] certaine to the Arts of Philosophie and the tongues,[j] and[k] certain to that studie in which they intend chiefly to travell for the profite of the Commonwealth. Which time being expired, we meane in every course, the children should[l] either proceed to farther knowledge, or else they must be set[m] to some handie craft or to some other profitable exercise, providing alwaies that first they have further[n] knowledge of Christian Religion;[22] To wit, the knowledge of Gods Law and Commandments, the use and office of the same; the chiefe Articles of the[o] beleefe, the right forme to pray unto God; the number, use and effect of the Sacraments; the true knowledge of Christ Jesus, of his Office and Natures and such others,[p] without[q] the knowledge

[b] *all Schollis*   [c] *Ministeris*   [d-d] *with the best learned*   [e] Not in Laing MS
[f] *tak*   [g] *A certane tyme*   [h-h] *ane certane tyme*   [i] *tongue*
[j-j] *ane certane tyme to the Artis, Philosophie and to the Toungis*   [k] *and a*
[l] *must*   [m] *sent*   [n] *the form of*   [o] *our*
[p] Laing in a footnote states that the 1621 text has *suche other points*, but this is not so in the St Andrews copy.
[q] *as without*

[20] The proposals of the foregoing paragraphs are unmistakably dependent upon Bucer, *De Regno Christi*, 2.48, *Opera Latina*, 15.236ff, who advocated education for every child according to his ability to learn in order to play his part in the commonwealth; that no child be allowed to be raised in idleness; that the Church should assist poor parents in providing for the education of their children if they have the aptitude for learning; that children with ability to acquire great learning must be required to pursue their studies *ad ampliora Ecclesiae et reipublicae ministeria*. The 'discreet, grave, and learned men' correspond to Bucer's *viri . . . summa pietate, sapientia et prudentia praestantes*, who were to be in charge of arranging for the education of the children. The quarterly visitation of the school by the minister and elders is not recorded in any extant session register for this early period.

[21] The graded programme of education briefly outlined here and repeated in greater detail in the following section on pp. 134ff is based on that of the educational reformers of the sixteenth century; see further *supra*, notes 11 and 13, and Introduction, pp. 54ff.

[22] Cf. Bucer, *De Regno Christi*, 2.48, *Opera Latina*, 15.240: 'Porro qui ex pueris lectionem iam et scriptionem cum fidei nostrae catechismo edoctis, aut etiam ex iis, qui artibus iam liberalibus discendis fuerint aliquamdiu applicati, apparebunt non esse a Domino ad ampliorem percipiendam doctrinam literariam effecti, hi aliis adhibeantur artibus, quisque ei, ad quam esse cuius ingenium videbitur magis congruens et aptum.'

wherof neither any*r* man deserves to be called a Christian,*r* neither ought any to be admitted to the participation of the Lords Table; and therefore thir principles ought and must be learned in the youthhead.[23]

The Times appointed to every course[24]

Two yeares we thinke more than sufficient to learne to read perfectly, to answer to the Catechisme and to have some entres in the first rudiments of Grammer, to the full accomplishment whereof (we meane of Grammer) we thinke other three years or foure at most sufficient[25] to the Arts, to wit, Logick and Rhetorick, and to the Greek tongue 4 years,[26] and the rest till the age of 24,

r—r deservith man to be named a Christiane

[23] This explanation of what is understood by 'the form of Christian Religion' summarises the main topics treated in the Catechism. See further Torrance, *School of Faith*, xii ff, 3ff, 237ff, and *Confession of Faith*, cap. XXIII.

[24] The programme of progressive education outlined under this heading closely follows that currently being effected on the Continent under the influence of the educational reforms put forward by André Gouvea, Jean Sturm and Claude Baduel. In 1538 Sturm had published his *Liber de literarum ludis recte aperiendis* and Baduel two years later his *De Collegio et Universitate Nemausensi*, two works which moulded the educational reforms effected in Lausanne in 1547 and Geneva in 1559, and of which the authors of this section of the Book of Discipline were, it may be deduced, fully informed. (Gaufrès, *Claude Baduel*, 39ff, 56ff, 180ff; Vuilleumier, *Histoire*, 1.408ff; Borgeaud, *L'Académie de Calvin*, 21ff, 626ff; Le Coultre, *Maturin Cordier*, 203f; Bourchenin, *Les Académies Protestantes*, 191ff.)

[25] The time allotted to primary and elementary education varied slightly among the educational reform programmes. Sturm devoted eight classes, as did Baduel at Nîmes, while Calvin assigned seven to the *scola privata* at Geneva, but the curriculum was similar to all three. (Bourchenin, *Les Académies Protestantes*, 62ff, 156; Gaufrès, *Claude Baduel*, 41, 56ff, 295; Borgeaud, *L'Académie de Calvin*, 38, 43f, 628f.) Two years for primary education was the average time spent on this stage in sixteenth-century Scotland, but the length of time thereafter at grammar school, and before entering university, varied. It is interesting to note that at Leith in 1572 it was agreed that none be admitted a bursar in grammar under seven years or over fourteen years, and that a pupil should not be allowed to hold a bursary for longer than seven years. (*BUK*, 1.214, 228f.; Durkan, 'Education in the Century of the Reformation' in McRoberts, *Essays on the Scottish Reformation*, 146, 151.)

[26] According to the programme proposed for Nîmes the arts course extended over the years from fifteen to twenty, but the *Leges Academiae Genevenses* did not lay down regulations of this nature. The subject matter of the arts course is, however, the same. In proposing four years for the arts course the authors of the Book of Discipline were not departing from the time strictly required for the Master's degree at the mediaeval universities. The Statutes of St Leonard's College go further than the older Faculty of Arts regulations, which would have allowed a student to begin his course as early as the age of twelve years, and require that no one be admitted under fifteen or above twenty-one years of age. The Statutes of the Faculty of Arts of St Andrews of 1570 did not permit a student to begin

to be spent in that study wherein the learner would profit the Church[s] or commonwealth, be it in the lawes, physick or divinitie.[27] Which time of 24 years being spent in the Schools, the learner must be removed to serve the Church or commonwealth,[28] unlesse hee bee found a necessary reader[29] in this[t] same Colledge or Universitie. If God shall move your hearts to establish and execute this order and put these things in practise your whole realme, we doubt not, within few years will serve it[u] selfe of true preachers and of other officers necessary for the[v] commonwealth.[30]

[s] See *supra*, p. 129 n.*a*.　　[t] *the*　　[u] *the*　　[v] *your*

his course until fourteen or to graduate as Master of Arts until he had reached his twentieth year. The Assembly at Leith ordained that none be admitted a bursar in Arts under the age of fourteen and that it be tenable for no more than five years. (Bourchenin, *Les Académies Protestantes*, 157ff; Gaufrès, *Claude Baduel*, 41, 47, 295f; Dunlop, *Acta Facultatis Artium*, lxxxii; Hannay, *Statutes* 35, 87, 92; Herkless and Hannay, *College of St Leonard*, 146, 161; *BUK*, 1.214.)

[27] According to Baduel's programme for Nîmes the young man at twenty had received all the instruction that could be gained at the arts college and was prepared to embark upon one or other of the higher studies, Medicine, Laws or Theology. Limits of this nature were not laid down for Geneva where at first the only higher study was that of Theology. According to the Statutes of Theology at St Andrews of 1561, revised immediately after the Reformation, the student was expected to have finished his course for the Bachelor of Divinity degree and to be ready to begin his course for the doctorate on completion of his twenty-fifth year. It is interesting to note that the authors of this section of the Book of Discipline did not contemplate the continuation of the course after the completion of the four years for the B.D. degree, unless a period of 'necessary regency' were required. The Assembly at Leith in 1572 agreed that none be admitted to higher studies without the M.A. degree and that a bursary for that purpose should not be held for more than six years. (Gaufrès, *Claude Baduel*, 41, 46, 296; Hannay, *Statutes*, 125f; *BUK*, 1.214; see note 29.)

[28] According to canon law ordination to the priesthood could not take place until the twenty-fifth year of age, but dispensations were on occasion granted. In 1572 the Assembly decreed that none be admitted to the office of a minister within the age of twenty-three years complete. Nevertheless, it would appear that men much younger had been admitted ministers. (*BUK* 1.25, 211; *Miscellany of the Spalding Club*, 4.99, 5.60ff; Keith, *History*, 3.45, Winzet, *Works*, 1.101.)

[29] An allusion to the requirement of the mediaeval university educational system whereby a student on graduating was obliged to spend two further years in 'necessary regency'. The post-Reformation statutes of the St Andrews Faculty of Arts do not require a period of necessary regency, which had in fact not been in operation for some considerable time previously, but those of the Faculty of Theology do. (Rashdall, *Medieval Universities*, 1.409, 464f, 473; Dunlop, *Acta Facultatis Artium*, cxxi f; Hannay, *Statutes*, 19f, 73ff, 125ff; Pantin, 'The Conception of the Universities in England in the period of the Renaissance' in *Les Universités européennes du XIVe au XVIIIe siècle*, 103ff.)

[30] This dual purpose of education was frequently stressed by the educational

reformers of the sixteenth century. The final sentence here echoes Baduel's appeal to the magistrates of Nîmes in 1548. 'Cette éducation première, où le savoir se mêle à la piété et à la vertu, apporte au corps entier de la cité et de l'Eglise la force que vous lui apportez vous-même, sage Président, après l'avoir puisée dans une institution pareille.' (Gaufrès, *Claude Baduel*, 160, cf. 296.)

Of^a the Erection of Universities

The Grammer Schoole^b being erected,^{c} and of the tongues (as we have said[1]) next we think it necessary there be 3 Universities in this whole realme, established in 3^d townes accustomed. The first in S. Androes,[2] the second in Glasgow[3] and the third in Aberdein.[4]

And in the first University and principal, viz.^{e} S. Androes, that^f there be 3 colledges;[5] and in the first colledge, which is the entry of the University,[6] there be 4 classes or seages,[7] the first to the

^{a} Not in Laing MS ^{b} *Schollis*
^{c} In Laing MS *being eretected* is placed after *tongues* ^{d} *the* ^{e} *whiche is*
^{f} Not in Laing MS

[1] i.e., the schools in the towns, and the colleges (in which the Arts . . . together with the tongues were to be taught) in the 'notable towns' mentioned *supra*, p. 131.

[2] The University of St Andrews was founded in 1412 by Bishop Wardlaw. See further, Cant, *University of St Andrews*.

[3] The University of Glasgow was founded by Bishop Turnbull in 1451. See further Mackie, *University of Glasgow*.

[4] The University of Aberdeen was founded by Bishop Elphinstone in 1494. See further Rait, *Universities of Aberdeen*.

[5] In 1560 the University of St Andrews comprised St Salvator's College, founded in 1450, St Leonard's College, founded in 1512, and St Mary's College, erected on an earlier foundation in 1537. (Cant, *University of St Andrews*, 22ff, 27ff, 33ff; Cant, *College of St Salvator*; Herkless and Hannay, *College of St Leonard*.)

[6] The proposal that one of the colleges should form an entrance to university studies was at this time new for St Andrews where hitherto students had been free to commence their studies in any one of the three colleges. The reformers may have been influenced by earlier conflicts between the Faculty of Arts and the colleges, or by developments at Glasgow where 'the college' which was controlled by the Faculty of Arts became 'from the moment of its foundation . . . the core of the life of the University', and at Aberdeen, where 'the University was established from the beginning on the basis of a single well organised college'. But some of them were undoubtedly influenced by contemporary developments in education on the Continent and wished to see one of the St Andrews Colleges become an arts college or academy on lines similar to those that had been followed at Strasbourg, Basel, and Zürich, and were presently being implemented in Geneva. (Cant, *College of St Salvator*, 32ff, 42ff; Dunlop, *Acta Facultatis Artium*, cix; Mackie, *University of Glasgow*, 42ff, 51ff; Rait, *Universities of Aberdeen*, 30ff; and Introduction, pp. 54ff.)

[7] i.e., forms, *ordines*.

new Supposts[8] shall be onely *Dialecticae,*[g][9] next onely *Mathematicae,*[h][10] the third of Physick onely,[11] the fourth of medicine.[12] And in the second colledge, two classes or seages; the first of[i] Morall philosophy,[13] the second of[i] the lawes.[14] And in the third colledge two classes or seages; the first of[i] the tongues, to wit, Greek and Hebrue, the 2 of[i] divinity.[15]

Of Readers[16] *and of the degrees and*[j] *time of Study*[j]

Item: in the first colledge and first[k] classe shall be a reader of *Dialectica,*[l] who shall accomplish his course thereof in a[m] yeare.[17]

[g] *Dialectique*   [h] *Mathematique*   [i] *in*   [j–j] *off Tyme and Studye*
[k] *and in the first*   [l] *Dialectique*   [m] *one*

[8] A term used for all members of a university, both graduate and undergraduate.

[9] See *infra,* note 17.   [10] See *infra,* note 18.   [11] See *infra,* note 19.

[12] See *infra,* note 21.   [13] See *infra,* note 22.   [14] See *infra,* note 23.

[15] See *infra,* notes 24 and 25. The 'basic principles' of the scheme outlined here came to nothing at the time, but were redrafted in a revised scheme attributed to George Buchanan in 1563, and 'were eventually effected at St Andrews in 1579'. (Cant, *University of St Andrews,* 44ff; see further Introduction, p. 73.)

[16] Instruction in the mediaeval university had been for the most part in the hands of regents who took their class of pupils through the successive stages of the curriculum and prepared them for the examinations and disputations. The sixteenth century witnessed the emergence of the specialist lector or reader. Prior to 1560 attempts were made to introduce this reform in method at St Andrews, but it would appear without much success. It had, however, become normal practice in most of the colleges and academies on the Continent, which had been influenced by the educational ideas of Sturm, and his fellow reformers. (Rashdall, *Medieval Universities,* 2.283f, 308f, 321f, 409f; Cant, *University of St Andrews,* 32, 52f; Dunlop, *Acta Facultatis Artium,* cxxiii ff; Borgeaud, *L'Académie de Calvin,* 53; Gaufrès, *Claude Baduel,* 59ff.)

[17] Dialectic or logic had in the mediaeval development of academic studies become by the end of the fifteenth century the primary study of the arts course and was so recognised in the contemporary statutes of the Faculty of Arts of St Andrews which were revised in 1561–62. No attempt had been made by the educational reformers to replace it but rather to deepen and purify the study of the subject (with which Rhetoric was combined) by requiring the student to come prepared with a knowledge of Greek to what were in origin Greek sciences. Dialectic along with rhetoric formed the course of instruction given by the Professor of Philosophy in the upper school, *schola publica,* of the reformed Colleges on the Continent, which some members of the two senior classes of the lower school, *schola privata,* might be permitted to attend. It was this course of study that Andrew Melville provided for first-year arts students at Glasgow in 1574 and of which his nephew gives the following details: 'he teatched tham the Greik grammaer, the Dialectic of Ramus, the Rhetoric of Taleus, with the practise thairof in Greik and Latin authors, namlie, Homer, Hesiod, Phocilides, Theognides, Pythagoras, Isocrates, Pindarus, Virgill, Horace, Theocritus etc.'. But as a student in St Leonard's College in 1571 in his first year James Melville had been taken by his regent through the traditional course of Rhetoric and

In *Mathematica*,[n] which is the second classe, shall be a reader which shall compleat his course of *Arithmetica*,[o] Geometrie, Cosmography and Astrologie in one[p] year.[18] In the third classe shall be a reader of naturall philosophy, who shall compleat his course in one[q] year.[19] And who after thir 3 years by triall and examination, shall be found sufficiently instructed in the foresaid sciences, shall be Laureat and Graduat in philosophy.[20] In the

[n] *In the Mathematique*   [o] *Arithmetique*   [p] *ane*   [q] *a*

Dialectic based on Latin texts. (Dunlop, *Acta Facultatis Artium*, lxxxiv, 416f; Hannay, *Statutes*, 61; Rashdall, *Medieval Universities*, 1.240, 440ff, 490; Schmidt, 'Mémoire de Jean Sturm' in *Bulletin Historique et Littéraire du Société de l'Histoire du Protestantisme Français*, 25 (1876), 499 ff; Bourchenin, *Les Académies Protestantes*, 91, 233, 241; Le Coultre, *Maturin Cordier*, 481ff; Gaufrès, *Claude Baduel*, 47ff; Borgeaud, *L'Académie de Calvin*, 52, 632; Melvill, *Diary*, 26f, 49.)

[18] In the mediaeval curriculum Mathematics was studied towards the end of the course for licence and was retained in this place in the revised Statutes for St Andrews in 1561–62. Nevertheless, as a student in St Leonard's College in 1572, James Melville, in his second year, received instruction not from his regent but from the Principal of the College in 'the four speaces of Arithmetic' (*i.e.*, Arithmetic, Geometry, Cosmography and Astrology). In the *Leges Scholae Lausanensis* and the *Leges Scholae Genevensis* the subject is so defined and was the responsibility of one of the public professors of Arts. At Glasgow Andrew Melville immediately following the dialectic course 'enterit to the Elements of Euclid, the Arithmetic and Geometrie of Ramus, the Geographie of Dyonisius, the Tables of Hunter and the Astrologie of Aratus'. (Rashdall, *Medieval Universities* 1.248f, 440ff, 490ff; Dunlop, *Acta Facultatis Artium*, lxxxvii f, 416f; Bourchenin, *Les Académies Protestantes*, 91, 241f; Le Coultre, *Maturin Cordier*, 487; Melvill, *Diary*, 27, 49.)

[19] Natural Philosophy or Physics traditionally formed part of the study of the third year of the late mediaeval Arts curriculum. The revised Statutes for St Andrews in 1561–62 do not assign the subject to a particular year, but James Melville studied during his third year at St Leonard's College five books of Aristotle's *Ethics* and eight books of the *Physics*. At Glasgow Andrew Melville taught the same subjects for the same year. They retained the same place in the Arts course followed at the Protestant Colleges on the Continent. (Rashdall, *Medieval Universities*, 1.444, 3.152ff; Dunlop, *Acta Facultatis Artium*, lxxxiv, lxxxviii, 181, 418f; Bourchenin, *Les Académies Protestantes*, 233, 242; Le Coultre, *Maturin Cordier*, 487; Melvill, *Diary*, 28, 49.)

[20] In the section entitled 'The Times appointed to every Course' *supra*, p. 134, four years were allotted to the Arts course, but this appears not infrequently to have been shortened to three and a half years, and students were tempted not to take the full fourth year on account of the obligations of further residence which could be imposed on graduands. Traditional practice placed the 'bachelor act' (as the culmination of the process of determination was called) towards the end of the third year. 'The baccalaureat never became a full university degree but merely a Faculty certificate of fitness, awarded by the Dean and qualifying the holder to pass to the higher stage of study necessary for his attainment of the teacher's licence and his inception into the Faculty as a master of Arts.' The 'trial and examination' (*temptamen et examen*) were the terms applied to the examination

fourth classe shall be a reader of medicine, who shall compleat his course in 5 yeares, after the study of the which time, being by examination found sufficient, they shall be graduat in medicine.[21] Item: in the second colledge, in the first classe, one reader onely in the Ethicks, Oeconomics and Politicks, who shall compleat his course in the space of one yeare.[22] In the second classe shall bee two readers in the Municipall and Roman lawes, who shall compleat his course[r] in 4 yeares, after which time being by

[r] thair courses

---

that followed determination. It would, perhaps, appear that the authors of this part of the Book of Discipline were at this point doing away with the fourth year of study as a requirement for graduation, or stating in telescopic fashion what normally took place over the last eighteen months of the academic course. As will be seen later (note 22) it was proposed that the study of Moral Philosophy, which traditionally formed part of the fourth-year course, be taken out of the graduation course and regarded as a propaedeutic for students of law and theology. Dr Dunlop has pointed out that the religious changes 'made little difference to the system of examinations and that the temporary statutes drawn up in 1561–62 were largely based upon current practice'. (Rashdall, *Medieval Universities*, 1.435ff; 462ff; Dunlop, *Acta Facultatis Artium*, xc ff, xcvii ff; Mackie, *University of Glasgow*, 30ff, 50; Melvill, *Diary*, 28.)

[21] By its foundation charters the University of St Andrews was entitled to teach and grant degrees in Medicine and the subject 'may have been taught intermittently'. A Professor of Medicine was not appointed until 1722, although according to the *Nova Fundatio* of 1579 'the Provost [of St Salvator's] was to be "professor of Medicine", and in 1588 Provost James Martine claimed to have given such instruction'. It may be noted that the almost contemporary plans for the Academy of Geneva included provision for a reader in medicine. The degree of Doctor of Medicine normally required at least five years' standing in the study, but not necessarily pursued at one academic centre. (Cant, *University of St Andrews*, 4, 9, 44ff, 85ff; Cant, *College of St Salvator*, 172, 174; Buist, 'Medicine' in *Votiva Tabella*, 197ff; Dunlop, *Acta Facultatis Artium*, clvii ff; Borgeaud, *L'Académie de Calvin*, 627; Rashdall, *Medieval Universities*, 1.233ff, 435ff; Bourchenin, *Les Académies Protestantes*, 233.)

[22] In the mediaeval Arts curriculum the study of Moral Philosophy on the basis of the three works mentioned here was reserved for the final stages of the course and they were listed among the 'extraordinary' books from the study of which dispensation might be granted. In the Statutes of St Andrews of 1561–62, two books of the *Ethics* were to be studied before the student proceeded to Natural Philosophy. As has been pointed out *supra*, note 19, James Melville studied the *Ethics* in his third year and it would appear from the course taught by Andrew Melville that Glasgow followed the same order. At the reformed colleges on the Continent the course in Moral Philosophy was provided by the Professor of Greek, included the study of Aristotle, Plato, Plutarch and the works of some Christian philosophers, and did not come within the province of the Arts or Philosophy professor. (Dunlop, *Acta Facultatis Artium*, lxxxviii ff, 417; Hannay, *Statutes*, 60ff; Melvill, *Diary*, 28, 49; Le Coultre, *Maturin Cordier*, 486; Borgeaud, *L'Académie de Calvin*, 66; Bourchenin, *Les Académies Protestantes*, 240, 242; Mackie, *University of Glasgow*, 34f.)

examination found sufficient, they shall be graduate in the lawes.[23] Item: in the third Colledge,[24] in the first classe, one reader of the Hebrew and another of the Greek tongue, who shall compleat the Grammar[s] thereof in 3 moneths,[t] and the remanent of the yeare the reader of the hebrew shall interpret one book of Moses, the Prophets or the Psalms, so that this[u] course and classe shall continue one year. The reader of the Greek shall interpret some book of Plato, together with some place of the new testament.[25] In[v] the second classe shall be two readers in divinitie, the one in the new Testament, the other in the old, who shall compleat their course in five yeares:[26] after which time who shall be found by

[s] *grammeris*   [t] *half ane yeare*   [u] *his*   [v] *And in*

[23] By the foundation charter the University was empowered to teach and grant degrees in Civil Law. 'That there was any teaching in Civil Law seems improbable in a university so strongly clerical in character as St Andrews.' Degrees were obtained in Civil Law in the days of Cardinal Beaton but by private examination. For information concerning the study of law at St Andrews see further Dunlop, *Acta Facultatis Artium*, cliii ff; and Cant, *University of St Andrews*, 4, 9, 48f. It is interesting to note that James Melville during the third and fourth years of his Arts course and in addition to what was required of him, attended lectures by the Commissary William Skene on 'Cicero, *de Legibus* and divers parts of the *Institutions* of Justinian' which undoubtedly formed the basis of instruction in Roman Law; he also attended the 'Consistorie' with his teacher who showed his pupils 'the practise in judgment of that which he teached in the scholles'. It may, therefore, be assumed that Skene also gave instruction in municipal or statute law. At the mediaeval universities the length of the course of study for the degree in civil law appears to have differed considerably from one centre to another. It should be noted that the protestant continental educational reformers of the sixteenth century attributed considerable importance to the study of civil law and that from the beginning plans for the provision of a professor were projected at Geneva and effected soon thereafter. (Melvill, *Diary*, 29; Borgeaud, *L'Académie de Calvin*, 88ff, 626; Bourchenin, *Les Académies Protestantes*, 233ff.)

[24] The arrangement proposed for this third college closely follows the plans laid down for the Academy of Geneva with the exception of the Arts Professor for whose work provision had already been made in the first College. Of the St Andrews Faculty of Theology prior to the outbreak of the Reformation comparatively little is known. The best account is found in Dunlop, *Acta Facultatis Artium*, cxxxix ff, but see also Hannay, *Statutes*, 67ff; Cant, *University of St Andrews*, 4, 9ff, 23f, 33ff, 44ff.

[25] At Geneva the Professor of Hebrew read a book of the Old Testament with the aid of the Rabinical Commentaries and gave instruction in Hebrew Garmmar; the Professor of Greek read from the philosophical or ethical works of Aristotle, Plato, Plutarch, or some Christian philosopher, and also from the Greek poets, orators and historians. There is no indication that he read or commented upon any part of the New Testament. (Borgeaud, *L'Académie de Calvin*, 631, 44, 65f; Bourchenin, *Les Académies Protestantes*, 90, 105ff, 233.)

[26] The plans of the Academy of Geneva, which were obviously in the minds of the authors of this section, provided for two Professors of Theology, but in 1559 lectures were being given by Calvin and Beza, who were not entitled public

examination sufficient, they[w] shall be graduate in divinitie.

Item, wee thinke expedient that none be admitted to the first colledge, and to bee suppots of the universitie, unlesse he have from the master of the schoole and[x] minister of the town where he was instructed in the tongues ane testimonie of his learning, docility, age and parentage:[27] and likewise triall be[y] taken by certain examinators depute by the Rector and Principalls of the same.[28] And if he be found sufficiently instructed in the *Dialectica*,[z] he shall incontinent the[a] same year be promoted to the classe of *Mathematica*.[b] [29]

Item, that none be admitted to the classe of [c] Medicine but he that shall have his testimonial of his time well spent in *Dialectica*,[z] *Mathematica*[b] and Physick, and of his docility in the last.

[w] Not in Laing MS   [x] and the   [y] to be   [z] in Dialectick   [a] that
[b] Mathematicque   [c] of the

---

professors, but regarded this academic work as an extension of their ecclesiastical and pastoral functions. The proposals put forward here made very little, if any, impression upon those who were engaged in revising the divinity statutes at St Andrews. Little, it would appear, was altered apart from the substitution of the Bible along with the Apocrypha in place of the *Sentences* of Peter Lombard. The length of the course was fixed at four years, which was the time required for obtaining the Bachelor's degree in theology. The *Nova Fundatio* of 1553 of St Mary's College had allowed six years for the course. The plans of the authors of the Book of Discipline were amplified in the *New Foundation* of 1579. (Borgeaud, *L'Académie de Calvin*, 53, 632; Bourchenin, *Les Académies Protestantes*, 23, 86ff, 232ff; Rashdall, *Medieval Universities*, 1.471ff; Dunlop, *Acta Facultatis Artium*, cxliii, cxxxix ff; Hannay, *Statutes*, 67ff, 80ff, 118, 125; Cant, 48ff; *Evidence*, 3.183f, 363.)

[27] No one, it would appear, was to be given admission to the arts college who had not completed the full grammar school course as outlined on pp. 133f. This course included Greek (already being taught in some schools) as well as the traditional Latin.

[28] In the mediaeval university 'the only qualification necessary for entering the University was a knowledge of Latin Grammar'. The Faculty of Arts in St Andrews determined in 1495 that no 'grammaticus sive scolaris' be received under a regent in Arts unless he had been examined and found qualified in the presence of the Dean by four regents at least and the master of the grammar school. According to the revised statutes of 1561–62 no one was to be admitted to the Dialectics course without an ability to read and write Latin and without examination by the Rector, the Dean of Faculty and three examiners appointed by common consent of the whole *academia*. No other language qualification was required. (Dunlop, *Acta Facultatis Artium*, lxxxi, lxxxix, 254, 416; Hannay, *Statutes*, 35ff; Hannay, *College of St Leonard*, 146, 160f; cf. Patrick, *Statutes*, 109.)

[29] According to the programme of studies of the educational reformers of the sixteenth century it was possible to begin the study of Dialectic and Rhetoric in the final class of the grammar school and thus to have covered some of the ground of the first-year Arts course. (Gaufrès, *Claude Baduel*, 47ff, 56f; Borgeaud, *L'Académie de Calvin*, 629; Bourchenin, *Les Académies Protestantes*, 192ff, 198f.)

Item, that none be admitted unto the classe of the lawes, but he that shall have sufficient testimonialls of his time wel spent in *Dialectica,*[z] *Mathematica,*[b] *Physica,*[d] Ethicks, Oeconomicks and Politickes and of his docilitie in the last.

Item: that none be admitted unto the classe and seage of divinity,[e] but he that shall have sufficient testimonialls of his time well spent in *Dialectica,*[z] *Mathematica,*[b] *Phisica,*[d] *Ethica,* *Oeconomica* and *Politica*[f] and the Hebrew tongue, and of his docilitie in the morall Philosophy and the Hebrew tongue. But neither shall such as apply[g] them to heare the lawes, be compelled to heare medicine, nether such as apply them to heare divinitie, be compelled to heare either Medicine or yet the lawes.[30]

Item: in the second University, which is Glasgow, shall be two colledges onely: in the first shall be a classe of *Dialectica,*[z] another of *Mathematica,*[b] and the third of[h] Phisica,[d] ordered in all sorts as S. Androes.[31]

Item: in the second, foure classes, the first of Morall philosophy, Ethicks, Oeconomicks and Physick.[i] [32] The second, of the Municipal and Roman lawes.[33] The third, of the Hebrew tongue, the fourth, of[j] divinitie, which shal be ordered in al sorts to[k] that[k] we have written in the order of the Universitie of S. Androes.[34]

[z] *in Dialectick*	[b] *Mathematicque*	[d] *Phisicque*	[e] *Divines*
[f] *Oeconomique, Morall Philosophie*		[g] *will apply*	[h] *and the third in*
[i] *Pollitiques*	[j] *in*	[k–k] *conform to it*	

[30] It was the general rule that students must pass in courses already taken before they proceeded to read for a degree in one of the higher faculties of Medicine, Laws or Theology. At St Andrews statutes had been passed in 1525 which submitted all students to an 'examination of fitness' at the beginning of every session. (Dunlop, *Acta Facultatis Artium,* I n., 349; Hannay, *Statutes,* 108ff.)

[31] See *supra,* p. 139 and n.20. The proposal that there be an arts college as in St Andrews but without Medicine reflects the actual situation in Glasgow prior to the Reformation where the study of Medicine permitted by the foundation charters 'never really began'. (Mackie, *University of Glasgow,* 25ff, 28f.)

[32] Laing's reading must obviously be accepted as correct. The three subjects mentioned combined to form the study of Moral Philosophy. See *supra,* p. 140, n.22.

[33] By its charters the University of Glasgow had been empowered to teach Canon and Civil Law and Theology, but Civil Law was 'beyond the competence' of the new foundation and Canon Law, although taught originally, disappeared in the early sixteenth century. (Mackie, *University of Glasgow,* 25ff.)

[34] There is 'no proof that much teaching [of theology] was done at the University proper in the first half of the sixteenth century'. It is probably of no significance that Greek is not mentioned. (Mackie, *University of Glasgow,* 26f.) For an account of the effects of the Reformation on the University of Glasgow, see Mackie, *University of Glasgow,* 55ff.

The third Universitie of Aberdein shall be conforme to this
Universitie of Glasgow in all sorts.[35]
Item: we think needfull that there be chosen of the bodie of the
University to every Colledge, a principall[l] man of learning, discretion and diligence,[36] who shall receive the whole rents of the
Colledge and distribute the same according to the erection of the
Colledge,[37] and shall dayly hearken the dyet counts,[m] [38] adjoyning
to him weekly one of the readers or regents,[39] above whom[40] he
shall take[n] attendance upon their diligence, as well in their reading
as exercising[o] of the yowth in the matter taught, upon the policie
and uphold of the place,[41] and for the punishment of crimes shall

[l] Not in Laing MS   [m] comptis   [n] Not in Laing MS   [o] exercitioun

[35] For the history of the University of Aberdeen during the period of the
Reformation see Rait, *Universities of Aberdeen*, 93ff; and Henderson, *Founding of
Marischal College*, 52f.

[36] These words repeat the qualifications required in the person to be elected
Principal of St Leonard's College, according to the *Statutes* – *virum gravem,
prudentem et doctum*. Herkless and Hannay, *College of St Leonard*, 150f.

[37] i.e., in accordance with the charters of foundation and endowment. See for
example the foundation charters of St Leonard's College in Herkless and Hannay,
College of St Leonard, 129ff, 138ff. The foundation charters of St Salvator's College
do not give instructions of this nature, but full details are to be found in the
Nova Fundatio et Erectio of St Mary's College of James Hamilton in 1553, and it is
probably this document the authors of this section of the Book of Discipline had
in mind. At Glasgow, according to the Statutes promulgated in 1482 a *bursar* or
receptor was elected annually to receive the University revenue, and at Aberdeen,
the foundation charters of the College of St Mary ('King's College') also made
provision for an annually elected procurator who was to receive the revenues and
distribute them according to the terms of erection. (*Evidence*, 3.362ff; *Munimenta
Alme Universitatis Glasguensis*, 2.11; *Fasti Aberdonenses*, 53ff, 86ff, 265ff.)

[38] The Statutes of St Leonard's College ordained that 'the principal should
each day after supper receive the daily account of the expenses from the Provisor,
with the assistance of one or two persons on the foundation'. The *Nova Erectio* of
St Mary's College advised *ut commodius exequatur* that the Principal should
receive *per se vel substitum* daily accounts from the Provisor, and that there be a
conference with the principal members of the college four times a year for the
ratification of the accounts. The Aberdeen Visitation of 1549 required that daily
accounts be kept by the *economus* and that his books be examined at least once a
month by the Principal and Sub-principal. (Herkless and Hannay, *College of St
Leonard*, 152, 170, 199, 211; *Evidence*, 3.365; *Fasti Aberdonenses*, 266f.)

[39] This is the first occurrence of the word 'regent'. Here and in the remainder
of the section it does not denote a separate grade of academic teacher but rather
denotes a lapse into traditional usage and should therefore be regarded as a
synonym for reader. (See *supra*, p. 138 and n.16.)

[40] i.e., over the readers or regents of the college of which he is Principal.

[41] These duties and responsibilities of the Principal are common to the foundation documents of the St Andrews, Glasgow and Aberdeen Colleges, but the
words most nearly approximate to the Statutes of St Leonard's College and the

hold a weekly convention with the whole members of the Colledge.[42] He shall be countable yerely to the Superintendent, Rector, and the[p] principals convened about the first of November.[43] His election shall be in this sort. There shall be three of the most sufficient men of the Universitie (not principalls already[q] nominate by the members of the Colledge) sworn to follow their consciences whose Principall is departed, and publickly proponed through the whole Universitie. After the which time 8 daies, by the Superintendent himselfe, or his speciall Procurator with the Rector and the rest of the principals as a chapter convenit, shall confirme one of the three they think most sufficient, being before sworn to do the same with a single eye but respect to fead or favour.[44]

[p] and rest of the   [q] In Laing MS the parenthesis closes here.

Nova Fundatio of St Mary's College. (Herkless and Hannay, *College of St Leonard*, 150ff, 168ff; *Evidence*, 3.362ff.)

[42] The Statutes of St Leonard's College ordained that every Friday a 'Chapter be held to correct excesses, in which the faults and omissions of all are to be duly punished'. (Herkless and Hannay, *College of St Leonard*, 156, 175.)

[43] The foundation charters of St Salvator's College required an 'annual inspection or visitation of the College by the Rector – if not a member of the house – or Archdeacon, or some special deputy of the University' along with assessors or advisers, but no specific date was mentioned. The Statutes of St Leonard's College provided for an annual visitation by the Sub-prior, the third prior and one other canon during the octave of St Leonard (6th to 13th November). The *Nova Fundatio* of St Mary's College required the Rector, and the six others (the Official of the Diocese, the Archdeacon, the Principal of St Salvator's College, the Sub-prior, the Provincials of the Dominicans, and of the Franciscans) who shared the rights of presentation to the principalship, to visit the College every year *circiter Calendas Novembris* and receive full accounts of its affairs. The provision for the visitation of the College of St Mary ('King's College'), Aberdeen were similar to those for St Salvator's and again no time of year is mentioned. (Cant, *College of St Salvator*, 19, 32, 37f, 44, 59, 77; Herkless and Hannay, *College of St Leonard*, 156, 175; *Evidence*, 3.365; *Fasti Aberdonenses*, x, xxv, 58, 102; Rait, *Universities of Aberdeen*, 36.) The Committee of visitation in all probability was derived from that appointed for St Mary's College, St Andrews. There was, however, no precedent for including the Superintendent if he was thought to have succeeded to the place of the Archbishop-Chancellor, but it is more likely that he was regarded as having succeeded to the office of either the Official or the Archdeacon. The place of the Sub-prior may have been regarded as being filled by the Principal of St Leonard's College. As the Provincials of the Dominicans and Franciscans, according to the reformers, no longer existed their function clearly lapsed.

[44] When the office of Provost of St Salvator's College fell vacant, the next senior member of the College succeeded to it; in St Leonard's the Principal was to be chosen by the Prior from the Chapter of Canons; in St Mary's College the right of presentation belonged to the six *praesentatores* mentioned *supra*, note 43, along with the Rector of the University. In the *Nova Fundatio* the following order is laid down. On the request of the senior members of the College the

Item: In every Colledge we think needfull at^r least, a steward, a cooke, a gardiner, and Porter, who shall be subject to discipline of the principall, as the rest.[45]

Item: That every Universitie have a beddall subject to serve at all times throughout the whole Universitie, as the Rector and Principall shall command.[46]

Item: that every Universitie have a Rector[47] chosen from yeare to

^r at the least

Rector is to summon a meeting of the *praesentatores* who are to swear to act in good faith in selecting a person eminently suitable for the office (*virum maxime idoneum praefecturae obeundae*) and present him to the Archbishop for appointment. At Aberdeen, according to the *Processus Fundationis* of Bishop Gavin Douglas in 1523, the Principal of the College was to be elected by the Rector, four pro-curators of the nations, the canonist, civilist, mediciner, sub-principal, regent in arts, grammarian, six students of theology and the cantor and sacrist. The order proposed by the authors of the Book of Discipline, whereby the members of the College were empowered to draw up a leet of three from the members of the University, and seek the appointment of one of them by the Superintendent, Rector and other Principals, acting together as a court of appointment, would appear to have no Scottish academic precedent. However, as was pointed out in note 43 the Court of appointment may have its origin in the six *praesentatores* of St Mary's College. (Cant, *College of St Salvator*, 56f, 73; Herkless and Hannay, *College of St Leonard*, 150f, 168; *Evidence*, 3.364; *Fasti Aberdonenses*, 98ff.)

[45] The extant foundation documents of St Salvator's College and St Leonard's and those of Glasgow and Aberdeen Universities either mention specifically their officers or presuppose their existence, but in the *Nova Fundatio* of St Mary's College three of them, *Provisor sive Dispensator, Coquus* and *Janitor* are stated to be part of the foundation and to be subject to the Principal. The Provisor is to be a priest and is to be paid £10 a year, and the cook and the porter six marks. A gardener is not mentioned but it may be that the office was to be combined with that of cook or porter as at a later period. The manuscript accounts of St Leonard's College show that there was from 1549 a gardener on the Foundation. For this information I am indebted to Mr R. G. Cant and Mr R. N. Smart. (Herkless and Hannay, *College of St Leonard*, 149ff, 150ff, 166ff; *Evidence*, 3.363; Rait, *Universities of Aberdeen*, 36, 39, 90; *Fasti Aberdonenses*, 55f, 265ff; *Munimenta Alme Universitatis Glasguensis*, 2.11; Mackie, *University of Glasgow*, 16, 23.)

[46] In the mediaeval university the university beadle was an important official who accompanied the rector on all public occasions and was also responsible for the publication of university announcements. Interesting information of the beadle's duties, responsibilities, and income are to be found in the printed *munimenta* of St Andrews, Glasgow and Aberdeen. There may be detected in the injunction that the beadle was to serve 'throughout the whole University' an echo of a previous conflict of loyalties in St Andrews. (Rashdall, *Medieval Universities*, 1.191f, 420; Hannay, *Statutes*, 99; Dunlop, *Acta Facultatis Artium*, cxxvi ff; *Munimenta Alme Universitatis Glasguensis*, 2.5, 9, 11f, 32; Mackie, *University of Glasgow*, 13, 16f; *Fasti Aberdonenses*, 271.)

[47] The office of rector underwent considerable development during the history of mediaeval universities, but by the time of the foundation of the Scottish universities he is clearly the most important person, the chief ruler and magistrate. He was always elected for one year at a time but appears to have been frequently

yeare as shall follow. The Principalls being convened with the whole Regents[48] chapterly shall be sworn that every man in his roume shall nominate such a one^s as his conscience shall testifie to be most sufficient to beare such charge and dignity:[49] and three of them that shall be oftest nominated shall be put in edict publickly 15 daies before Michaelmaes and then shall on Michaelmas[50] even convene the whole principalls, regents and supposts that are graduat, or at the least studyed their time in Ethicks, oeconomicks and politickes and na others yonger,[51] and every one^t [52] first protest^u in Gods presence to follow the sincere dytment of their

^{s} *suche one* ^{t} *everie natioun* ^{u} *first protestand*

---

reappointed. (Rashdall, *Medieval Universities*, 1.177ff, 312ff, 402ff; Cant, *University of St Andrews*, 6ff; Dunlop, *Acta Facultatis Artium*; Mackie, *University of Glasgow*, 14ff; Rait, *Universities of Aberdeen*, 36ff.)

[48] See *supra*, note 39.

[49] The proposal that the principals of colleges and the teaching masters should draw up a list of nominees for the office of rector has no precedent in the history of the rectorship in Scotland. See further *infra*, note 52.

[50] 'The statutory date for the election of the Rector at St Andrews from 1471 to 1579 was the last of February and this date was only departed from in special circumstances.' At Glasgow the date was the feast of St Crispin and St Crispian, 25th October, one week after the official opening of the session. The statutory date for the election of the Rector of Aberdeen is not known. It is not clear why the authors of the Book of Discipline should have wished to alter the St Andrews practice, but they may have considered 28th September more convenient than a date in the middle of the academic year. (Anderson, *Early Records*, xiii; Cant, *University of St Andrews*, 5ff; *Munimenta Alme Universitatis Glasguensis*, 2.6; Mackie, *University of Glasgow*, 14.)

[51] All members of the university were eligible to take part in the election of the rector at Glasgow and Aberdeen, and had been so entitled at St Andrews until 1475. In that year 'a statute was made confining the right to vote . . . to doctors, masters, licentiates, bachelors of the various faculties and to the members of religious communities, priors and priests', and continued in force until 1625. The proposal of the Book of Discipline would have confined the vote to those who had studied for four years at least. (Cant, *University of St Andrews*, 7; Anderson, *Early Records*, xiv; Dunlop, *Acta Facultatis Artium*, xxxiii; *Evidence*, 3.233; *Munimenta Alme Universitatis Glasguensis*, 2.5; Mackie, *University of Glasgow*, 17ff; see *supra*, p. 140.)

[52] At St Andrews 'the Rector was not elected by a direct poll of those entitled to vote, but indirectly by four intrants specially chosen for the purpose by the four nations [into which all those who were incorporated were divided]. The successful candidates for the post of Intrant would no doubt be charged by their respective Nations to vote for a particular person.' A similar procedure was followed at Glasgow and at Aberdeen. (Anderson, *Early Records*, xiii ff; Cant, *University of St Andrews*, 7f; Dunlop, *Acta Facultatis Artium*, xiii, xxxiii, lxiv; *Evidence*, 3.233. On voting by Nations see Rashdall, *Medieval Universities*, 1.311ff, 405ff, and Index *sub* 'Nations'; Kibre, *The Nations in the Medieval Universities*; *Munimenta Alme Universitatis Glasguensis*, 2.6, 8, 43; Mackie, *University of Glasgow*, 14f, 17; Rait, *Universities of Aberdeen*, 37.)

conscience shall nominate[v] of the three, and he that hath most votes shall be confirmed by the Superintendent and Principals,[w] [53] and his duety with an exhortation proponed unto him, and this to be the 28 day of September and thereafter tryall[x] to be taken *hinc inde* of his just and godly government and of the rests[y] lawful submission and obedience.[54] He shall be propyned by[z] the universitie at his entry with a new garment,[55] bearing *insignia Magistratus*,[56] and be holden monethly to visite every Colledge and with his presence decore and examine the lections and exercise thereof.[57] His assessors shall be a lawyer and a theologe,[58] with

v ane of the said thre   *w Principall*   *x aithis*   *y remanentis*   *z to*

[53] Formal ratification or confirmation of the election of the rector by the archbishop-chancellor and the principals of the colleges is not mentioned in any extant document for the mediaeval period, but is unlikely except for the chancellor as the office pre-dates existence of the colleges. The authors of this section, however, may merely be anxious to ensure that the local resident dignitaries should preside at the election, and take part in the ceremony of installation. Unfortunately no details of a pre-Reformation installation are extant. An interesting account of procedure in the middle of the nineteenth century and while the system of voting by nations was still in operation at St Andrews is given in Roger, *History of St Andrews*, 130f.

[54] The taking of an oath of office was normal practice for university officials. The form of oath used at the University of Glasgow is printed in *Munimenta Alme Universitatis Glasguensis*, 2.6, 42; that used at St Andrews at a late date is printed in *Evidence*, 3.233. The formal requirement of 'Lawful submission and obedience' on the part of electors may represent ecclesiastical rather than academic usage. (Cf. 'The Form and Order for the Election of Superintendents', Dickinson, *Knox's History*, 2.272; Laing, *Knox's Works*, 2.144ff.)

[55] The presentation of the newly elected rector to the university robed in the official gown of office no doubt formed, as it still does, part of the installation ceremony. Details of the St Andrews rector's gown from the mediaeval period have not survived but there is every reason to believe that the original form has survived and is still used. Description of the gowns worn by the Rector of the University of Glasgow is preserved in the Statutes of 1482. (*Munimenta Alme Universitatis Glasguensis*, 2.7, 75, 106; cf. Mackie, *University of Glasgow*, 15, 49.)

[56] It is not known what this symbol of office was in the ceremony of installation. It may, however, be inferred from the Glasgow Statutes that it was the rector's *Album* or *Librum Conclusionum*. See Roger, *History of St Andrews*, 130f.

[57] There would appear to be no mediaeval precedent for this procedure, which, as was noted above, provided for an annual visitation of the colleges by the rector. See note 43.

[58] At St Andrews 'on the same day or the day following [the election of the Rector] assessors were chosen to assist the Rector in the discharge of his duties, as also deputies [usually four] to act for him in his absence'. They were 'usually nominated by the Nations, but actually appointed by himself'. In the period immediately preceding and following the Reformation the assessors regularly numbered three from every nation. I am indebted to Mr R. G. Cant and Mr R. N. Smart for this information. The Statutes of the University of Glasgow provided that the rector have the advice of four deputies who were, as at St Andrews, elected

whose advice he shall decide all questions civill betwixt the members of the Universitie.[59] If any without the Universitie persue a member thereof or he[a] be persued by a member of the same, he shall assist the provost and baillies in these cases, or other Judges competent to see justice be ministred. In likewise if any of the Universitie be criminally persued, he shall assist the Judges competent and see that justice be ministred.[60]

We think expedient that in every colledge in every University there be 24 bursars,[61] devided equally in all the classes and seges as is above expremit, that is in S. Androes 72 bursars; in Glasgow 48 bursars,[62] in Aberdine 48,[63] to be susteined onely in meat upon

[a] Not in Laing MS

---

immediately after the election of the rector. (Anderson, *Early Records*, xiii ff; Cant, *University of St Andrews*, 6f; *Munimenta Alme Universitatis Glasguensis*, 2.7f, 43; Mackie, *University of Glasgow*, 15ff; see also Rashdall, *Medieval Universities*, 1.405.) The legal jurisdiction enjoyed by the rector over the incorporated members of the university would render advisable the presence of a lawyer on his court. It may, however, be that the authors are here referring not to the regularly appointed assessors but to those required for judicial causes only.

[59] The jurisdiction over all incorporated members of the university was granted in the foundation charters to the rector at all three Scottish universities. (*Evidence*, 3.173f, 178ff; *Munimenta Alme Universitatis Glasguensis*, 1.7ff; *Fasti Aberdonenses*, 13f; cf. Rashdall, *Medieval Universities*, 405f; see further *infra*, pp. 153f.)

[60] See further *infra*, p. 153 and n.72.

[61] The foundation charters and endowment of St Salvator's College provided for the maintenance of thirteen founded persons. If the four readers proposed by the reformers were to be supported by the foundation then places were left for only seven scholars. The income to provide for the additional seventeen, it was probably intended, should be derived from the numerous chaplaincies (over thirty by 1475 and 'considerably increased by the time of the Reformation') with which the College Church had been endowed. The foundation charters of St Leonard's College provided for twenty scholars in arts, six in theology, with the Principal and four chaplains two of whom were to be regents, thirty-three persons in all. If the College supported three or four readers, there should still have been places left on the foundation for the number of students proposed. The foundation charters of St Mary's College provided for the support of thirty-six founded persons, including the provisor, cook, and porter. There should therefore have been funds to support the number of masters and bursars proposed. In suggesting twenty-four bursars for every college the reformers, as far as St Andrews was concerned, were probably making a conservative estimate of the number that the colleges could have been expected to support. (Cant, *College of St Salvator*, 14, 21ff; Herkless and Hannay, *College of St Leonard*, 128f, 138f; Evidence, 3.362.)

[62] The financial position of Glasgow on the eve of the Reformation was very unsatisfactory. The proposals therefore may represent for this university an ideal rather than an immediate possibility. (See further, Mackie, *University of Glasgow*, 55ff.)

[63] The foundation charter of the College of St Mary (King's College), Aberdeen, provided for thirty-six persons in 1505, but this was increased in 1531 to forty-two persons, and there were eight chaplains of the choir for whom provision had

the charges of the Colledge and to be admitted at the examination of the Ministrie and chaptour of principalls in the University,[64] as well in the docility of the persons offered, as of the abilitie of their parents to sustaine them themselves,[65] and not to burden the Commonwealth with them.

Of the Stipends and Expenses necessary

Item. We thinke expedient that the Universities be doted with temporall lands, with rents and revenewes of the Bishopricks temporalitie and of the Kirkes collegiat, so farre as their ordinary charges shall require, and therefore that it would please your Hon[ours] by advice of your Hon[ours] Coun[sell] and vote of Parliam[ent] to do the same.[66] And to the effect the same may be shortly exped,[b] we have recollected the summes we think necessarie for the same.

Imprimis: for the ordinary stipend of the dialectician Reader, the Mathematician, Physician and morall philosopher,[c] we thinke sufficient an hundred pounds for every one of them.

Item: for the stipend of every Reader in Medicine and Lawes a hundreth thirty three pounds 6s. 8d.

Item: to every Reader in Hebrew, Greek and Divinitie, 200 p.

Item: to every principall of a Colledge 200 pounds.

Item: to every steward 16 pounds.[d]

[b] expediat [c] Philosophie [d] of fie

---

been made. Although the precise details of the revenue of the University of Aberdeen and its College were in all probability not known to the authors of this section of the Book of Discipline, the number of bursars which was proposed would not appear to have been unreasonable, provided the sources of the revenue were secured for the reformation programme. (*Fasti Aberdonenses*, 53ff, 80ff, 122.)

[64] See *supra*, p. 142 and n.28.

[65] The foundation charter of St Salvator's College specifically mentions that the six poor scholars must be the children of parents who could not support them (*quibus eciam parentes eorum nequeunt subvenire*). The Statutes of St Leonard's College required that those who seek admission on the foundation be examined in scholastic attainment and in their poverty 'in things temporal'. The *Nova Fundatio* of St Mary's College of 1553 expressly requires students on the foundation to swear before admission that they had no means of support (*nec sacerdotium, nec patrimonium, aliasve fortunae opes, quibus in studiis sufficienter nutriri possint*). Similar conditions are laid down in foundation charters of the College of St Mary (King's College), Aberdeen. (Cant, *College of St Salvator*, 55, 62, 72; Herkless and Hannay, *College of St Leonard*, 146, 160; *Evidence*, 3.363f; *Fasti Aberdonenses*, 55, 84; for the meaning of 'poor scholar' in colleges see further, Rashdall, *Medieval Universities*, 3.411ff.)

[66] Cf. *infra*, pp. 161f and n.39 where it is proposed that these sources of revenue be also used for the maintenance of the superintendents. See also Introduction, p. 60.

Item: to every gardiner, to every cooke and porter, to ilk one of them ten merkes.

Item: to the buird of every bursar without the classe[e] of Theologie[e] 20 pounds.

Item: in the classe of Theologie which will be onely twelve persons in S. androes, 24 p.

Summe of yearly and ordinary expences in the Universitie of S. androes 3976 p.[f]

Summe of yearly and ordinary expences of Glasgow 2922 p.

Abberdine as much.

Summe of the ordinary charges of the whole [9640 p.][g]

Item: the Beddalls stipend shall be of every intrant and suppost of the University 2 shillings; of every one graduate in Philosophie 3 shillings; of every one graduate in medicine or lawes 4 shillings; in Theologie 5 shillings; all bursars being excepted.[67]

Item; we have thought good for building and upholding of the places, a generall collect be made; and that every Earles sonn at his entry to the university shall give 40 shil. and likewise at every Graduation 40 shil.

Item; each[h] Lords sonne likewise at such time 30 shil.; each

[e–e] *Classes of Theologie and Medicine*   [f] *extendis to 3796*
[g] No figure is given in the text of the St Andrews copy.   [h] *Everie*

[67] At St Andrews the beadle had from the earliest days a fixed stipend from the Faculty of Arts, but there are repeated injunctions that he be paid his *cota* by students. The revised Statutes of 1561–62 list the sums due to the beadle (styled *apparitor*) as follows: two shillings if *potens*, on reception, eighteen pence if *pauper*; at the time of the baccalaureate seven shillings if *potens*, and forty pence if *pauper*; at responsions two shillings if *potens* and eighteen pence if *pauper*. On graduation every new master was required to pay him eight shillings. The Statutes of 1570 require two shillings for the beadle from every student before determination, eight pence before licence and four shillings on graduation. This section of the Statutes also contains in practically the same words a requirement of the Glasgow Statutes of 1482 that the beadle *ut diligentius serviat* receive from every student sixpence every year at All Saints. The Glasgow Statutes also require the payment of eight pence by every determinant becoming a bachelor. Later Statutes promulgated during the reign of James VI require two shillings to be paid by all students every year. A list of beadle's fees, similar to those for St Andrews and Glasgow, is noted in the report of the Visitation of Aberdeen in 1549. In the immediate Post-Reformation Statutes of the Faculty of Theology of St Andrews the beadle is to be paid first a half mark (six shillings and eight pence) and subsequently on graduation *tria nobilia* (one gold noble equalled half a mark) *vel saltem aliquod decens vestimentum*. No figures are extant for students in other faculties. (Hannay, *Statutes*, 39, 64, 94, 123; Dunlop, *Acta Facultatis Artium*, xiii, cxxvi; *Munimenta Alme Universitatis Glasguensis*, 2.30, 50f; Mackie, *University of Glasgow*, 23, 38; *Fasti Aberdonenses*, 271; see also Daly, *Medieval University*, 45f, 54f.)

freeholding Barons sonne 20 shil.; every fewar and substantious Gentlemans sonne 1 mark. Item; every substantious husband and Burges sonne at each time 10 shil.

Item: every one of the rest, not[i] excepting the bursars 5 shil. at each time.[68]

And that this be gathered in a common box, put in keeping to the principall of the Theologians, every principall having a key thereof,[69] to be counted each year once with the rest of principalls to be laid in the same about the 15 day of Nov[ember][70] in presence of the Superintendent, Rector and whole[j] Principalls, and with[k] their whole consent, or at least the most part of them,

[i] Not in Laing MS   [j] the hoill   [k] at

[68] The system of payments made by students appears to have been complicated. Sums were due to the rector, the dean, the examiners, and, as we have seen, the beadle, as well as the faculty. The variation in scale of the individual charges according to one's social standing appears to have been introduced late in the fifteenth or early in the sixteenth century. According to a scale of charges applicable to rich graduands only and written on the first flyleaf of the Faculty of Arts Bursar's book at St Andrews, the total amount payable to the Faculty and Rector was 42s. 6d., and this scale was still in force in 1578. The Statutes of 1561–62 also set down a scale of fees which amount to 21s. and again in 1570 another set which amount to 34s. 6d. Similar fees appear to have been charged at Glasgow. The report of the Visitation held at Aberdeen in 1549 stated that the fee to be paid by those who are to be created bachelors and masters was not to exceed thirteen shillings for a rich person unless he was the holder of a benefice, the son of an earl or of a rich lord, and then the maximum was twenty shillings. Those of lesser means were to be charged at the discretion of the regents. It would therefore appear that the authors of this section of the Book of Discipline in providing general regulations were attempting to simplify a complicated system, but yet not to impose any exaggerated increase or decrease in fees. (Anderson, *Early Records*, xxxii; Hannay, *Statutes*, 64, 94; Mackie, *University of Glasgow*, 38f; *Fasti Aberdonenses*, 269f.)

[69] The common chest of St Leonard's was required to have two keys, one in the hands of the Principal and the other in the hands of the sacrist. The *Nova Fundatio* of St Mary's College required that the sums for the maintenance of the fabric be kept in an *aerarium publicum*, which was to have four locks and keys, one to be kept by each of the four senior members of the College. The Foundation Charters of the College of St Mary (King's College), Aberdeen, required that the sums for the repair of the buildings be kept in a chest with three locks and three keys, one held by the rector, one by the Principal and one by the Sub-principal. There is no reference to a University Chest in the extant published documents at St Andrews, but the Faculty of Arts had a common *cista* with three keys. It would appear that the authors of this part of the Book of Discipline envisaged that the property of the colleges would be held by the university which would be responsible for the maintenance of its fabric and not by the individual colleges. (Herkless and Hannay, *College of St Leonard*, 200, 203; *Evidence*, 3.364; *Fasti Aberdonenses*, 60, 97f. 266; Dunlop, *Acta Facultatis Artium*, 181.)

[70] The last day of October was the regular date for the ending of the financial year and auditing of accounts at St Andrews in the first half of the sixteenth century. (For this information I am indebted to Mr R. N. Smart.)

referred[1] and imploied only upon the building and upholding of the places and repairing of the same, ever as[m] necessitie shall require. And therfore the Rector with his assistants[n] shall be holden to visit the places each yeare once, incontinent after he be promoted upon the last of October or thereby.[71]

Of the priviledges of the Universitie

Seing we desire that Innocencie should[o] defend us rather then priviledge, we think that each person of the universitie should answer before the Provost and Bailiffs[p] of each town, where the Universities are, of all crimes whereof they are accused, onely that the Rector be assessor to them in the said actions.[72] In civill

[1] *reservit*   [m] *as ever*   [n] *assistance*   [o] *shall*   [p] *Baillies*

[71] *i.e.*, at the time of the annual visitation of the colleges, see *supra*, p. 145 and n.43.

[72] During the Middle Ages 'certain rights, privileges and immunities', including the right to be tried in ecclesiastical courts and exemption from the jurisdiction of the local civil courts and magistrates, had been secured by the universities. The Foundation Charter of the University of St Andrews given by Bishop Wardlaw in 1411–12 and confirmed by Pope Benedict XIII stated: *Volumus etiam et concedimus quod omnes causae civiles, actiones, et quaestiones scolarium contra quoscunque, tam de civitate nostra quam de regalia et aliis terris nostris ad eorundem scolarium voluntatem coram rectore vestro audiantur, et per ipsum, summarie et de plano procedentem secundum juris exigentiam terminentur. Insuper concedimus vobis, quod inviti non teneamini comparare coram quocunque judice, ecclesiastico vel seculari, quam praedicto rectore vestro, super quibuscunque contractibus vel civilibus quaestionibus, sed in hoc sit cuilibet vestrum electio coram quo maluerit judice ecclesiastico litigandi.* These privileges were readjusted and modified by Bishop Kennedy in 1444, but still left members of the University in a position of privilege both as pursuers and defenders. Under the papal bull of Pope Nicholas V founding the University of Glasgow in 1451 members of the University were to enjoy all the privileges of the University of Bologna but these were, as regards the rectorial jurisdiction, subsequently defined 'with modification after the letter and spirit of the revision made in 1444 by Kennedy'. In 1461 the Bishop of Glasgow 'extended the civil and criminal authority of the Rector until it equalled his own, at the same time allowing the defender in every suit a choice of courts' The foundation charters of the University of Aberdeen conferred on the members of that university without particular specification all the privileges and immunities conceded to the other universities.

As the reformers were strongly opposed to the exercise of clerical privilege and immunity, it was natural that scholarly privilege should also be attacked. The permitting of the rector to act as assessor in criminal cases in which a member of the university was concerned when he was brought before the burgh courts reflects the agreement arrived at in Bishop Kennedy's time whereby the provost of the burgh was permitted to be present *non tamen est judex sed ut assessor* at the hearing of a cause which had been brought before the rector's court and in which a citizen was involved. (Kibre, *Scholarly Privileges in the Middle Ages*, 46ff; Rashdall, *Medieval Universities*, 2.305ff, 312; *Evidence*, 3.173, 176ff; Dunlop, *Life and Times of James Kennedy*, 271ff; Mackie, *University of Glasgow*, 18f; *Munimenta Alme Universitatis Glasguensis*, 1.16; *Fasti Aberdonenses*, 6, 33ff; Calvin, *Institutes*, 4.11.15;

L

matters, if the question be betwixt members of the universitie, on each side making their residence and exercise therein for the time, in that case the partie called shal not be holden to answer, but onely before the Rector and his assessors heretofore exprimed.[73] In all other cases of civill pursuit, the generall rule of the law to be observed, *actor sequatur forum rei etc.*[74]

Item: that the Rector and all inferiour members of the universitie be exempted from all taxations, imposts, charges of warr or any other charge that may onerate or abstract him or them from the care of his[q] office, such as tutorie, curatorie,[r] or any such like that are established or hereafter shall be established in our Commonweale;[75] to the effect that (without trouble)[s] they may wait on the upbringing of the youth in learning and[t] bestow their[t] time onely in that most necessarie exercise.

All other things touching the books to be read in ilk classe, and all such like particular affaires we referre to the discretion of the Masters, Principals and Regents, with their well advised coun-

---

q thair   *r* Laing MS adds *Deaconrie*   *s* but *Trubill*
t–t that othir bestow his

Anderson, 'The Beginnings of St Andrews University', *SHR*, 8 (1910–11), 333ff; Hannay, 'Early University Institutions at St Andrews and Glasgow: A comparative Study', *SHR*, 11 (1913–14), 270ff; and *supra*, p. 149.)

[73] See pp. 148f. This privilege had been granted in the foundation charter of Bishop Wardlaw and had not been affected by the subsequent agreement in the time of Bishop Kennedy. *Item jurisdictionem, punitionem et correctionem in injuriam vobis vel in vos delinquentes, sive sint clerici sivi laici, eidem rectori concedimus dummodo ad atrocem injuriam non sit processum.* (*Evidence*, 3.173.)

[74] *i.e.*, 'The pursuer shall follow the forum of the defender.' This maxim of Roman law had been adopted and generally followed in Scots law. (Green, *Encyclopaedia of the Laws of Scotland*, 9.528, §4.) It is interesting to note that in answer to a question of the Royal Commissioners relative to the privileges of the University of St Andrews, the Senatus Academicus stated that 'By a contract between the city and University of an ancient date and still in force, it is provided that if any of the citizens do injury to the person or property of anyone connected with the University any process relative to the injury must be brought before the Provost and magistrates of the city as judges in the case. But if on the other hand a member of the University does injury to a citizen the complaint against him must be laid before the Rector and his Assessors, as the judges of the delinquency.' (*Evidence*, 3.256f, 258.)

[75] These privileges were granted to the University of St Andrews by James I in 1432–33 and confirmed by his successors including James VI in 1579 and again in 1621. They were also granted to the University of Glasgow by James II in 1453, and confirmed by his successors, including James VI in 1579; and to the University of Aberdeen by James IV in 1497 and confirmed by James VI in 1579. (*Evidence*, 3.178ff; *Munimenta Alme Universitatis Glasguensis*, 1.6, 25f, 47f, 54f, 60, 126; Mackie, *University of Glasgow*, 18, 21f; *Fasti Aberdonenses*, 11ff, 79.)

sell;[u] [76] not doubting but if God shall grant quietnesse and give your Wisedomes grace to set forward letters in the sort prescribed, ye shall leave wisedome and learning to your posterity, a treasure more to be esteemed then any earthly treasure ye are able to amasse[v] for them, which without wisedome are more able to be their ruin and confusion, then help and[w] comfort. And as this is most true, so we leave it with the rest of the commodities to be weighed by your honours wisedome, and set forwards by your authority to the most high advancement of this Commonwealth committed to your charge.

[u] *counsallis*   [v] *provide*   [w] *or*

[76] This is the first and only reference to any kind of academic council (or councils) in the universities, and it may be that the authors of the Book of Discipline had in mind the continuation of the faculties, and in particular the Faculty of Arts, which had hitherto been responsible for the selection of books to be read and the programme of examinations. (See for example, Dunlop, *Acta Facultatis Artium*, lxxxi ff; Hannay, *Statutes*, 11ff; *Munimenta Alme Universitatis Glasguensis*, 2.25ff.)

Of the Rents[1] and Patrimonie[2] of the Church[a]

Thir two sorts of men, that is to say, Ministers and the poore, together with the Schooles, when order shall be taken thereanent, must be susteyned upon the charges of the Kirk; and therefore provision must be made how and by[b] whom such summes must be lifted.[3] But before we enter in this head, we must crave of your Honours, in the name of the eternall God and of his Son Christ Jesus, that ye have respect to your poore brethren, the Labourers and Manurers of the ground, who by thir cruell beastes the Papists have before[c] been[d] opprest, that their life to them hath been dolorous and bitter.[4] If ye will have God authour and approver of this[e] reformation, ye must not follow their foote-steps, but ye must have compassion of [f] your brethren, appointing them to pay[g] reasonable teinds,[5] that they may finde[h] some benefite of Christ Jesus now preached unto them.

With the griefe of our hearts we heare that some Gentlemen are now as cruell over their tenants, as ever were the Papists, requiring of them whatsoever they afore payed to the Kirk, so

---

[a] *Kirk*. See *supra*, p. 113 n.d.   [b] *of*   [c] Not in Laing MS   [d] *so*
[e] *youre*   [f] *upoun*   [g] *been so*   [h] *feill*

[1] *i.e.*, the income derived from lands and other properties belonging to the Church which were feued or set in tack.

[2] By this term the authors seem to have intended the teinds; it is so defined authoritatively in an Act of Parliament of 1567, but on p. 112 *supra* the word is obviously given a broader connotation corresponding to 'charges of the Kirk' in line 3 *infra* by which is to be understood the total revenue of the Church. (*APS*, 3.24; *CSP Scot.*, 2.292; Duncan, *Parochial Ecclesiastical Law*, 275, 277.)

[3] See *infra*, pp. 158f, 174ff.

[4] The suffering of the 'humbler members of society' not only as a result of the exaction of offerings and mortuary dues, but also from 'the unreasonable exaction of teinds' is well attested in contemporary literature. See further, Donaldson, *Scottish Reformation*, 47f; Fleming, *Reformation in Scotland*, 157ff.

[5] Or tithes. In Scotland teinds were generally though not exclusively derived from the fruits of the ground (such as grain) animals and their produce and were regarded as the endowment or main source of income of the parish priest. (Patrick, *Statutes*, 21ff, 40, 46, 49, 54. For a full account see Connell, *A Treatise on Tithes*, 2nd edition, 1.75ff.)

that the Papistical tyrannie shal onely be changed into the
tyrannie of the lord and[i] laird.[6] We dare not flatter your Honours,
neither yet is it profitable for you that we so doe. If we[j] permit
cruelty[k] to be used, neither shall yee who by your authoritie
ought to gainestand such oppression, nor yet[l] they that use the
same escape Gods heavie and fearefull judgements. The Gentlemen, Barones, Earles, Lords and others, must be content to live
upon their just rents,[7] and suffer the Kirk to be restored to her
liberty;[8] that in her restitution, the poore, who heretofore by the
cruell Papists have been spoiled and oppressed, may now receive
some comfort and relaxation;[m] [9] that their teinds[10] and other
exactions be[n] cleane discharged, and no more[o] taken in times comming. The[p] uppermost claith,[q] [11] corps-present,[q] [12] clerk-maile,[13]

[i] or of the   [j] you   [k] suche creualtie   [l] Not in Laing MS
[m] The rest of this paragraph is in the Laing MS an *additio* introduced by the
words *Concludit be the Lordis*
[n] to be   [o] never to be   [p] cuming; as the   [q] the clerk-maill

[6] The authors refer both to those who had purchased from the ecclesiastical
authorities leases or tacks of the teinds and those who had benefited from the
secularisation of Church property, which were so marked a feature of the early
sixteenth century. Complaints of ill treatment of their tenants at the hands of
barons, lairds and others are voiced by Sir David Lindsay and Sir Richard Maitland in their poetic works and by the General Assemblies in their supplications to
the Queen. (Lindsay, *Works*, 2.249, 255; *The Poems of Sir Richard Maitland*, 42f,
163; Patrick, *Statutes*, 182 n.; Connell, *Treatise on Tithes*, 58ff; Duncan, *Parochial
Ecclesiastical Law*, 275; Donaldson, *Scottish Reformation*, 37ff.)

[7] i.e., the exact rents to which they were legally entitled.

[8] i.e., the free enjoyment of her revenues.

[9] The right of the poor to share in the revenue of the Church was maintained
in canon law.

[10] The Lords in making this addition were not requiring the abolition of
teinds in general, but only those that were an oppression to the poor as mentioned
in the following sentence.

[11] The uppermost cloth was 'sometimes the uppermost cloth on the bed,
sometimes the outermost garment of the deceased'. It was exacted as a mortuary
due in accordance with the Statutes of the Scottish Church. Sir David Lindsay
and many other contemporary writers complained against the extortionate exaction of mortuary dues by the clergy from the poor. (Patrick, *Statutes*, 46f, 50,
158, 178 n.2; Lindsay, *Works*, 1.332, 338, 2.197, 259, 353, 3.427.)

[12] A mortuary or funeral fine or present (in theory for teinds unpaid during the
deceased person's life) exacted by or given to the parson or vicar on the death of a
parishioner – 'usually a cow or the upmost cloth'. (Lindsay, *Works*, 2.319, 3.317.
See also references given in previous note.)

[13] A tax due to the parish clerk. On the office of parish clerk see McKay, 'The
Election of Parish Clerks in Medieval Scotland', *Innes Review*, 18 (1967), 25–35.
In January 1570 Edinburgh Town Council summoned a meeting of 'the hale
dekynnis' in order that arrangements be made for the uplifting of 'the clerk male'

the Pasche offering,[r] [14] teind-aile and all handlings upland,[15] can neither be required nor received of good[s] conscience.[16]

Neither do we judge it to proceed of [t] justice that any[u] man should[v] possesse the teinds of another, but we think it a most reasonable thing that every man have the use of his own teinds,[17] provided that he answer to the Deacons and Treasurers[18] of the Kirk, of that which justice[w] shall be appointed to him. We require the[x] Deacons and Treasurers rather to receive the rents then[y] the Ministers themselves; because that of the teinds must not onely the Minister[z] be susteined but also the poore and schooles. And therefore we think it expedient[a] that common Treasurers: to wit Deacons[b] be appointed from yeare to yeare, to receive the whole rents appertaining to the Kirk, and that commandement be given

---

[r] *offeringis*   [s] *godlie*   [t] *frome*   [u] *one*   [v] *sall*   [w] *justlie*
[x] Not in Laing MS. In the margin the Laing MS *additio* reads: *The Lordis aggreis with this heid of the reseaving of the deaconis.*
[y] *nor*   [z] *Ministeris*   [a] *most expedient*   [b] *the deacons*

---

which 'in tyme of papistrie' had been given to 'the perroch clerk' for the benefit of the reader. (*Edinburgh Burgh Records A.D. 1557–1571*, 267.)

[14] The Easter offerings are defined as that 'quhilk is takin fra men and women for distribution of the sacrament of the blessit Body and Blud of Jesus Christ' in the 'Articles proponit to the Quene Regent' by some of the Lords and Barons in 1559. (Patrick, *Statutes*, 158, cf. 185f and 42.)

[15] Teind-aile was one of the small teinds and may have been rarely exacted. 'Handlings' may refer to other small 'Takings' from the countryside. A clue to the range of such exactions may be found in the petition of the General Assembly of August 1574 in which the Regent was requested 'in speciall to discharge teind sybowis, leiks, keale, onzoons, be ane act of Secret Counsell, quhill and Parliament be conveinit, that they may be simpliciter discharged'. (*BUK*, 1.306.)

[16] See Introduction, p. 65.

[17] It had become the practice for gentlemen to acquire from the Church the right to gather the teind for a fixed sum of money, and in this way the tenant or farmer was only answerable indirectly to the Church. The reformers wished to remove the middle man who was given to recoup himself by imposing heavy payments on the occupiers and workers of the land, and to restore the practice whereby the person who worked the land was directly responsible to the Church. In 1559 the Provincial Council sought to have the burden alleviated by enacting that teinds at the disposal of the churchmen be collected by the churchmen themselves or 'let and leased to none but tillers and cultivators of the lands', or, if the churchmen had difficulty in collecting the teinds, let for three years at most. The Council also sought to ensure that when the tacksmen had to be employed the bargain be such that the teinds could 'be let to the tillers and husbandmen at a moderate price'. The proposal of the Book of Discipline was, however, not to prove acceptable to the barons and gentlemen who formed a main support for the reform movement amongst the laity. (Patrick, *Statutes*, 179ff, cf. 97, 141; Donaldson, *Scottish Reformation*, 40 ff.)

[18] See *infra*, pp. 174ff.

that none be permitted either to receive or yet to intromet with anything apperteining to the sustentation of the persons foresaid, but such as by common consent of the Kirk are thereto appointed.

If any think this prejudiciall to the tackes and assedations of them that now possesse the teinds, let them understand that their[c] unjust possession is no possession before God; for they of whom they received their title and presupposed right or[d] warrant were[d] theeves and murtherers and had no power so to alienate the patrimonie and common good of the Kirk.[19] And yet we are not so extreame, but that we wish just recompence to be made to such as have deburset summes of money to the[e] unjust possessors, so that it hath not bene done[f] of late dayes in prejudice of the Kirk. But such as are found and known to be done of plaine collusion, in no wayes ought to be maintained by[g] you. And for that purpose we thinke it most expedient that whosoever have assedation of teinds and[h] kirks, be openly warned to produce their assedation and assurance, that cognition being taken, the just taksmen may have the[i] just and reasonable recompence for the yeares that are to runne, the profite of the yeares past being considered and deduced,[j] and the unjust and surmised may be served accordingly, so that the kirk in the end may receive[k] her libertie and freedom, and that onely for the reliefe of the poore.[20]

[c] ane   [d-d] war and ar   [e] those   [f] Not in Laing MS   [g] of   [h] or
[i] ane   [j] deducted   [k] recover

[19] The leasing of teinds, as pointed out *supra*, note 17, had increased considerably in the sixteenth century and had given rise to concern. Here the authors of the Book of Discipline are insisting, as did the opponents of the practice in the provincial councils, on the Church's inalienable right to teinds, and on the illegality of this particular form of 'secularisation' or alienation. The reformers were basing the claims of the reformed Church to the teinds on the traditional basis expressed in canon law. In a letter to the Regent in 1571 Erskine of Dun maintained that 'all benefices of tithes or having tithes joined or annexed thereto (which is taken up of the people's labours) have the offices joined to them; which office is the preaching of the Evangell, and ministration of the sacraments. And this office is spirituall, and therefore belongeth to the Kirk, who onlie hath the distribution and ministration of spiritual things.' (Calderwood, *History*, 3.156f; cf. Connell, *Treatise on Tithes*, 1.86ff.)

[20] The proposal that some form of compensation should be paid to those who had bought the right to collect the teinds and were consequently 'unjust', *i.e.*, illegal, 'possessors' (provided that they had not done so recently in the hope of making financial gain out of the troubled religious situation), indicates that the authors of the Book of Discipline had no wish to defraud those who had purchased such leases in good faith.

Your Honours may easily understand that we speake not now for ourselves, but in favour of[l] the Labourers defrauded and opprest by the priests, and by their confederate pensioners;[21] for while that the Priests Pensioner his idle belly is delicately fed, the poore, to whom the[m] portion of that appertaines was pyned with hunger, and moreover the true labourer[n] was compelled to pay that which he[o] ought not. For the labourer is neither debtor to the dumb dogg,[22] called the Bishop, neither yet to his hired pensioner, but is debter onely to the kirk. And the kirk is bound[p] to sustaine and nourish of her charges the persons before mentioned, to wit, the Ministers of the word, the poore and the teachers of the youth.

But now to return to the former head.[23] The summes able to sustaine the forenamed persons and to furnish all things appertaining to the preservation of good order and policie within the Kirk, must be lifted off the tenths,[q] [24] to wit, the tenth sheafe,[25] hay,[26] hemp,[27] lint,[28] fishes, tenth calfe, tenth lamb, tenth wooll, tenth folle, tenth cheese.[r] And because that we know that the tenth[s] reasonably taken as is before expressed,[29] will not suffice to discharge the former necessitie, we think that all things dotted to

[l] of the poor and   [m] a   [n] laboraris   [o] Not in Laing MS   [p] onlie bund
[q] teyndis
[r] Laing MS has *teynd* before each item, a slightly different order, and at the end of the sentence, *etc.*
[s] tythes

[21] *i.e.*, the tacksmen or purchasers of leases.

[22] A common contemporary reformed opinion of bishops who were rarely known to preach. Cf. Isaiah 56.10. On the occurrence of this phrase in the writings of both Roman Catholic Scottish reformers and the Scottish Protestant reformers see J. K. Hewison's note in Winzet, *Works*, 2.100.

[23] *i.e.*, to the topic raised at the beginning of the section on p. 156; see further Introduction, p. 27.

[24] On the claims of the reformed Church to the teinds see *supra*, note 19. The right of the Church to the teinds continued to be upheld until settlement was finally reached in 1633. The list that follows includes both 'parsonage' and 'vicarage' teinds. (Connell, *Treatise on Tithes*, 86ff, 344; Duncan, *Parochial Ecclesiastical Law*, 273f.)

[25] *i.e.*, grain raised from seed sown on cultivated ground such as wheat, oats, barley, and bere.

[26] Natural grass cut for winter feeding.

[27] The plant from the fibre of which ropes and sails were made.

[28] The flax plant as just pulled or in the early stages of manufacture into yarn. See *Dictionary of the Older Scottish Tongue, sub voce.*

[29] *Supra*, p. 156.

hospitalitie[30] and[t] annuall rents[31] both in burgh and land[32] pertaining to the[u] Priests, Chantorie Colleges,[33] Chappellanries[34] and[v] the Freeries of all orders,[35] to the sisters of the Seenes,[36] and[w] such others[37] be reteined still in[w] the use of the kirk or kirks within the Townes and[x] parishes where they were doted.[38] Furthermore, to the upholding of the Universities, and sustentation of the Super-

[t] all   [u] Not in Laing MS   [v] and to
[w-w] and to all utheris of that Ordour, and suche utheris within this Realme be receaved still to
[x] or

[30] i.e. endowments for the maintenance of hospitals for the poor or the aged. Cf. Dickinson, Knox's History, 2.304 nn. 3 and 4. For a detailed list of the mediaeval hospitals see Easson, Medieval Religious Houses, Scotland, 134–165, and also Durkan, 'Care of the Poor: Pre-Reformation Hospitals', McRoberts, Essays on the Scottish Reformation, 116–128.

[31] A rent or duty, usually paid annually, for the support of a priest who offered anniversary masses for the repose of the soul of the founder (or others mentioned by him) at particular altars within a church.

[32] i.e., in rural areas.

[33] Laing by inserting a comma read these two words as referring to different foundations and in this he was followed by Dickinson, who for Laing's 'chanterie' read 'chantries'. The Dictionary of the Older Scottish Tongue, sub Chanterie, omits the comma and supports this reading by citing APS, 3.489, 563, where reference is made to the Chapel Royal at Stirling and 'uther chantorie colleges'. For a detailed list of such foundations see Easson, Medieval Religious Houses, Scotland, 173–188; see also Cant, College of St Salvator, 169.

[34] Foundations for the endowment of priests whose primary function was the saying of masses at particular altars for the souls of the dead.

[35] For details of the various orders of friars in Scotland at the time of the Reformation see Easson, Medieval Religious Houses, Scotland, 96–119.

[36] The only Scottish Convent of Dominican Nuns, the Order of St Katherine of Sienna, was founded in 1517 and 'situated a short distance to the south of Edinburgh'. Throughout its brief existence it had maintained for itself a high reputation. (Laing, Knox's Works, 2.224 n.2; Dickinson, Knox's History, 2.304 n.; Easson, Medieval Religious Houses, Scotland, 128; Donaldson, Scottish Reformation, 8; Donaldson, Thirds of Benefices, xviii.)

[37] For details of female religious houses in Scotland see Easson, Medieval Religious Houses, Scotland, 120–130.

[38] In February 1562 the Privy Council decided that the revenues of chaplinaries, prebends and friaries within burghs should be wholly devoted to hospitals, schools and 'other godly uses' and friaries as yet undemolished should be carefully preserved by the burghs for educational and other purposes'. RPC Scot., 1.202; Keith, History, 3.366; Laing, Knox's Works, 2.308f; Donaldson, Thirds of Benefices, xi; Easson, Medieval Religious Houses, Scotland, has gathered together under separate houses considerable information of what became of monastic property in Scotland in the immediate post-Reformation period. For information on the application of revenue from ecclesiastical sources for students see Anderson, Early Records, 297ff, and Donaldson, Thirds of Benefices, on for example pp. 230, 235, 242, 246.

intendents, the whole revenue of the temporalitie of the Bishops, Deanes and Archdeanes lands, and of ^{y} all rents of lands pertaining to the Cathedrall kirks whatsoever.[39] And further, merchants and rich craftsmen in free Burghs, having^z nothing to do with the manuring of the ground, must take^a some provision of ^{b} their cities, townes and^c dwelling places for to support the need of the kirk.^{d} [40]

To the ministers and failing thereof the readers, must be restored their Manses and^e Gleibs,[41] for else they cannot serve the^f flocke at all times as their dutie is. If any Gleib exceed six akers of

---

^{y} Not in Laing MS　　^{z} _who have_　　^{a} _mak_　　^{b} _in_　　^{c} _or_
^{d} Margin _Aggreit alsua be the Lordis._　　^{e} _and thair_　　^{f} _thair_

---

[39] See _supra_, p. 150, note 66. The 'temporality', as distinct from the 'spirituality' (teinds and the like) mainly consisted of estate lands and the revenues that were derived from them. The sources of revenue for the most part remained in the hands of their pre-Reformation possessors, but were subsequently annexed to the Crown.

[40] This recommendation was undoubtedly made out of a sense of fairness. In the period immediately prior to the Reformation the citizens of burghs had shown considerable interest in both the burgh church and the burgh school on which they expended considerable sums of money. As has been pointed out in the Introduction, pp. 5f, the burghs had also played a considerable part in supporting the Reform movement; it is not therefore surprising to find that many of them undertook from 1559 onwards the maintenance of the burgh parish ministers. It is significant that in January 1567 the Privy Council appointed commissioners to set yearly tax upon burghs for the 'sustentation of the ministrie' which was to be gathered by the ministers themselves or 'thair Collectouris or Chamberlanis'. In order to assist the burghs in raising the required sums the Privy Council granted to them 'the annuellis of Alteragis, Chapellaneries and Obittis within the same' if they were already vacant or whenever they should become vacant by the death of the present possessor; any surplus was to be distributed to the poor and the hospitals of the burgh 'be the avyise of the minister and eldaris thairof'. (Rankin, 'Scottish Burgh Churches in the 15th Century' in _RSCHS_, 7 (1941), 63–75; Donaldson, _Thirds_, ix n.3; _RPC Scot._, 1.497f; Keith, _History_, 3.160f.)

[41] According to canon law the provision of manses was an essential requirement in the erection of a parish. Their introduction into Scotland has been attributed to the thirteenth century and the existence of both rector's and vicar's manses in the first half of the sixteenth century is well established. There was, however, no basis in the statute law of Scotland which guaranteed to benefice holders the provision of a manse. Nevertheless the reformers in laying claim to the possessions of the mediaeval Church repeatedly requested the return of manses to the new incumbents. To this request all the Lords who signed the Book of Discipline except four agreed. See the _additio_ referred to in textual note _h_. (_Decretalium Gregorii Lib. III, De censibus_, Tit. XXXIX, cap. 1, _Corpus iuris canonici_, 2.662; Duncan, _Parochial Ecclesiastical Law_, 352; Patrick, _Statutes_, 12, 68, 97, 141f, 169, 181; _APS_, 2.539; 3.38, 73.)

ground[g] the rest to remain in the hands of the possessours, till order bee taken therein.[h] [42]

The receivers and collectors of these rents and duties must be Deacons[i] or Thesaurers appointed from yeare to yeare in every kirk, and[j] by the[k] common consent, and free election of the kirk.[43] The Deacons must[l] distribute no part of that which is collected but by command[m] of the ministers and Elders. And that[n] they may command nothing to be delivered, but as the kirk hath before determined, to wit, the Deacons shal of the first part[o] pay the summes either quarterly, or from halfe yeare to halfe yeare, to the ministers, which the kirk hath appointed. The same they shall doe to the Schoolmasters, Readers and Hospitall,[p] if any bee, receiving alwayes an acquittance[q] for their discharge.[44]

If any extraordinarie summes be[r] to be delivered, then must the Ministers, Elders and Deacons, consult whether the deliverance of such[s] summes, doth stand with the common utilitie of the kirk or not. And if they do universally condiscend and agree upon[t] the affirmative or negative then because they are in credite and office for the yeare, they may doe as best seemes,[u] but if there be any[v] controversie amongst themselves, the whole Kirk

[g] *land*
[h] The Laing MS has the following *additio* inserted in the margin: *The Lordis condiscendis that the Manse and Yairdis be restorit to the Ministeris: and all the Lordis consentis that the Ministeris have sex aikeris of landis, except Merscheall, Mortoun, Glencarne, and Cassillis, quhair Mansses ar of gret quantitie.* It was not incorporated in the 1621 text. See further Dickinson, *Knox's History*, 1.cii f, and Introduction, pp. 12, 30, 65f.
[i] *the Deaconis*   [j] *and that*   [k] Not in Laing MS   [l] *may*
[m] *commandiment*   [n] Not in Laing MS   [o] Not in Laing MS
[p] *Hospitalis*   [q] *acquettances*   [r] *lie*   [s] *thei*   [t] *eathir upon*
[u] *seameth unto them*   [v] Not in Laing MS

[42] The General Assembly in May 1561 petitioned Parliament to take action against those who had of 'late obtained feus of vicarages and parsonages, manses and kirkyards, and that six acres (if so much there be) of the glebe, be always reserved to the minister, according to the appointment of the Book of Discipline; and that every minister may have letters thereupon'. At the Parliament, held in June 1563 an act was passed prohibiting the feuing of manses and glebes by parsons or vicars without special licence from the Queen, and ordained that the person appointed to 'serve and minister' at any kirk should have the principal manse of the parson or vicar. (*BUK*, 1.8f; Dickinson, *Knox's History*, 1.360, 2.79; *APS*, 2.539.)

[43] See *supra*, p. 158, and *infra*, pp. 174ff.

[44] From the extant early records of kirk sessions it appears that the financial responsibilities of the deacons were largely confined to the distribution of the congregational alms for the poor. See *StAKSR*, 2, Index *sub* Deacons, and Calderwood, *Kirk of the Canagait*, 7, 13, 19, and Index *sub* Poor.

must be made privy and, after that the matter be proponed[w] and the reasons,[x] the judgment of the Kirk with the Ministers consent shall prevaile.[45]

The Deacons shall be compelled and bound to make accounts to the Minister[y] and Elders of that which they received,[z] as oft as the policie shall appoint: and the Elders, when they are changed (which must be every yeare)[46] must cleare their counts before such auditers as the Kirk shall appoint: and both the Deacons and Elders being changed shall deliver to them that shall be new[a] elected all summes of mony, cornes and other profites resting in their hands. The tickets wherof must be delivered to the Superintendents in their visitation,[47] and by them to the great councell of the Kirk,[48] that aswell the aboundance as the indigence of everie kirk may be evidently known, that a reasonable equality may be had throughout this[b] whole Realm.[49] If this order be perfectly[c] kept, corruption cannot suddenly enter. For the free and yearly election of Deacons and Elders shall suffer none to usurpe a perpetuall domination[d] over the Kirk, the knowledge of the rentall shall suffer[e] them to receive no more then wherof they shall be bound to make accounts; the deliverance of money[f] to the new officers shall not suffer private men to use in their private business that which appertaines to the publick affaires of the Kirk.

[w] exponed   [x] reasonis hearde   [y] Ministeris   [z] have receaved   [a] now
[b] the   [c] preciselie   [d] dominioun   [e] suffice   [f] the money

[45] See Introduction, pp. 68f.

[46] Infra, pp. 175ff.

[47] Bucer recommended that the deacons should keep a record of expenses in a book and render an account of all receipts to the 'bishop and presbytery'. (De Regno Christi, 2.14; Opera Latina, 15.145.)

[48] See Introduction, pp. 69f.

[49] A similar recommendation that the churches with abundance should help those in need was made by Bucer in De Regno Christi, 2.13; Opera Latina, 15.136f.

THE SEVENTH HEAD

Of Ecclesiastical Discipline

As that no Commonwealth can flourish or long indure without good lawes and sharpe execution of the same, so neither can the Kirk of God be brought to purity neither yet be retained in the same without the order of Ecclesiastical Discipline,[1] which stands in reproving and correcting of the*a* faults, which the civill sword either doth neglect or not*b* punish;[2] Blasphemie,[3] adulterie,[4] murder,[5]

a these   *b doeth eather neglect, eather may not*

[1] Cf. *Forme of Prayers*, 1556, in which a section is entitled 'The Order of Ecclesiastical Discipline', and Calvin, *Institutes*, 4.12.1. In *Forme of Prayers* and the *Confession of Faith*, cap. XVIII, ecclesiastical discipline is stated to be the third distinguishing mark of the Church. (Laing, *Knox's Works*, 4.203f, 172.)

[2] On the relation of the civil government to the Church as set forth in the Book of Discipline see Introduction, pp. 62ff. The responsibility of the state to bring its laws into line with the law of God is argued at length by Bucer, *De Regno Christi*, 2.60, *Opera Latina*, 15.287–292.

[3] According to Leviticus 24.16 the blasphemer is to be put to death. Calvin in his commentary on Deuteronomy 13 vigorously defended the infliction of the death penalty for this offence and added 'in a well constituted polity, profane men are by no means to be tolerated by whom religion is subverted'. Knox in his writings repeatedly called for the infliction of the death penalty on blasphemers and in May 1562 the General Assembly petitioned for the punishment of 'horibill vices' and stated that the 'eternal God in his Parliament hes pronounced death to be the punishment for adulterie and blasphemie'. In Scotland it was regarded as criminal by common law, but in the seventeenth century the death penalty was prescribed by statute. (Calvin, *Harmony of the Pentateuch*, 2.74; Bucer, *De Regno Christi*, 2.60, *Opera Latina*, 15.287; Laing, *Knox's Works*, 4.501, 5.89, 167, 222, 224ff, 231, 2.340; *BUK*, 1.21, *Green's Ency. of Scots Law*, 2.151.)

[4] The death penalty was required by Leviticus 20.10 (cf. Deuteronomy 22.22 and Ezekiel 16.38–40). Knox, following Calvin and Bucer, vigorously advocated the punishment of the offence by death. (Calvin, *Institutes*, 20.2.16, *Harmony of the Pentateuch*, 2.76, 3.77ff; Bucer, *De Regno Christi*, 2.60, *Opera Latina*, 15.287; Laing, *Knox's Works*, 2.340, 383, 475.) On the Act of Parliament passed in 1563 see *infra*, p. 196, n.63, and *Green's Ency. of Scots Law*, 1.139.

[5] Various forms of murder were punished by death in the Old Testament; Exodus 21.12, Leviticus 24.17, Deuteronomy 19.11–13; see also Leviticus 20.2, Numbers 35.27 and Exodus 21.29. Murder was a criminal offence punishable by death in Scotland; in 1540 an Act was passed re-enforcing former statutes. The General Assembly in 1565 clearly defined the rights of the Church as far as the slander was concerned and sought not to infringe the province of the civil magistrate. (*APS*, 2.372; *BUK*, 1.74f.)

perjurie[6] and other crimes capitall,[7] worthy of death, ought not properly to fall under censure of the Kirk; because all such open transgressors of Gods lawes ought to be taken away by the civill sword. But drunkenness,[8] excesse[9] be it in apparel, or be it in eating and drinking, fornication,[10] oppressing of the poore

[6] In regarding perjury as a capital crime the Book of Discipline was going beyond the teaching of Calvin, who noted that 'False testimony was punished by damages similar and equal to injury among the Jews'. Bucer regarded the giving of false testimony *in causa capitali* as a capital offence in accordance with Deuteronomy 19.16–21. In 1562 the General Assembly petitioned that it be punished as a vice 'commanded by the law of God to be punished'. Under pre-Reformation statutes in Scotland severe corporal pains and even banishment were authorised penalties. Hume gives several instances of capital punishment following conviction of perjury in the seventeenth century. (Calvin, *Institutes*, 4.20.16, cf. *Harmony of the Pentateuch*, 3.185f; Bucer, *De Regno Christi*, 2.60, *Opera Latina*, 15.287f, 289f; *BUK*, 1.19; Hume, *Commentaries on the Law of Scotland*, 2.150 ff.)

[7] Capital crimes mentioned by Bucer apart from those listed here included the introduction of false doctrine (Deuteronomy 13.6–10, 17.2–5), the violation of the Sabbath (Exodus 31.14–15, 35.2, Numbers 15.32–36), rebellion against the authority of parents (Deuteronomy 21.18–21), rape and kidnapping (Deuteronomy 22.20–25, 24.7). (*De Regno Christi*, 2.60, *Opera Latina*, 15.287f, 289f.)

[8] The denunciation of drunkenness in Scripture is too well known to require specification. In Scotland it was a punishable offence by a statute of 1436. In 1573 the General Assembly ordained that 'committers of drunkenness' should be admonished and if they did not amend their ways they should be repelled from the 'table of the Lord', but maintained that 'Magistrates may inflict a pecuniall pain for the same, while order be tane in Parliament'. It was not until the seventeenth century that statutes were passed against excessive drinking. (*BUK*, 1.284; Hume, *Commentaries on the Law of Scotland*, 2.334.)

[9] Moderation in all things formed an important element in Calvin's teaching and preaching. Bucer recommended that a law be passed by the state against luxury, pomp, excess in buildings, clothing, ornaments of the body, food and drink, in England, as had been enacted in reformed cities on the Continent. In Geneva offences of this nature were dealt with in the Consistory and this became the practice in Scotland. (Wallace, *Calvin's Doctrine of the Christian Life*, 170ff.; Bucer, *De Regno Christi*, 2.55, *Opera Latina*, 15.261; McNeill, *History and Character of Calvinism*, 135 ff; *StAKSR*, 1.xlix ff.)

[10] Sins of the flesh are unsparingly denounced throughout the Scriptures, but little account is taken of the distinction between fornication and adultery. In December 1560 the General Assembly had 'appointed that to the punishment of fornication the law of God be observit', two years later it petitioned for the punishment of this offence by the state, and in 1566 passed an Act excommunicating offenders who did not declare their repentance. Parliament passed an Act in December 1567, but the matter continued to be dealt with by kirk sessions. Fleming noted that the sin of fornication outnumbered all the faults and failings with which the session had to deal. The fault was for Calvin a sin of special gravity 'since the body of a Christian is in a real sense a member of Christ and the temple of the Holy Ghost'. (*BUK*, 1.5, 19; Dickinson, *Knox's History*, 2.138; Laing, *Knox's Works*, 2.538; *CSP Scot.*, 2, no. 124; *APS*, 3.25f; *RPC Scot.*, 1.297f; see also Hume, *Commentaries on the Law of Scotland*, 2.332ff; Wallace, *Calvin's Doctrine of the Christian Life*, 174 n.4; *StAKSR*, 1.xlv.)

by exactions,[11] deceiving of them in buying and*c* selling by wrang met and*d* measure,[12] wanton words and licentious living tending to slander,[13] doe openly*e* appertaine to the kirk of God to punish them,*f* as God's word commands.[14]

But because this accursed Papistrie hath brought in such confusion into the world, that neither was vertue rightly praised neither yet vice severely punished, the kirk of God is compelled to draw the sword which of God she hath received, against such open and manifest contemners,*g* cursing and excommunicating all such, as well as those whom the civill sword ought to punish, as the other, from all participation with her in prayers and Sacraments, till open repentance appeare manifestly in them.*h* [15] As*i* the order[16] and proceeding to excommunication*i* ought to be slow and grave, so being once pronounced against any person of what estate or*j* condition that ever they be, it must be kept with all severity. For lawes made and not kept, engender contempt of virtue, and brings in confusion and liberty to sinne. And therefore this order we thinke expedient to be observed afore and after excommunication.

First, if the offence be secret or*k* known to few men*l* and rather

c or   *d or*   *e propirlie*   *f the same*   *g offendaris*
h Margin, *Consented on be the Counsall.*
i-i As the ordour of Excommunication and proceiding to the same
j and   *k and*   *l* Not in Laing *MS*

[11] The care of the poor and their protection was regarded as the particular concern of the Church and its courts; see *infra*, note 12, and *supra*, pp. 112ff, and pp. 156f.

[12] It was as part of its concern for the poor that this matter was regarded as falling within the province of the Church. It should be noted that the General Assembly in December 1560 had referred to Parliament 'the petition of weights and measures'. This subject had repeatedly come before Parliament prior to the Reformation and as recently as 1555. In 1563 a new commission was appointed and previous statutes re-enforced. The matter, however, continued to be a concern well into the next century; by an Act of 1607 sheriffs and magistrates were to try users of false weights and measures. (*BUK*, 1.5; *APS*, 2.496f, 504f, 4.374.)

[13] The Reformers, no doubt, had in mind 1 Corinthians 15.33, 'Evil communications corrupt good manners.' Loose talk was severely denounced by Calvin. See further, Wallace, *Calvin's Doctrine of the Christian Life*, 174f, and *StAKSR*, I.lii, 104–111, and Index *sub* Slander; and Calderwood, *Kirk of the Canagait*, Index *sub* Slander.

[14] *i.e.*, in accordance with Matthew 18.15–18; see *infra*, note 17.

[15] The doctrine set forth in this sentence follows, Calvin, *Institutes*, 4.11.3ff. See also 'The Order of Excommunication' (Laing, *Knox's Works*, 6.449ff.)

[16] See *infra* pp. 171f.

stands in suspicion then in manifest probation, the offender ought
to be privately admonished to absteine from all appearance of
evill, which if he promise to doe and declare himself sober,
honest, and one that feares God, and feares to offend his brethren,
then may the secret admonition suffice for his correction. But if
he either contemne the admonition or after promise made do
shew himself no more circumspect then he was before, then must
the Minister admonish him, to whom if he be found inobedient
they must proceed according to the rule of Christ, as after shall be
declared.[17]

If the crime be publick,[18] and such as is heynous, as fornication,
drunkennesse, fighting, common swearing or execration, then
ought the offender to be called in[m] presence of the Minister,
Elders and Deacons,[19] where his sinne and trepasse[n] ought to be
declared and aggreged, so that his conscience may feele how farre
he hath offended God and what slander he hath raised in the
Kirk. If signes of unfaigned repentance appeare in[o] him, and if he
require to be admitted to publick repentance, the Minister[p] may
appoint unto him a day when the whole kirk convenes together,
that in presence of all he may testifie his[q] repentance, which
before[r] he professed. Which if he accept and with reverence
confesse[s] his sinne, doing[s] the same and earnestly desiring the
Congregation to pray to God with him for mercy, and to accept
him in their societie notwithstanding the[t] former offence; Then
the Kirk may and ought to[u] receive him as a penitent. For the
Kirk ought to be no more severe then God declares himselfe to
be, who witnesses thet in whatsoever houre a sinner unfainedly
repents and turnes from his wicked way, that he will not remember one of his iniquities.[20] And therefore ought the Kirk diligently
to advert that it excommunicate not those whom God absolves.[21]

If the offender called before the Ministerie[22] be found stubborn,

[m] in the   [n] offence   [o] into   [p] Ministerie   [q] the   [r] before thame
[s-s] do, confessing his syn and dampnyng   [t] his   [u] Not in Laing MS

[17] This paragraph closely follows *Institutes*, 4.12.2–6. By the 'rule of Christ' is
meant Matthew 18,15–17. See also *Ordonnances Ecclésiastiques*, *CR*, 10.1.29f,
116ff; Bergier, *Registres*, 1.12.

[18] This distinction is drawn by Calvin, *Institutes*, 4.12.4, cf. *Ordonnances Ecclésiastiques*, *CR*, 10.1; Bergier, *Registres*, 1.12.

[19] See Introduction, p. 68, and *infra*, pp. 178f.

[20] Cf. Psalm 103, Isaiah 43.25, Hebrews 8.12, 10.17.

[21] This point is also clearly made by Calvin, see *Institutes*, 4.12.6–13, and
Ordonnances Ecclésiastiques, *CR*, 10.1.30, 118ff; Bergier, *Registres*, 1.12f.

[22] See Introduction, p. 68.

hard-hearted or*v* in whom no signe of repentance appeares, then must he be demitted with an exhortation to consider the dangerous estate in which he stands, assuring him that*w* if they finde in*x* him no other tokens*y* of amendment of life, that they will be compelled to seek a further remedy. If he within a certaine space show his repentance to the Ministerie, they may*z* present him to the Kirk, as before is said.[23]

If*a* he continue not in his repentance,*a* then must the Kirk be advertised*b* that such crimes are committed amongst them, which by the Ministry hath bene reprehended, and the persons provoked to repent, whereof because no signes appeare unto them they could not but signifie unto the Kirk the crimes, but not the person, requiring them earnestly to call to God to move and touch the heart*c* of the offender,*c* so that suddenly and earnestly he*d* may repent.

If the person maligne, the*e* next day of publick Assembly,[24] the crime and the person must be both notified unto the Kirk, and their judgements*f* must be required, if that such crimes ought to be suffred unpunished among them; request also should*g* be made to the most discrete and*h* nearest friend*i* of the offender to travell with him to bring him to knowledge of himselfe, and of his dangerous estate, with a commandment given to all men to call to God for the conversion of the unpenitent. If a solemne and speciall prayer were drawne*j* for that purpose the thing should be more gravely done.[25]

The third Sonday the Minister ought to require, if the unpenitent have declared any signes of repentance to one*k* of the Ministrie; and if he have, then may the Minister appoint him to be examined by the whole Ministry, either then instantly, or*l* another day affixed to the Consistorie,[26] and if repentance appeare, as well for his*m* crime, as for*n* his long contempt, then he may be

v or one   *w* Not in Laing MS   *x* into   *y* tokin
z must   *a–a* But gif he continew in his impenitence   *b* admonisched
c–c heartis of the offendaris   *d* thei   *e* than the   *f* judgement   *g* wald
h and to the   *i* freindis   *j* maid and drawin   *k* ony   *l* or at
m of the   *n* of

[23] See *supra*, p. 168 and *infra* n.27.

[24] *i.e.*, when the whole church assembled for public worship.

[25] In 'The Ordoure of Excommunication and of Public Repentance' drawn up by John Knox at the request of the General Assembly and published in 1569 there is provided a 'Prayer for the Obstinate' to be used on the Sunday after the third public admonition. (Laing, *Knox's Works*, 6.390, 460, 462f; *BUK*, 1.37.)

[26] See Introduction, p. 68.

M

presented to the Kirk and make his confession to[o] be accepted as before is said. But if no man signifie his repentance, then ought he to be excommunicated, and by the mouth of the Minister, and[p] consent of the Ministry and commandement of the Kirk must such a contemner be pronounced excommunicate from God, and from[q] all society of the Kirk.[q] [27]

After which sentence may no person (his wife and family onely excepted) have any kind of conversation with him, be it in eating and drinking, buying and[r] selling; yea in saluting or talking with him except that it be at[s] commandement or licence of the Ministerie for his conversion, that he, by such meanes confounded, seeing himselfe abhorred of the godly and faithfull, may have occasion to repent and so be saved.[28] The sentence of[t] excommunication must be published universally throughout the Realme, lest that any man should pretend ignorance.

His children begotten and[u] borne after that sentence and before his repentance may not be admitted to Baptisme, till either they be of age to require the same, or else that the mother, or some of his speciall friends, members of the Kirk, offer and present the child, abhorring and damning the iniquity and obstinate contempt of the impenitent.

If any man should think[v] it severe that the child should be punished for the iniquitie of the father; let him[w] understand that the Sacraments appertaine to[x] the faithfull and[y] their seed, but such as stubbornly contemne all godly admonition and obstinately remaine in their iniquitie, cannot be accounted amongst the faithfull.[29]

[o] and to   [p] Not in Laing MS   [q–q] from the society of his Churche   [r] or
[s] at the   [t] of his   [u] or   [v] Yf ony think   [w] thame   [x] onlie to
[y] and to

[27] This is in accordance with Calvin's teaching, Institutes, 4.12.7. 'Paul's course of action for excommunicating a man is the lawful one, provided the elders do not do it by themselves alone, but with the knowledge and approval of the Church; in this way the multitude of the people does not decide the action but observes as witness and guardian so that nothing may be done according to the whim of a few.' Bucer, De Regno Christi, 1.4 and 9, Opera Latina, 15.40, 49, 75f, also emphasised the ultimate responsibility of the Church in this matter. Cf. Forme of Prayers, 1556, Laing, Knox's Works, 4.174, 205f; The Order of Excommunication, 6.466f; StAKSR, 1.194ff.

[28] The corrective view of excommunication is emphasised by Calvin and Bucer. (Institutes, 4.12.10; Ordonnances Ecclésiastiques, CR, 10.1.30; De Regno Christi, 1.9, Opera Latina, 15.78.)

[29] Cf. Calvin, Institutes, 4.16.6; Wallace, Calvin's Doctrine of the Word and Sacrament, 192ff. Confession of Faith, cap. XXIII. In 1570 the General Assembly

The Order for Publick Offenders

Wee have spoken nothing of them that commit horrible crimes, as murtherers, manslayers, adulterers; for such, as we have said,[30] the civill sword ought to punish to dead.[z] But in case they be permitted to live, then must the kirk, as is before said,[31] draw the sword, which of God she hath received, holding them as accursed even in their very[a] fact. The offender being first called and order of the Kirk used against him in the same manner as the persons for[b] their obstinate impenitency are publickly excommunicate. So that the obstinate impenitent after the sentence of excommunication and the murtherer or adulterer stand in one case, as concerning the judgement of the Kirk.[c] That is, neither of both may be received in the fellowship of the kirk to prayers or Sacraments (but to hearing the word they may)[32] till first they offer themselves to the Ministrie, humbly requiring the Ministers and Elders to pray to God for them, and also to be intercessors to the Kirk that they may be admitted to publick repentance, and[d] to the fruition of the benefits of Christ Jesus, distributed to the members of his bodie.[e]

If this request be humbly made, then may not the Ministers refuse to signifie the same unto the Kirk the next day of publicke preaching, the Minister giving exhortation to the kirk, to pray to God to perform the worke which he appeares to have begun, working in the heart of the offender, unfaigned repentance of his grievous crime and offence[f] and feeling of his great mercy by the operation of the[g] holy Spirit. Thereafter one day ought publickly to be assigned unto him to give open profession[h] of his offence and contempt, and so to make[i] publick satisfaction to the Kirk of God, which day the offender[j] must appeare in presence of the whole Kirk, with[k] his own mouth damning his own impiety,

[z] *death*   [a] Not in Laing MS   [b] *that for obstinate*   [c] Not in Laing MS
[d] *and so*   [e] Margin *Consented to be the Lordis*   [f] *and the sence*   [g] *his*
[h] *Confession*   [i] *make ane*   [j] *offenderis*   [k] *and with*

ordained that 'The children of excommunicat persons to be recivit be a faithfull member of the Kirk to baptisme'. (*BUK*, 1.170.)

[30] See *supra*, p. 165.   [31] See *supra*, pp. 167f.

[32] In the Articles drawn up by Calvin for the organisation of the Church in Geneva in 1537 the duty of continuing to come to church is strongly stated, but it is not mentioned in the *Ordonnances Ecclésiastiques* of 1541; it is, nevertheless, in agreement with his view of excommunication as a remedial and corrective discipline. (*CR*, 10.1.10, *Institutes*, 4.12.10.)

publickly confessing the same: Desiring God of his mercy and grace and his Congregation, that it would[l] please them to receive[m] him in their society, as before is said. The Minist[er] must examine him diligently whether he findes a hatred or[n] displeasure of his sinne, as well of his contempt, as of his crime;[o] which if he confesse, he must travell with him to see what hope he hath of Gods mercies[p] and if he find him reasonably instructed in the knowledge of Christ Jesus, in the vertue of his death, then may the Minister comfort him with[q] Gods infallible promises, and demand of the Kirk if they be content to receive that creature of God whom Satan before had[r] drawen in his nettes, in the society of their bodie, seeing that he delcared[s] himselfe penitent. Which if the Kirk grant, as they cannot[t] justly deny the same, then ought the Minister in publick prayer commend[u] him to God, confesse the sinne of that offender before the[v] whole Kirk desiring mercy and grace for Christ Jesus sake. Which prayer being ended, the Minister ought to exhort the Kirk to receive that penitent brother in their favours, as they require God to receive themselves when they offend.[w] And in signe of their consent, the Elders and chiefe men of the Kirk[33] shall take the penitent by the hand, and one or two in the name of the rest[x] shall kisse and imbrace him with[y] reverence and gravitie, as a member of Christ Jesus.

Which being done, the Minister shall exhort the received that[z] he take[z] diligent heed in times comming that Sathan trap him not in such crimes, admonishing him that he will not cease to tempt and trie by[a] all meanes possible to bring him from that obedience which he hath given to God and to the ordinance of Jesus Christ.[b] The exhortation being ended the Minister ought to give publick thankes unto God for the conversion of their brother and for all[c] benefites which we receive of[d] Christ Jesus, praying for the increase and continuance of the same.

[l] *will*   [m] *accept*   [n] *and*   [o] *contempt* and *crime* are transposed
[p] *mercy*   [q] *by*   [r] *before have*   [s] *declairis*   [t] *may not*
[u] *to commend*   [v] *and of the*   [w] *have offendit*   [x] *whole*   [y] *with all*
[z-z] *reconciled to tak*   [a] Not in Laing MS   [b] *his Sone Christ Jesus*
[c] *the*   [d] *by*

[33] In the *Order of Excommunication* (Laing, *Knox's Works*, 6.460) 'the Eldaris and Deacons, with Ministers (if anie be) in the name of the hole Church' receive the reconciled person by the hand and embrace him. Similar instructions for the receiving of a woman who had committed murder, which were issued by the superintendent, are given in Calderwood, *Kirk of the Canagait*, 36.

If the penitent after he hath offered himselfe unto the Minis-terie or to the Kirk be found ignorant of [e] the principall points of our Religion, and chiefly in the Articles[f] of Justification[34] and of the Office of Christ Jesus,[35] then ought he to be exactly instructed before he be received. For a mocking of God it is to receive them to[g] repentance, who know not wherein standeth their remedie, when they repent their sinne.

Persons subject to Discipline[h]

To discipline must all the estates within this Realm be subject,[i] as well the Rulers, as they that are ruled; yea and the Preachers themselves, as well as the poore[j] within the Kirk.[36] And because the eye and mouth of the Kirk ought to be most single and irreprehensible, the life and conversation of the minister[k] ought to[l] be diligently[l] tryed, whereof we shall speak after that we have spoken of the election of Elders and Deacons, who must assist the Minister[m] in all publick affaires of the Kirk.[n] [37]

[e] in   [f] article   [g] in   [h] Margin *Consented to likewise*
[i] Adds *yf they offend*   [j] *poorest*   [k] *Ministers*   [l–l] *most diligentlie to be*
[m] *Ministeris*   [n] *Churche etc.*

[34] *i.e.*, the doctrine of Justification by Faith. There is no article on this topic in the *Confession of Faith*, as is to be found in the Augsburg Confession (Art. IV) and the Confession of Geneva 1536 (Art. XI); but it is clearly stated in the Geneva Catechism which was authoritative in Scotland and underlies chapters XII to XV of the *Confession of Faith*.

[35] In the Geneva *Confession* three articles are devoted to this subject; it also occupies a considerable portion of the *Catechism* and is covered in chapters VI to XI of the *Confession of Faith*. See *supra* p. 98 and pp. 133f and n.23.

[36] Cf. Calvin, *Institutes*, 4.12.7, 'As no one was exempt from this discipline, both princes and common people submitted to it. And rightly! For it was estab-lished by Christ, to whom it is fitting that all royal scepters and crowns submit'. The subjection of everyone to ecclesiastical discipline was strongly emphasised by Knox in 1559 in his *Brief Exhortation to England*. For an example of stern disciplin-ing of a minister see further the case of Paul Methven. See also the public repent-ance in St Giles required of the Lord Treasurer of Scotland in 1563. (Laing, *Knox's Works*, 2.364ff; Dickinson, *Knox's History*, 2.66f, 187f; *CSP Scot.*, 2, no. 45 p. 33.) In 1573 the General Assembly found it necessary to state that 'Great men offending in sick crymes as deserves sackcloath, should receive the samein als weill as the poore'. (Laing, *Knox's Works*, 6.516, 519f, *BUK*, 1.284.)

[37] See *infra* pp. 176f.

Touching the Election of Elders and Deacons*[a] [1]

Men of best knowledge in Gods word and*[b] cleanest life, men faithfull and of most honest conversation that can be found in the kirk, must be nominate to be in election, and their names*[e] must be publickly read to the whole Kirk by the minister, giving them advertisement that from amongst them must be chosen Elders and Deacons. If any of these*[d] nominate be noted with publick infamie,[2] he ought to be repelled. For it is not seemly that the servant of corruption shall have authoritie to judge in the kirk of God. If any man know other*[e] of better qualities within the kirk then these that be nominate, let them be put in election, that the kirke may have the choyce.[3] If the kirk*[f] be of smaller number then that Seniors[4] and Deacons can be chosen from amongst

[a] *Deaconis etc.*   *[b]* *of*   *[c]* *and the names of the same*   *[d]* *the*   *[e]* *utheris*
[f] *Yf churcheis*

[1] See also *Forme of Prayers*, 1556, Laing, *Knox's Works*, 4.176, and 'The Ordour for the Electioun of Elderis and Deaconis in the Privie Kirk of Edinburgh'. (*Ibid.*, 2.151ff.; Dickinson, *Knox's History*, 2.277ff.) For a popular account of the development of the eldership see Henderson, *Scottish Ruling Elder*, 11ff.

[2] *Supra*, p. 100.

[3] The responsibilities of the congregation to share in the nomination and to elect the elders is clearly set out in 'The Ordour' mentioned in the previous note. In the *Ordonnances Ecclésiastiques* of 1541 provision was made for the appointment of elders from the city's councils. Nomination was to be made by the Little Council which was to confer with the ministers in the matter. Thereafter those nominated were to be approved by the Council of Two Hundred. Calvin regarded this as a temporary measure and strove to acquire more power for the ministers and the congregation in the nomination and by 1561 the congregation were given the liberty to make their views known. Calvin's endeavour to have the consistory regarded as an ecclesiastical court, composed of prominent members of the church, led to this decision and to that made in the previous year whereby a magistrate, if elected, took his place 'en qualite d'Ancien, pour gouverner l'Eglise, sans y porter baston'. The General Assembly in December 1560 appointed that the election of the minister, elders and deacons be 'in the public kirk' and that 'the premonition' be made on the Sunday preceeding the day of the election. (*CR*, 10.1.22f, 120f; see also Macgregor, *Scottish Presbyterian Polity*, 41; *BUK*, 1.5.)

[4] On the use of this word as a synonym for elder see Introduction, p. 36.

them, then may they well be joyned to the next adjacent kirks,*g*
for the pluralitie of kirks without ministers and order, shall
rather hurt then edifie.*h* 5

The election of Elders and Deacons ought to be used every
yeare once, which we judge to bee most convenient at*i* the first
day of August, lest of *j* long continuance of such officers men
presume upon the liberty of the kirk.6 It hurteth not that one be
received*k* in office moe years then one, so that he be appointed
yearly by common and free election, provided alwayes that the
Deacons and*l* Thesaurers be not compelled to receive the office
againe for the space of 3 yeares.7 How the votes and suffrages may
be best received, so that every man may give his vote freely every
severall kirk may take such order as best seemes*m* them.8

The elders being elected must be admonished of their office,
which is to assist the ministers*n* in all publike affaires of the kirk,
to wit, in*o* determining and judging*o* causes, in giving admonition
to the licentious liver, in having respect to the manners and

---

g Churche   *h* Margin, *What churches may be joined let the policy judge.*
i Not in Laing MS   *j* *that by*   *k* *one man be reteaned*
l Not in Laing MS   *m* *to thame*   *n* *Minister*   *o–o* *in judgeing and decernyng*

5 Donaldson, 'The Church Courts' in *An Introduction to Scottish Legal History*,
The Stair Society, 20.371, points out that more than a generation elapsed before
every parish had its session and that in some remote parishes only in the early
seventeenth century and under the direction of the bishops does it seem that
sessions were at length set up. See also *Scottish Reformation*, 222.

6 According to the *Ordonnances Ecclésiastiques* the elders were required to report
at the end of each year of office to the magistrates, who would decide whether
they were to continue or not. It was, however, stated that they were not to be
replaced frequently without due cause. Yearly election was also the practice in
the English congregation at Geneva of which Knox was one of the ministers. In
'The Ordour' (see note 1) the reason given for relieving the elders was that the
task was too demanding to be held for a longer period. In St Andrews the election
took place in October and elders were often re-elected to office. In the Kirk of
the Canongate the election for the years 1564–67 took place in August; elders
were sometimes re-elected after a lapse of at least one year. (*C.R*, 10.1.23, 102;
Mitchell, *Livre des Anglois*, 11ff; Laing, *Knox's Works*, 4.151f, Dickinson, *Knox's
History*, 2.277; *StAKSR*, 1.1ff; Calderwood, *Kirk of the Canagait*, 5, 26, 51, 72f.
For further development see Donaldson, *Scottish Reformation*, 222.)

7 An examination of the *St Andrews Kirk Session Register* shows that although
changes in the lists of deacons were regularly made some deacons held office for
longer periods than three years.

8 Details of the procedure followed in St Andrews are given in the *Register*
1.1f, but it appears that there was no general suffrage; nevertheless in the Register
of the Kirk of the Canongate the votes of the whole congregation were counted
'every one standing in order as thay war wottit with moniest lyttes'. (Calderwood,
Kirk of the Canagait, 26, 48, 71f.)

conversation of al men within their charge.⁹ For by the gravitie of the Seniors the*ᵖ* light and unbridled life of the licentious must be corrected and bridled.

Yea the Seniors ought to take heed to the like*ᵍ* manners, diligence and study of their ministers.¹⁰ If he be worthy of admonition, they must admonish him; of correction, they must correct him; and if he be worthy of deposition, they with consent of the kirk and Superintendent, may depose him, so that his crime deserve so.¹¹ If a minister be light of*ʳ* conversation, by his Elders and Deacons*ˢ* ¹² he ought to be admonished. If he be negligent in study or one that vaikes not upon his charge or*ᵗ* flock or one that propones not faithfull*ᵘ* doctrine he deserves sharper admonition and correction. To the which if he be found stubborn and inobedient then may the Seniors of the*ᵛ* kirk complain to the ministry of the two next adjacent kirks, where men of greater gravitie are.¹³ To whose admonition if he be found inobedient, he ought to be discharged of his ministry till his repentance appeare and a place be vakand for him.¹⁴

ᵖ aught the   ᵍ life,   ʳ in   ˢ Elderis and Seniouris   ᵗ and   ᵘ frutefull
ᵛ one

⁹ Similar summaries of the duties of elders were given in Calvin, *Institutes*, 4.3.8, *Ordonnances Ecclésiastiques*, (*CR*, 10.1.22, 100), and in *La Discipline ecclésiastique*, 1559, §21, cf. also *The Forme of Prayers*, 1556 (Laing, *Knox's Works*, 4.176.) In June 1562 the General Assembly found it necessary to stress that the minister required every elder to assist him 'in all his lawfull assemblies'. After the election of elders and deacons in the Canongate Church in August 1566, the office-bearers were reminded of their responsibilities at the first meeting as follows: 'To seik the puris silwer and mak compt at the quarteris. The secund, to wisie the seke and puris and to schew the same to the minister and elderis. Thirdlie, that thay passe to the buriall of the puris alls weill as to the ryche. Fourthlie, to segnifie unto the olklie assemble all faltis that ar sclanderous to Godis word.' (Calderwood, *Kirk of the Canagait*, 51; *BUK*, 1.16.)

¹⁰ In *Forme of Prayers*, 1556, the exercise of discipline over the minister by the consistory is given prominent expression, and by the General Assembly in June 1562. (Laing, *Knox's Works*, 4.178; *BUK*, 1.14.) For examples see Calderwood, *Kirk of the Canagait*, 13. This paragraph is discussed in the Introduction, pp. 36ff.

¹¹ In the deposition and excommunication of Paul Methven in 1562–63 the procedure here outlined appears to have been followed. (*BUK*, 1.31.)

¹² The text is difficult: perhaps the Laing MS reading should be preferred. On the membership of the kirk session and the place of the deacons in it see Introduction, p. 68, and *infra*, p. 179, n.23.

¹³ Appeal to neighbouring churches in cases of difficulty is in line with Calvin's teaching. (*Institutes*, 4.3.7.) See also *La Discipline ecclésiastique*, 1559, §18, and *supra*, pp. 68f.

¹⁴ A striking feature of this section is the independence of the Church in the matter of ministerial discipline. In the draft of the *Ordonnances Ecclésiastiques*, 1541, Calvin sought to have the investigation of offences committed by the ministers

If any Minister be deprehended in any notable crime, as whore-dome, adulterie, man-slaughter,[w] perjurie, teaching of heresie or any other[x] deserving[x] death[15] or that[y] may be a note of perpetuall infamie, he ought to be deposed for ever. By heresie we mean pernicious doctrine plainly taught and openly[z] defended against the foundations[a] and principles of our faith: and such a crime we judge to deserve perpetual deposition from the ministry. For most dangerous we know it to be to commit the flocke to a man infected with the pestilence of heresie.

Some crimes deserve deposition for a time and while the person give declaration of greater gravitie and honesty. And[b] if a minister be deprehended, drinking,[c] brawling or fighting, an open slanderer, or[d] infamer of his neighbours,[e] factious and a sower of discord, he must[f] be commanded to ceasse from his ministry, till he declare some sign[g] of repentance, upon the which the Kirk shall abide him the space of 20 dayes or further, as the kirk shall think expedient, before they proceed to a new election.

Every inferiour kirk[16] shall by one of their Seniors and one of their deacons, once in the yeare notifie unto the ministers[h] of the Superintendents kirk, the life, maners, study and diligence of their ministers to the end the[i] discretion of some may correct the levitie[j] of others.[17]

[w] murther, man-slauchter,   [x-x] such as deserve   [y] Not in Laing MS
[z] obstinatlie   [a] foundatioun   [b] as   [c] dronk, in   [d] ane   [e] nychtbour
[f] may   [g] the signis   [h] ministerie   [i] that the   [j] lenitie

---

in the hands of the ministers and elders who would in turn report to the magistrates if they considered the delinquent's behaviour merited deposition. The Council, however, altered the draft so that offences against the civil law should be dealt with directly by the magistrates and the delinquent minister deposed while on other offences it was agreed that investigation by the ecclesiastical authority take precedence. The French *Discipline ecclésiastique* also asserts the independence of the Church and in addition the right of appeal to the provincial synod. (*CR*, 10.1.20, 97f; *La Discipline ecclésiastique*, §§15–18.)

[15] See *supra*, pp. 165f.

[16] *i.e.*, local congregation, see Introduction, p. 68.

[17] The 'ministrie' of the superintendent's chief town formed his council. See *supra*, p. 96 n.4. Donaldson, *Scottish Reformation*, 124, writes that the 'germ' of the Synod 'may possibly be detected' in this clause. In December 1562 the General Assembly ordained that the superintendents appoint synods twice in the year and that they give 'sufficient advertisement to the particular kirks, that the minister with ane elder or deacon may repaire toward the place appointed to consult upon the comon affaires of their Dioceses'. It should be noted that the *Corpus Iuris Civilis*, Novellae CXXIII, 10, required that bishops hold two synods annually, and that Bucer recommended that this be done. See further, *De Regno Christi*, 2.12, *Opera Latina*, 15.129. The supervision by the superintendent over all ministers

Not onely must[k] the life and maners of ministers come under censure and judgment of the kirk, but also of their wives, children and familie,[18] judgement must be taken, that he neither live riotously neither yet avaritiously; yea respect must be had, how they spend the stipend appointed to their living. If a reasonable stipend be appointed, and they live avaritiously, they must be admonished to live as they receive, for as excesse and superfluitie is not tolerable in a minister, so is avarice and the carefull sollicitude of money,[l] utterly to be damned in Christs servants, and especially in them that are fed upon the charge of the kirk. We judge it unseemly and untollerable that ministers shall be buirded in common Ale-houses or in Tavernes, neither yet must a minister be permitted to frequent and commonly haunt the court, unlesse it be for a time when he is either sent by the kirk, either yet called for by the authoritie for his counsell and judgment in civill affaires,[m] neither yet must he be one of the councell, be he judged never so apt for the purpose.[19] But either must he cease from the ministery (which at his own pleasure he may not do)[20] or else from bearing charge in civill affaires, unlesse it be to assist the parliament if they[n] be called.

The office of[o] Deacons, as before is sayd,[p] [21] is to receive the rents etc,[q] gather the almes of the kirk, to keep and distribute the same, as by the ministers and[r] kirk shall be appointed.[22] They

[k] *may*   [l] *money and geir*
[m] In the Laing MS the words *in civill affaires* follow *counsall* in the same line
[n] *he*   [o] *of the*   [p] *declared*   [q] *and*   [r] *ministerie of the*

---

in his diocese had been emphasised by the General Assembly in June 1562; It is noteworthy that the disciplinary power of superintendents is stated in quite different terms in the 'Head' entitled 'Of Superintendents', *supra*, p. 123; see also Introduction, pp. 50f, 68f. (*BUK*, 1.15f, 29; cf. *La Discipline ecclésiastique*, §3.)

[18] The disciplining of the minister's family is not mentioned in the *Ordonnances Ecclésiastiques* or *La Discipline ecclésiastique*.

[19] Knox had made the same point in his 'Brief Exhortation' published in 1559. (Laing, *Knox's Works*, 5.519.) Cf. Calvin, *Commentaries on the Epistles to Timothy*, CTS, 210f. The matter was raised in the General Assembly in 1564 and in 1569 Adam Bothwell, Bishop of Orkney, was brought before the Assembly and charged, among other things. with exercising the office of a temporal judge, 'as a Lord of the Session'. In 1571 an exception was made by the Assembly in the person of Robert Pont and in the following year it was clearly stated that this exception alone was to be permitted. (*BUK*, 1.52, 162ff, 206, 264, 267.)

[20] See *supra*, p. 103.

[21] See *supra*, p. 158 and p. 163 and *Forme of Prayers*, 1556. (Laing, *Knox's Works*, 4.176.)

[22] The responsibility of deacons for collecting and distributing of alms according to the wishes of the kirk session and for rendering regular accounts is clearly

may also assist in judgement with the Ministers and Elders[23] and may be admitted to read in[s] assembly, if they be required and able[t] thereto.[24]

The Elders and Deacons with their wives and houshold should[u] be under the same censure that is prescribed for the ministers; for they must be carefull over their office, and seeing they are judges over others manners,[v] their own conversation ought to be irreprehensible. They must be sober,[w] lovers and maintainers[x] of concord and peace, and finally they ought to be examples[y] of godlines to others. And if the contrary thereof appeare, they must be admonished thereof [z] by the Ministers[a] or some of their brethren of the ministery, if the fault be secret; and if the fault be open and known, they[b] must be rebuked before the ministery and the same order kept against the Senior and[c] Deacon, that before is described against the Minister.[25]

We think it not necessary that any publick stipend shall be appointed either to the Elders or yet to the Deacons, because their travell continues but for a yeare, and also because that they are not so occupied with the affaires of the kirk but that reasonably they may attend upon their domesticall businesse.

[s] *in the*   [t] *and be found abill*   [u] *houshaldis must*
[v] *to the maneris of uthiris*   [w] Adds *humill*   [x] *interteinaris*   [y] *the exempill*
[z] Not in Laing MS   [a] *Minister*   [b] *it*   [c] *or*

---

illustrated in Calderwood, *Kirk of the Canagait, passim*. See also Bucer, *De Regno Christi*, 2.14, *Opera Latina*, 15.144f.

[23] This is not stated to be part of the duties of deacons in *Forme of Prayers* or in *Ordonnances Ecclésiastiques* or in Calvin's *Institutes*, but they did share in the work of the consistory in the French Church. Bucer, *De Regno Christi*, 1.14, 2.14, *Opera Latina*, 15.87f, 145f, noted that the deacons mentioned in Acts 6.1–6 assisted in the exercise of discipline and the administration of the Sacraments in addition to their service to the poor. (MacGregor, *Scottish Presbyterian Polity*, 41f.) Fleming, *StAKSR*, 1.xxiv, noted that 'From several incidental references, it is evident that the deacons were not only present at meetings of the session, but were counted members of that body'. See also Henderson, *Scottish Ruling Elder*, 68f.

[24] Cf. *La Discipline ecclésiastique*, §24: 'En l'absence du Ministre, ou lors qu'il sera malade, ou aura quelque autre nécessité, le diacre pourra faire les prières et lire quelque passage de l'Escriture sans forme de prédication.'

[25] See *supra*, pp. 176f. for examples of rigorous disciplining of an elder see *BUK*, 1.14, 98f; and Calderwood, *Kirk of the Canagait*, 24, 32, 43, 62.

Concerning the Policie of the Kirk

Policie, wee call an exercise of the kirk in such things as may bring the rude and ignorant to knowledge or else inflame the learned to greater fervencie, or to reteine the kirk in good order. And thereof there bee two sorts the one utterly necessarie, as that the word be truly preached, the sacraments rightly ministred, common prayers publickly made, that the children and rude persons be instructed in the chiefe points of religion and that offences be corrected and punished. These things be[a] so necessarie that without the same there is no face of a visible kirk.[1] The other is profitable but not meerly[b] necessarie:[b] that Psalms should be sung;[2] that certain places of the Scripture be[c] read when there is no sermon; that this day or that, few or many, in the week, the kirk should assemble. Of these and such others we cannot see how a certaine order can be established. For in some kirks the Psalmes may conveniently be sung, in others perchance they cannot. Some kirkes convene[d] every day, some twice, some thrice in the week, some perchance but once. In this[e] and such like must every particular kirk by their[f] consent appoint their owne policie.[3]

In great townes we thinke expedient that every day there be

[a] we say be   [b–b] of mere necessitie as   [c] suld be   [d] may convene
[e] these   [f] thair awin

[1] See *supra*, pp. 87ff. In the *Confession of Faith*, cap. XVIII, three notes or marks of the Church are specified. The offering of public prayers and the instruction of children were, nevertheless, regarded as essential by the leaders of the reformed Churches. (Calvin, *Institutes*, 3.20.29–33, 4.19.13 and n.27, LCC edition, and Benoit edition notes 3 and 4.)

[2] Congregational singing was introduced in Protestant Churches by Martin Luther, but Zwingli had opposed it in Zürich. Calvin, however, affirmed its place in public worship in 1537 and again in 1541. In the 1561 edition of the *Ordonnances Ecclésiastiques* an entire section was devoted to it. The singing of Psalms and hymns at Protestant worship in Scotland began prior to 1560. Fleming (*Reformation in Scotland*, 302ff) provided detailed information of the various editions of the Psalms in English metre used in the Church in Scotland in the second half of the sixteenth century. (*CR*, 10.1.6, 12, 26, 104; Calvin, *Institutes*, 3.10.31 with notes in *LCC* edition; Vuilleumier, *Histoire*, 1.329–335; McMillan, *Worship*, 16ff, 74ff; *StAKSR*, 1.40 n.).

[3] *Les Ordonnances Ecclésiastiques de 1561* contain a similar clause. (*CR*, 10.1.99.)

either sermon or*g* common prayers with some exercise of reading of Scriptures.[4] What day the publick Sermon is, we can neither require nor greatly approve that the common prayers be publickly used, lest that wee shal either foster the people in superstition, who come to*h* prayers, as they come to the Masse, or else give them occasion, that*i* they think them no prayers but which be made before and after Sermons.*i* [5]

In every notable town we require that one day beside the Sonday be appointed to the Sermon and prayers, which during the time of Sermon, must be kept free from all exercise of labour, as well of the Maister as of the Servant.*j* [6] In smaller townes, as wee have said,[7] the common consent of the Kirk must put order, but the Sonday must straitly be kept both before and after noone in all townes.[8] Before noone must the word be preached and

g or ellis   *h* the Prayeris
i–i to think that those be no prayeris whiche ar maid before and efter Sermon
j servandis

[4] This was general reformed practice in Switzerland. *Les Ordonnances Ecclésiastiques de 1561* provided for a sermon every working day in the three city parish churches: 'Les iours ouvriers qu'il y ait presche tous les iours es tros parroisses. ... Mais que les prieres soyent faites specialement le iour de mercredi, si non que ci apres fust establi autre iour selon l'opportunite du temps.' (*CR*, 10.1.99, cf. 21; see also Vuilleumier, *Histoire*, 1.319.) Daily services, with sermon on at least one day, became the practice in the main towns of Scotland. (McMillan, *Worship*, 136ff, 144ff.)

[5] On this topic see the discussion in McMillan, *Worship*, 148f.

[6] What the difference was between 'great' towns and 'notable' towns is not made clear; in all probability the 'great' towns were the cities of the superintendents. McMillan, *Worship*, 146ff, points out that in many towns there were two preaching days during the week other than Sundays.

[7] See *supra*, p. 180.

[8] *i.e.*, the two services must be held and the people required to attend and for this purpose the closing of markets, taverns and shops was to be made obligatory. As early as 2nd October 1559 the town council of Dundee had passed a burgh act enforcing the observance of Sunday and Edinburgh followed with a similar act in October 1560. In 1562 the General Assembly made supplication to the Queen 'for punishing of all vyces commanded be the law of God to be punished' including the breaking of 'the Sabbath day in keiping of commoun mercatts'. Two years later the Privy Council sought to give effect to this petition by re-enforcing an Act of 1503 prohibiting the holding of markets and fairs on holy days; this action was approved by Parliament in 1567, and the following year an Act was passed 'anent the keeping of the Saboath day'. But difficulty appears to have been encountered in having this Act observed, for the Privy Council in 1569 again sought to have it enforced. From 1568 Sabbath breakers begin to appear before the Kirk Session of St Andrews, and are usually accused of breaking it in time of sermon. By 1570 both the General Assemblies and this Kirk Session become more insistent on Sabbath observance and in 1579 another Act was passed by Parliament for the 'dischargeing of mercattis and labouring on Sundayis

Sacraments ministred, as also marriage solemnized,[9] if occasion offer: after noone must the yong children be publickly examined in their Catechisme in the audience of the people,[10] wherof[k] the Minister must take great diligence as well to cause the people[l] understand the questions proponed as[m] answers, and that[n] doctrine that may bee collected thereof.

The order and how much is appointed for every Sonday is already distinguished in the[o] book of our common order, which Catechism is the most perfect that ever yet was used in the kirk;[11] and after noone[p] may Baptisme be ministred,[12] when occasion is offered of great travell before noone. It is also to be observed, that prayers be[q] after noone upon[r] Sonday where there is neither preaching nor catechisme.

It appertaines to the pollicie of the kirk to appoint the times when the Sacraments shall be ministred. Baptisme may be ministred whensoever the word is preached, but we think it more expedient that it be ministred upon[s] Sonday, or upon the day of prayers onely after the Sermon, partly to remove this grosse errour, by the which many are[t] deceived, thinking[t] that children be damned if they die without Baptism, and partly to make the people have[u] greater reverence to the administration of the sacraments then they have;[u] for we see the people begin already to

[k] *in doing whereof*   [l] *to understand*   [m] *as the*   [n] *the*   [o] *oure*
[p] *At efter noon also*   [q] *be used at*   [r] *upoun the*   [s] *upoun the*
[t-t] *deceaved, think*
[u-u] *assist the administratioun of that sacrament with greater reverence than thei do*

---

or playing and drinking in tyme of Sermone'. (Fleming, *Reformation in Scotland*, 295ff; *BUK*, 1.19, 30; *RPC Scot.*, 1.269, 687, 2.64, 390; *APS*, 3.38, 56, 138; *StAKSR*, 1.xliv ff, and Index *sub* Sabbath-breaking.) On the attitude of reformed Churches in Switzerland see the interesting discussion in Vuilleumier, *Histoire*, 1.319ff, and Calvin, *Institutes*, 2.8.33, 34 and *CR*, 6.62ff; Bucer, *De Regno Christi*, 2.10, *Opera Latina*, 15.114ff.

[9] See *infra*, p. 196 n.60.

[10] This was the practice in Geneva and in other reformed Churches of Switzerland. (*CR*, 10.1.20, 28, 99, 115; Vuilleumier, *Histoire*, 1.353ff.) It is recorded as having been followed in Aberdeen and St Andrews. *Selections from the Records of the Kirk Session, Presbytery and Synod of Aberdeen*, Spalding Club, 23; *StAKSR*, 848; Melvill, *Diary*, 22; McMillan, *Worship*, 133ff.

[11] A translation of the Catechism composed by Calvin for use in Geneva appeared with the *Forme of Prayers*, 1556, and 'with practically every edition of the Book of Common Order up to 1611'. The French original has footnotes which divide the work into sections for fifty-five Sundays and these divisions were repeated in the English versions. (*CR*, 6.8ff; Torrance, *School of Faith*, 3ff; McMillan, *Worship*, 133ff.)

[12] See the following note.

wax weary by reason of the frequent repetition of those promises.[13]

Foure times in the yeare we think sufficient to the administration of the Lords Table,[14] which we desire to be distincted that the superstition of times[15] may be avoided so far as may be. For[v] your Honours are not ignorant how superstitiously the people runne to that action at Pasche,[16] even as if[w] the time gave vertue

[v] Not in Laing MS   [w] Not in Laing MS

[13] The administration of baptism in church in face of the congregation and at the time of sermon was the rule in Geneva and in reformed Churches generally and was in conformity with the teaching of Calvin. The doctrine of the mediaeval Church that infants who die without receiving baptism were consigned to limbo was rejected by Calvin and Calvinists. Sunday became the regular day for the administration of this Sacrament. (*CR*, 10.1.26, 103; Bergier, *Registres*, 1.8f; Laing, *Knox's Works*, 4.186f; Dickinson, *Knox's History*, 2.313; Vuilleumier, *Histoire*, 1.340ff; Calvin, *Institutes*, 4.15.19, 20, with notes in both *LCC* and Benoit editions; Herminjard, 9.65.)

[14] In accordance with his theology of the Sacrament Calvin favoured a frequent celebration of the Lord's Supper – 'very often and at least once a week'. In the draft *Ordonnances* of 1541 he sought to have it once a month but the civic authorities decreed that it be administered four times in the year. This decision was repeated in the 1561 revision of the *Ordonnances* and reflects the practice during Knox's residence. Of the reformed cities of Switzerland only Basel provided for a weekly celebration; in other German-speaking areas three times a year was normal. The *Forme of Prayers* states that the sacrament 'commonlye is used once a monthe, or so oft as the congregation shall thinke expedient'. In 1562 the General Assembly ordained that the Communion be 'ministrat four tymes in the yeir within burrowes and twyse in the yeir to landwart'. But it appears that celebrations were much less frequent in practice. (Calvin, *Institutes*, 4.17.43, 44; Bergier, *Registres*, 1.9f; *CR*, 10.1.25, 104; Vuilleumier, *Histoire*, 1.343f; Laing, *Knox's Works*, 4.191; *BUK*, 1.30, 58; McMillan, *Worship*, 190ff; Henderson, *Scottish Ruling Elder*, 44; Donaldson, *Scottish Reformation*, 82f.)

[15] In the section in the *Institutes* referred to in note 8, Calvin wrote strongly against the 'superstitious' observance of days but did 'not condemn churches that have other solemn days for their meetings, provided there be no superstition' (2.8.33, 34). He was not, however, opposed to the celebration of the Lord's Supper on the main festivals of the Christian year and *Les Ordonnances Ecclésiastiques de 1561* decreed that on the Sunday nearest to Christmas, on Easter, on Pentecost and on the first Sunday in September the Sacrament should be so observed. In this matter of festivals as is seen above pp. 88f, the Scottish reformers were more radical but undoubtedly the principal reason for disregarding them here was the 'Calvinistic' fear of superstitious associations remaining in the minds of the people. In 1570, however, the General Assembly in answer to the question 'Whether the communion may be administered upon Pasch day or not?' replied, 'Why not, where superstition is removed?' (*CR*, 10.1.104; Vuilleumier, *Histoire*, 1.343; *StAKSR*, 1.388 n.; McMillan, *op. cit.*, 195f, 299f; *BUK*, 1.80, but cf. 1.346.)

[16] According to a canon of the Fourth Lateran Council (1215), confirmed by the Council of Trent, all members of the Church were required to receive communion at Easter. Calvin (*Institutes*, 4.17.44, 45, 46) vigorously denounced the practice of receiving communion only once a year. (See *Cath. Ency.*, 7.402.)

to the Sacrament, and how the rest of the whole yeare, they are careless and negligent, as if *ˣ* it appertained*ʸ* not unto them but at that time onely. We thinke therfore most expedient that the first Sonday of March be appointed for one time, *ᶻ* the first Sonday of June for another, the first Sonday of September for the third, the first Sonday of December for the fourth. We doe not deny but*ᵃ* any severall Kirk for reasonable causes may change the time and may minister oftner, but we study to represse*ᵇ* superstition.

All ministers must be admonished to be more carefull to instruct the ignorant then readie to serve*ᶜ* their appetite and to use more sharp examination then indulgence*ᶜ* in admitting to thir*ᵈ* great Mysteries*ᵈ* such as be ignorant of the use and vertue of the same. And therfore we think that the administration of the Table ought never to be without*ᵉ* examination passing before and*ᵉ* specially of them whose knowledge is suspect. We think that none are*ᶠ* to be admitted to this*ᵍ* Mysterie who can not formally say the Lords prayer, the Articles of the Beliefe, and declare the summe of the Law.[17]

Further, we think it a thing most expedient and necessary that every Kirk have the Bible in English,[18] and that the people be

---

ˣ as that   *ʸ apperteaneth*   *ᶻ* Not in Laing MS   *ᵃ but that*   *ᵇ suppresse*
ᶜ⁻ᶜ satisfie their appetites and more sharp in examinatioun then indulgent
ᵈ⁻ᵈ that great Mysterie   *ᵉ⁻ᵉ without that examinatioun pass before*
ᶠ ar apt to   *ᵍ that*

[17] The instruction and examination of intending communicants in the essential elements of the faith was regular practice in Lutheran and reformed Churches. The *St Andrews Kirk Session Register* and the *Buik of the Kirk of the Canagait* testify that the injunctions in this paragraph were observed. Henderson, *Scottish Ruling Elder*, 46ff, cites instances from other registers of the seventeenth century in which people were debarred from communion until they were able to 're-hearse the Lord's Prayer, Belief and Ten Commandments and to answer the ordinary Catechism'. In 1590 the General Assembly agreed that a uniform order be kept in examinations before communion and that a 'short Forme of Examinatioun be sett downe'. (*StAKSR*, 1.196 and n., and Index; *CR*, 10.1.54; Bergier, *Registres*, 1.16; *BUK*, 2.774; Calderwood, *Kirk of the Canagait*, Index *sub* Communicants; *Confession of Faith*, cap. XXIII.)

[18] A similar provision had been made for England in a series of Royal Injunctions in 1538, 1547, and 1559. It is generally agreed that the volume these injunctions prescribed was the Great Bible which became available in quantity late in 1539 and which was reprinted in 1562 and 1566. English Protestant exiles, supported by Knox while he was in Geneva, had been for some time preparing a new version; it was completed in 1560. There is no doubt that it was this version that Knox and his Scottish associates wished to have used in Scotland. Bruce, *The English Bible*, 92, states that 'In Scotland the Geneva Bible was from the beginning the version appointed to be read in churches'. A licence for a Scottish printing of this Bible was given in 1568, but the earliest printing of this version was published

commanded to convene and[h] heare the plaine reading and[i] interpretation of the Scripture, as the kirk shall appoint.[19] By[j] frequent reading, this grosse ignorance which in this[k] cursed Papistry hath overflowed all, may partly be removed. We thinke it most expedient that the Scripture be read in order: that is, that some one book of the old or[l] new Testament be begun and orderly read to the end. And the same we judge of preaching where the Minister for the[m] most part remaines in one place. For this skipping and divagation from place to place of Scripture, be it in reading or be it in preaching we judge not so profitable to edifie the Kirk as the continuall following of one[n] text.[20]

Every Master of houshold must be commanded either to instruct, or[o] cause to[o] be instructed his children, servants and family, in the principalls of the Christian Religion,[21] without the knowledge whereof ought none to be admitted to the Table of

[h] to   [i] or   [j] That be   [k] the   [l] and the   [m] Not in Laing MS
[n] ane   [o-o] or ellis caus

---

in Edinburgh in 1579. At the suggestion of the bishops, superintendents and visitors, the Privy Council in 1575 'issued a charge that five pounds should be contributed and collected in every parish for the purchase of a Bible'; and in 1579 Parliament passed an Act requiring that 'householders' purchase Bibles and Psalm books. (Gee and Hardy, *Documents illustrative of English Church History*, 275, 421; Bruce, *English Bible*, 67ff, 85ff; Greenslade, *Cambridge History of the Bible*, 151ff; BUK, 1.326ff, 346; Darlow and Moule, *Historical Catalogue of the Printed Editions of Holy Scripture*, 1.61, 89; APS, 3.139; RPC Scot., 2.545, 3.266, 484; Edgar, *History of Early Scottish Education*, 200f.)

[19] The reference is probably to the appointment of the times, but it may also indicate that the kirk session sometimes decided the passages that should be read and from which the minister should preach. See *infra*, note 20. (StAKSR, 2.856; McMillan, *Worship*, 121.)

[20] The practice of reading the Scriptures in order was introduced by Zwingli in Zürich in 1519 prior to the establishment of the Reformation in that city. Calvin and the other Swiss reformers followed his example and this in turn was accepted in Scotland where the kirk sessions appear to have regulated the order. On 29th December 1565 the minister of the Kirk of the Canongate consulted 'with the kirk quhat buk of the Scriptouris thai thocht expedient to be intratt for this present time, haifand endit the evangellis Luke, eefter ripe consoltatioun and inwocatioun of the name of God, desiris him to be gyne the Actis of the Appostellis, efter that he had endit the first chapter of Esay quhilk he was intrattand'. In 1597 we find the Kirk Session in St Andrews in reply to a request from the Town Council that Common Prayers be read each day, ordaining that 'ane chaptour of the New Testament and ane uther of the Auld' be read before noon every day except the days of public preaching, 'begynand at Genesis and Mathow with ane prayer befoir and eftir'. (Vuilleumier, *Histoire*, 326f; StAKSR, 2.829f; McMillan, *Worship*, 120f; Calderwood, *Kirk of the Canagait*, 36f.)

[21] Bucer recommended that a law be made requiring that parents educate their children in the Christian faith. (*De Regno Christi*, 2.9, *Opera Latina*, 15.114.)

N

the Lord Jesus. For such as be so dull and so ignorant that they can neither try themselves, nor yet know the dignitie and mysterie of that action cannot eate and drink of that Table worthily. And therefore of necessity we judge that^p everie yeare at the^q least publick examination be had by the Ministers and Elders of the knowledge of every person within the kirk; to wit, that every Master and Mistresse of houshold come themselves and their family so many as be come to maturity before the Minister^r and Elders and^s give confession of their faith.^{t} If they understand^t not, nor cannot rehearse the commandments of Gods law,^{u} know not how to pray, neither wherein their righteousnesse stands^v or consists they^v ought not to be admitted to the Lords table.^{22} And if they stubbornly contemne^w and suffer their children and servants to continue in wilful ignorance, the discipline of the Kirk must proceed against them to excommunication, and then must that matter be referred to the Civill Magistrate.^{23} For seeing that the just lives by his own faith,^{24} and^x Christ Jesus justifies by knowledge of himselfe,^{25} insufferable we judge it that men be^y permitted to live and continue in ignorance, as members of the Kirk.^{z}

Moreover men, women, children, would be exhorted to exercise themselves in Psalmes,^{a} that when the Kirk doth con-

---

^{p} it that ^{q} Not in Laing MS. ^{r} Ministeris ^{s} to
$^{t-t}$ and to ansueir to such cheaf points of Religioun as the Ministeris shall demand. Such as be ignorant in the Articulis of thair Faith; understand. ^{u} of God
$^{v-v}$ consistis ^{w} continew ^{x} and that ^{y} shall be ^{z} Churche of God
^{a} the Psalmes

---

^{22} This paragraph follows the practice which was set forth by *Les Ordonnances Ecclésiastiques de 1561* and which became normative in Scotland. Examination before Communion by the minister, one elder and one deacon was regularly arranged by the Kirk Session of the Canongate and the Kirk Session of St Andrews. In July 1570 the General Assembly ordained 'anent the tryall of zong children and how they are brough up be their parents in the true religion of Jesus Christ', that the ministers and elders shall throughout the realm examine all children within their parishes when they reach nine, twelve and fourteen years of age, in order that it be known if they have profited 'in the school of Christ'. (*CR*, 10.1.116f; Henderson, *Scottish Ruling Elder*, 45ff; Calderwood, *Kirk of the Canagait*, 23, 42, 47; *StAKSR*, Index *sub* Lord's Supper; *BUK*, 1.176.)

^{23} A similar regulation, but without mentioning excommunication, was included in the *Ordonnances Ecclésiastiques* of 1541 and 1561. (*CR*, 10.1.28, 116.)

^{24} Habakkuk 2.4. A literal translation of the Latin *justus autem in fide sua vivet*, and not that of either the Great Bible or the Geneva Bible.

^{25} Probably a reference to 2 Peter 2.20; cf. 1.3.

veene and sing, they may be the more able together with common hearts[b] and voyces[c] to praise God.[26]

In private houses we think[d] expedient that the most grave and discreet person use the common prayers at morn and night, for the comfort and instruction of others.[27] For seeing that we behold and see the hand of God now presently striking us with divers plagues, we thinke it a contempt of his judgements or[e] provocation of his anger more to be kindled against us, if we be not moved to repentance of our former unthankfulnesse, and to earnest invocation of his name whose onely power may and great mercy will if we unfainedly convert unto him, remove from us thir terrible plagues, which now for our iniquities hang over our heads.[28] 'Convert us, O Lord, and we shall be converted.'[29]

For Prophecying or Interpreting of the Scriptures[f] [30]

To the end that the Kirk of God may have a tryall of mens

[b] heart   [c] voice   [d] think it   [e] or ane
[f] For Preaching and Interpreting off Scripturis, etc.

[26] On the place of Psalms in Reformed worship see supra, p. 180 n.2.

[27] Knox in his Letter of Wholsome Counsel, 1556, emphasised the importance of instruction in religion in the home and of family worship 'in every house . . . once a day at least'. In the Forme of Prayers published in the same year was included 'A Fourme of Prayers to be used in Privat Houses Every Morninge and Evenynge'. Parliament ordained in 1579 that all gentlemen and householders should have a Bible and Psalm Book in the vulgar tongue in their homes for the better instruction of themselves and their families in the knowledge of God. Severe penalties were prescribed for defaulters. In 1596 the General Assembly in condemning 'ane universall caldness and decay of zeale in all Estates' referred to the lack of 'religious exercises' in families, both 'of prayer and of reiding of the Word'. (Laing, Knox's Works, 4.136f, 207f; APS, 3.139, cf. 211; BUK, 3.873.)

[28] See Introduction, p. 42. A similar statement was made by Bucer in an allusion to the defeat of the Lutherans in the Schmalcaldic War, De Regno Christi, 2. Cap. ult., Opera Latina, 15.303, cf. 41.

[29] Lamentations 5.21. A literal translation from the Latin and not that of the Great Bible or the Geneva Bible. Converte nos, O Domine, et nos convertemur.

[30] A much shorter section entitled 'Interpretation of the Scriptures' is given in Forme of Prayers, 1556. A weekly meeting for the study of a portion of Scripture led by ministers (appointed for this purpose at the previous meeting) formed an essential part of the organisation of a number of the Swiss Churches from 1537. The first part, consisting of the exposition, took place in public and at the end of this the congregation were allowed to ask questions. Thereafter the ministers met in private to continue discussion of the topics raised and to 'censure' the public performance of the ministers. This exercise was considered particularly valuable for young men and others who might wish to become ministers. When the weekly exercise was set up in St Andrews all masters and students in the three colleges were required to be present by a statute of the University dated 7th

knowledge, judgements, graces and utterances, as[g] also such that
have somewhat[g] profited in Gods word, may from time to time
grow in[h] more full perfection to serve the Kirk, as necessitie shall
require, it is more[i] expedient that in every towne where Schooles
and repaire of learned men are, there[j] be in one[j] certaine day
every week appointed to[k] that exercise which S. Paul calls prophecying; The order whereof is expressed by him in thir words:
'Let two or three Prophets speak, and let the rest judge. But if
anything be revealed to him that sits by, let the former keep
silence. Yee may one by one all prophesie that all may learne and
all may receive consolation. And the spirit,[l] that is, the judgements
of the Prophets are subject to the Prophets.'[31] By[m] which words
of the Apostle, it is evident that in[n] the Kirk of Corinth,[n] when
they[o] did assemble for that purpose, some place of Scripture was
read, upon the which one first gave his judgement to the instruction and consolation of the auditors: after whom did another
either confirme what the former had said or added what he had
omitted, or did gently correct or explaine more properly where
the whole veritie was not reveiled to the former. And in case
things[p] were hid from the one and from the other, liberty was
given for a[q] third to speak his judgement to[r] the edification of the
Kirk. Above which number of three (as appeares) they passed
not for avoiding of confusion.[32]

This exercise is a thing[s] most necessarie for the Kirk of God this
day in Scotland. For thereby, as said is, shall the Kirk have judgement and knowledge of the graces, gifts, and utterances of every
man within their body.[t] The simple and such as have somewhat
profited shall be encouraged daily to studie and to proceed in
knowledge; the kirk shall be edified. For this exercise must be

[g–g] and also that suche as somewhat have   [h] to   [i] most
[j–j] that thair be one   [k] Not in Laing MS   [l] Spreittis   [m] Off
[n–n] in Corinthus   [o] the Churche   [p] sum thingis   [q] to the   [r] for
[s] These Exercisses, we say, ar thingis   [t] awin body

January 1562. James Melville was deeply impressed by the weekly exercise at
Montrose in his youth. (Vuilleumier, *Histoire*, 1.286ff; Laing, *Knox's Works*,
4.178f; Ruchat, *Histoire de la Réformation de la Suisse*, 2.77, 4.417f, 5.158; *CR*,
10.1.18, 96; Herminjard, 4.263 n.10; Melvill, *Autobiography and Diary*, 22;
Dunlop, *Acta Facultatis Artium*, 416; MacGregor, *Scottish Presbyterian Polity*, 53ff;
Henderson, 'The Exercise' in *Burning Bush*, 42ff; McMillan, *Worship*, 366ff.)

[31] 1 Corinthians 14.29–32.

[32] This exposition follows that given by Calvin in his *Commentary on the
Epistle to the Corinthians*, 1.460ff.

patent to such as list to heare and learne;[33] and every man shall have liberty to utter and declare his minde and knowledge to the comfort and consolation[u] of the Kirk.[34]

But least of this profitable exercise, there arise[v] debate and strife, curious, peregrine and unprofitable questions are to be avoided. All interpretation disagreeing from the principles of our faith, repugning to charity or that stands in plaine contradiction with any other manifest place of Scripture, is to be rejected. The Interpreter in this[w] exercise may not take to himself the liberty of a publick Preacher,[35] (yea, although he be a Minister appointed) but he must bind himselfe to his text, that hee enter not in[x] digression, or in explaining[x] common places;[36] he may use no invective in that exercise, unlesse it be of[y] sobriety in confuting heresies; in exhortations of admonitions he must be short, that the time may bee spent in opening the minde of the Holy Ghost in that place; following[z] the sequele[a] and dependance of the text, and[b] observing such notes as may instruct and edifie the auditor for avoiding of contention: neither may the interpreter, nor any in[c] the Assemblie move any question in open audience, wherto himselfe is not able[d] to give resolution, without reasoning with another, but every man ought to speake his own judgement to the edification of the Kirk.

If any be noted with curiosity of[e] bringing in of[f] strange doctrine, he must be admonished by the Moderator,[g] Ministers and Elders immediately after the interpretation is ended.

The whole Ministers,[h] a number[h] of them that are of the Assembly, ought to convene together, where examination should be had, how the persons that did interprete, did handle and convey the matter (they themselves being removed) to[i] every man must bee[i] given his censure. After the which, the person[j]

[u] edificatioun   [v] But least that of a proffitable Exercise mycht aryise   [w] that
[x-x] by disgressioun in explanying   [y] with   [z] in following   [a] fyle   [b] and in
[c-c] neather yit any of   [d] content   [e] or   [f] any   [g] Moderatouris
[h-h] memberis and nomber   [i-i] till every man have   [j] persones

[33] From this sentence it is clear that these meetings, although public, were intended primarily, as in Switzerland (see *supra*, note 30), for ministers and for those who were considered suitable candidates for the ministry, and not, as in the churches of English exiles at Frankfurt and Geneva, for everyone of the congregation. See further Henderson, *The Burning Bush*, 44f.

[34] *i.e.*, everyone present should be able to contribute to the discussion.

[35] *i.e.*, he must 'open up' but not enter into the 'application' of the text.

[36] The common heads or *loci* of doctrine.

being called the faults (if any notable be found) are noted, and the person gently admonished.[37] In that[k] Assembly are all questions and doubts, if any arise,[k] resolved without contention.[38]

The Ministers of the Parish Kirks in[l] Landwart adjacent to every chiefe Town, and the Readers, if they have any gift of interpretation,[39] within sixe miles must concurre[m] and assist[m] these that prophecie within the townes, to the end that they themselves may either learne or[n] others may learne by them.[40] And moreover men in whom is[o] supposed to be any gift[p] which might edifie the Church, if they were well imployed,[q] must be charged by the Minister[r] and Elders, to joyne themselves with the[s] session and company of interpreters, to the end that the Kirk may judge whether they be able to serve to Gods glorie and to the profit of the Kirk in the vocation of Ministers or not.[41] And if

k–k *that last Assembly all questions and dowtis (yf any arryise) should be*
l *to*   m–m *assist and concur to*   n *or ellis*   o *ar*   p*giftis*   q *applyed*
r *Ministeris*   s *that*

[37] The text of this paragraph is in places corrupt and beyond restoration with certainty. The meaning appears to be that the ministers who formed the membership of the assembly or 'exercise' met in private session at the close of the public meeting to 'censure' the performance of those appointed to take the leading part in interpreting the prescribed passage. This action would be in agreement with an addition made to *Les Ordonnances Ecclésiastiques de 1561* which undoubtedly reflects the practice in Geneva, during Knox's ministry to the English congregation in that city, and in other parts of Switzerland. 'Et en la fin quand les Ministres se seront retirez chacun de la compagnie advertira ledict proposant de ce qui sera trouvé à redire, afin que telle censure lui serve de correction.' (*CR*, 10.1.96; Ruchat, *Histoire de la Réformation de la Suisse*, 4.484, 460; Vuilleumier, *Histoire*, 1.286f.; and *supra*, p. 187 n.30.)

[38] The possibility of contention arising was anticipated in the *Forme of Prayers*, 1556, which this section at this point closely follows, and in the *Ordonnances Ecclésiastiques* of 1541 and 1561; but while Knox and his associates planned that differences be settled as it were internally, Calvin provided for the calling in of the magistrates if reconciliation by the elders should fail. (*CR*, 10.1.18, 96; Niesel, *Theology of Calvin*, 45; Laing, *Knox's Works*, 4.179.)

[39] Those readers classed as exhorters. See *supra*, pp. 106, 111f.

[40] Similar provision for ministers serving rural congregations was made in Geneva and in other parts of Switzerland. The General Assembly in June 1565 received complaints against two ministers serving in rural areas for not attending 'the exercise of prophecying' in Linlithgow. In 1576 the General Assembly enacted that 'all Ministers and Reidars within aught myles or utherwayes at the good discretioun of the Visitor sall resort to the place of Exercise ilk day of Exercise'. (*CR*, 10.1.18, 96; *BUK*, 1.57, 366.)

[41] These meetings were attended by the readers and other candidates for the ministry and probably as in Switzerland by those former priests who continued

any be found disobedient, and not willing to communicate the gifts and speciall[t] graces of God with their brethren, after sufficient admonition, Discipline must proceed against them, provided that the civill Magistrate concurre with the judgement and election of the Kirk. For no man may be permitted as[u] best pleaseth him to live[u] within the Kirk of God, but every man must be constrained by fraternall admonition, and correction to bestow his labours, when of the Kirk he is[v] required to the edification of others.[42]

What day in the week is most convenient for that exercise, what books of Scripture shal be most profitable to reade, we refer to the judgement of every particular kirk, we mean to the wisedome of the Ministers and Elders.[43]

Of Marriage

Because that marriage, the blessed ordinance of God,[44] in this cursed Papistry, hath partly bene contemned,[45] and partly hath beene so infirmed, that the parties[w] conjoyned could never be assured in conscience,[x] if the Bishops and Prelates list to dissolve the same,[46] we have thought good to shew our

---

[t] *spirituall*   [u-u] *to leave as best pleaseth him*   [v] *they ar*   [w] *personis*
[x] *of continewance*

---

to draw their stipends. (Donaldson, *Scottish Reformation*, 204f; McCrie, *Life of Andrew Melville*, 438f; Vuilleumier, *Histoire*, 1.287.)

[42] In June 1562, for example, the General Assembly required two men who were deemed to have the necessary qualifications to enter the ministry. (*BUK*, 1.18.)

[43] Little is known about the early exercises as none of the extant manuscript registers begins until the 1580s, but from the records of the General Assembly it is clear that considerable difficulty was encountered in maintaining them. As early as December 1562 it was complained that in the area over which the Superintendent of Angus had charge 'the ministeris resort not to the exercise, according to the order set down in the Book of Discipline'. (*BUK*, 1.26, 270, 321, 331, 358, 366.)

[44] According to reformed teaching marriage is a divine ordinance, not a Sacrament. (Calvin, *Institutes*, 2.8.41ff, 4.19.34ff.)

[45] *e.g.*, by forbidding priests to marry and by regarding virginity as a state superior to marriage. (See Calvin, *Institutes*, 4.12.22–28, 4.13.3, 4.19.36.)

[46] Commenting on the reports of the *Officials' Courts*, 1512–1554, Walton wrote: 'Considering the wide range of impediments to marriage arising from consanguinity, affinity, and *cognatio spiritualis* (arising from baptism and confirmation) it is not surprising to find that suits for nullity of marriage are very numerous. The Archbishop of St Andrews, in a petition to the Pope in 1554 wrote that it was hardly possible in Scotland to find a spouse for a man or a woman "*honeste vel generose familie*" who was not within the prohibited degrees. But dispensations were of everyday occurrence.' Smith also comments that while relaxation from these restrictions could usually be obtained from the Pope 'the procedure

judgements how such confusion in times comming may be avoided.*ʸ 47*

And first publick inhibition must be made, that no person under the power or*ᶻ* obedience of others, such as sonns and daughters and*ᵃ* those that be under curators, neither men nor women, contract marriage privately, and without knowledge of*ᵇ* their parents, tutors or curators under whose power they are for the time.*ᵇ* Which if they doe, the censure and discipline of the Kirk to proceed against them.⁴⁸ If the son or daughter or other, have their heart touched with the desire of marriage, they are bound to give honour to their*ᶜ* parents, that they open unto them their affection, asking their*ᵈ* counsell and assistance, how that motion, which they judge to be of God, may be performed. If the father, friend or maister gainestand their request, and have no other cause then the common sort of men have, to wit, lacke of goods, and*ᵉ* because they are not so high borne, as they require, yet must not the parties whose hearts are touched, make any covenant till further declaration be made unto the Kirk of God, and therfore after that they have opened their mindes to their parents, or such others as have charge over them, they must declare it to the Minister*ᶠ* also or to the Civill Magistrate, requiring them to travell with their parents for their consent, which to doe they are bound. And if they, to wit, the Minister or Magistrate,*ᵍ* find no cause that is just*ʰ* why the mariage required, may not be fulfilled,

---

*ʸ be best avoyded   ᶻ and   ᵃ Not in Laing MS   ᵇ⁻ᵇ Not in Laing MS
 ᶜ the   ᵈ of them   ᵉ or   ᶠ ministrie   ᵍ Magistrate or Ministeris
 ʰ no just caus*

---

involved was costly and long, and many again, according to Archbishop Hamilton "contract marriage with their blood relations without obtaining any dispensations" and later "they seek divorces or repudiate their wives putting forward as a pretext the want of dispensations" '. In 1521 John Major complained that 'the Scots of the present day find occasion of divorce all too lightly'. (Walton, 'The Courts of the Officials and the Commissary Courts 1512–1830' in *An Introductory Survey of the Sources and Literature of Scots Law*, 136; Smith, 'The Transition to Modern Law' in *An Introduction to Scottish Legal History*, 35f; Fleming, *Reformation in Scotland*, 305; but see also Donaldson, 'The Church Courts' in *An Introduction to Scottish Legal History*, 365f; and Ireland, 'Husband and Wife; Divorce, Nullity of Marriage and Separation' in the same volume, pp. 90ff.)

⁴⁷ Bucer devoted a considerable part of the *De Regno Christi* to a discussion of marriage which is echoed in a number of the proposals put forward by the authors of the Book of Discipline (2.15–47, *Opera Latina*, 15.152–235). The foregoing paragraph summarises the main points of 2.15.

⁴⁸ Cf. Bucer, *De Regno Christi*, 2.18, *Opera Latina*, 15.157ff, where the relevant references to the *Corpus Iuris Civilis* and the *Corpus Iuris Canonici* are given.

then after sufficient admonition, to the father, friend, master, or superiour, that none of them resist the work of God, the Minister[i] or Magistrate may enter in the place of parents[j] and be consenting to their just requests may admit them to mariage.[49] For the worke of God ought not to be hindered, by the corrupt affections of worldly men. The work of God we call when two hearts, without filthinesse before committed, are so joyned and[k] both require and are content to live together in that holy band of Matrimony.

If any[l] commit fornication with that[m] woman he requires in Marriage they[m] doe both loose this foresaid benefit as well of the Kirk as of the Magistrate, for neither of both ought to be inter-cessors or advocates for filthy fornicators. But the father or neerest friend, whose daughter being a virgine is defloured, hath power by the law of God to compell the man that did that injurie, to marry his daughter:[50] and[n] if the father wil not accept him by reason of his offence, then may he require the dowrie of his daughter,[51] which if the offender be not able to pay, then ought the civill magistrate to punish his body by some other punishment.

And because whoredome, fornication, adulterie, are sinnes

---

[i] *Ministerie*   [j] *the parent*   [k] *that*   [l] *any man*
[m]–[m] *the woman whome he required in marriage then*   [n] *or*

[49] A similar provision was made in *La Discipline ecclésiastique*, §37. See also *Les Ordonnances Ecclésiastiques de 1561*. (*CR*, 10.1.105f, cf. 10.1.35.) Bucer, *De Regno Christi*, 2.18, *Opera Latina*, 15.160, proposed that if parents unreasonably refused consent then the 'magistrates ought to impose their authority in accordance with the provision of the *Corpus Iuris Civilis*. In June 1565 the General Assembly found that two minors had contracted marriage without following the above procedure and by a special committee appointed to examine the case declared that they had not lawfully proceeded. (*BUK*, 1.61f, 66, 72; see also *StAKSR*, 1.367.)

[50] For an example of this procedure and a citation of this part of the Book of Discipline see *StAKSR*, 1.220f, cf. 224.

[51] Exodus 22.16, 17, cf. Deuteronomy 22.28, 29. For examples of this pro-cedure see *StAKSR*, 1.lii, 186, 304, 357, 359. Nevertheless, the policy followed by the Church in these matters was not always consistent. In July 1570 the General Assembly in answer to the question 'Whither a man deflouring a virgine shall be constrained to marrie her, or, if paying her tocher, according to the discretione of the Kirke, he may be free to marrie whom he pleaseth in the Lord?', advised that 'the Kirk seek the consent of the magistratis to this law'. In the following year the Assembly thought that the offender had the liberty to marry, but four years later the Assembly in answer to the question whether the young offender should be compelled to marry or pay the dowry decided that 'There is no law establishit that the man should either marrie her or pay her tocher good'. (*BUK*, 1.180, 197, 345; Calderwood, *History*, 3.37.)

most common in this realme, we require of your Honors in the name of the eternal God, that severe punishment, according as God hath commanded,[52] bee executed against such wicked contemners.[o] [53] For we doubt not, but such enormities and crimes[p] openly committed, provoke the wrath of God, as the Apostle speaketh,[54] not onely upon the offenders, but upon such places where without punishment they are committed.

But to return to our former purpose.[q] Marriage ought not to be contracted amongst persons that have no election for lack of understanding.[55] And therefore we affirme that bairns and infants cannot lawfully be married in their minor age, to wit, the man within 14 yeares[r] and the woman 12 yeares at least.[s] Which if it have been,[t] and they have kept themselves[u] always separate, we cannot judge them to[v] adhere, as men and wives,[w] by reason of that promise which in Gods presence was no promise at all; but if in yeares of judgement they have embraced the one the other, then by reason of that[x] last consent they have ratified that which others have[y] permitted[y] for them in their youth-head.[56]

[o] *offendaris*   [p] *enorme crymes*   [q] Margin *Agrees to the head of marriage*
[r] *yeares of aige*   [s] *within twelf yearis at the least*
[t] *if it chance any to have bene*   [u] *thair bodyis*   [v] *bound to adhere*
[w] *man and wyiff*   [x] *thair*   [y-y] *did promeise*

[52] Leviticus, 20.10.

[53] See *supra*, p. 165 n.4, 10, and *infra*, p. 196, n.63.

[54] Ephesians 5.6, Colossians 3.6, 1 Corinthians 10.11.

[55] Cf. *Les Ordonnances Ecclésiastiques de 1561* (CR, 10.1.106) For a discussion of canon law in this matter see Esmein, *Le mariage en droit canonique*, 1.167ff.

[56] This passage should be compared with a remarkably similar passage in Peter Lombard, *Sentences*, IV.36.4. *Hoc etiam sciendum est quod pueri ante 14 annos et puellae ante 12 annos secundum leges matrimonium inire nequeunt. Quod si ante praedicta tempora copulam inierint, separari possunt, quamvis voluntate et assensu parentum juncti fuerint. Qui vero in pueritia copulati post annos pubertatis nolunt se delinquere, sed in conjunctione permanere jam ex hoc efficiuntur conjuges et deinceps nequeunt separari.* (Migne, *PL*, 192.931) The ages requisite to marriage according to canon law were accepted by the Scottish reformers. In 1568 the Superintendent of Fife prohibited the marriage of a thirteen-year-old boy until he had reached fourteen years. (*StAKSR*, 1.299.) In 1600 the General Assembly because 'inconveniences arises daylie through the untymeous marriage of young and tender persons . . . and that ther is no law nor statute of the Kirk, [made] as yet defyning the age of persons to be married . . . statute and ordainit, that no Minister within this realme presume to joyne in matrimonie [any persones], in tyme coming, except the man be of fourtein yeirs and the woman of twelve yeirs at the leist: ordaining lykewayes the commissioners of the Generall Assemblie to desyre this statute to be ratified in the Conventione'. (*BUK*, 3.953.) See also Scanlan, 'Husband and Wife: Pre-Reformation Canon Law of Marriage of the

In a reformed kirk marriage ought not to be secretly used but in open face and publick audience of the kirk,[57] and for avoyding of dangers, expedient it is that the band[z] [58] be publickly proclaimed 3 Sondayes, unlesse the persons be so[a] knowne, that no suspicion of danger may arise; and then may the time[b] be shortned at the discretion of the ministry. But no wayes[c] can we admit mariage to be used secretly[59] how honourable soever the persons be. The Sonday before noon[d] we think most expedient[e]

[z] *the bannes*   [a] Not in Laing MS   [b] *bannes*   [c] *in no wyse*
[d] sermon   [e] *convenient*

Officials' Courts', *An Introduction to Scottish Legal History*, 75; and Ireland, 'Divorce, Nullity of Marriage and Separation' in the same volume, p. 90. It is noteworthy that the *Ordonnances sur les mariages* made in Geneva in 1545 forbade marriage before the age of twenty-four for the man and twenty for the woman. (Bergier, *Registres*, 1.38f.)

[57] This injunction was not always followed. In March 1571 the General Assembly declared that 'trouble and slander had arisen' because the solemnisation of marriages was taking place in private houses and by ministers who were not the parish ministers of the contracting parties. It was therefore ordained that in future all marriages be performed in the face of the congregation, according to the established order, and inhibited all ministers and exhorters from solemnising marriages of those who were not parishioners without special licence. (*BUK*, 1.192; cf. 393.)

[58] The publication of banns, as a prenuptial inquiry to discover any impediments, became part of canon law after the fourth Lateran Council in 1215. The practice was retained by the Reformed Churches and in Scotland has been regulated from time to time by the General Assembly. As early as June 1560 the minister and elders of St Andrews had ordained an 'act' anent the registration of the proclamation of banns. (Scanlan, 'Pre-Reformation Canon Law of Marriage of the Officials' Courts', 73; Ireland, 'Post-Reformation Canon Law of Marriage of the Commissaries' Courts', 84ff; *NSH*, 1.434ff; McMillan, *Worship*, 271f; *StAKSR*, 1.42; Patrick, *Statutes*, 142f; *BUK*, 1.66, 72, 114, 185.)

[59] Clandestine and irregular marriages of various types had for centuries been a cause of grave scandal in the Church. The reformers were not wholly successful in accomplishing their aims. Canon law as formulated prior to the Council of Trent in 1563 continued to direct judgments in the Commissary Courts after their establishment in February of that year and irregular marriages did not cease. 'From the time of the Reformation until the 19th century', Ireland wrote, 'the history of the law of marriage is dominated by the efforts of church and government in the interests of public order and of the establishment, to suppress the celebration of marriage without prior publication of the parties' intention to marry, or by persons other than the ministers of the established Church.' (Walton. 'The Courts of the Officials and the Commissary Courts 1512–1830', *An Introductory Survey of the Sources and Literature of Scots Law*, 147; Esmein. *Le mariage en droit canonique*, 1.198ff, 2.148ff, 252; Scanlan, 'Husband and Wife: Pre-Reformation Canon Law of Marriage of the Officials' Courts', *An Introduction to Scottish Legal History*, 73; Ireland, 'Post-Reformation Canon Law of Marriage of the Comissaries' Courts', *An Introduction to Scottish Legal History*, 84.)

for mariage and it be*f* used no day else, without the consent of the whole ministrie.⁶⁰

Mariage once lawfully contracted, may not be dissolved at mans pleasure, as our master Christ Jesus doth witnes, unlesse adulterie be comitted;⁶¹ which being sufficiently proved in presence of the civill magistrate,⁶² the innocent (if they so require) ought to be pronounced free and the offender ought to suffer death, as God hath commanded.⁶³ If the civill sword foolishly

f it to be

⁶⁰ The celebration of marriage on Sunday was practised in Geneva and although this became general in Scotland it was not uniformally kept. The General Assembly in 1579 in reply to a question raised by the 'Synodall Assemblie of Sanct Andrews' decreed that marriages may take place on 'feriall dayes', and it would appear that the Geneva practice of permitting marriage on working days 'moyennant que ce soit au commencement du presche' was allowed. In 1584 the Kirk Session of Perth ordained that marriages could be celebrated on Thursdays 'in time of sermon as on Sunday' and in 1586 discharged 'all marriages to be made on Sundays in the morning in time coming'. The General Assembly decreed in 1610 that 'the celebration and solemnization of the holy band of matrimonie be refused to no Christians within this realme neither upon Sunday, nor upon any other day when the samine shall be required'. (*CR*, 10.1.26, 105, 108; *BUK*, 2.439, cf. 1.72, 114, 3.1101; 'Extracts from the Kirk Session Register of Perth', *Spottiswoode Miscellany*, 2.249, 253; Fraser, *Husband and Wife*, 1.241f; McMillan, *Worship*, 272ff; Bergier, *Registres*, 1.33, and *supra*, pp. 181f.)

⁶¹ On the basis of Matthew 3.9 and unaware, it would appear, of the exegetical difficulties connected with this passage and the parallel passage in Mark 10.2-12, the Scottish Reformers here regarded marriage as indissoluble except in a case of adultery. The mediaeval Church did not allow divorce *a vinculo* on the grounds of adultery but only a separation *a mensa et thoro*. Protestant and Reforming theologians regarded adultery as valid ground for divorce but some, including Calvin, extended the grounds for divorce to cover desertion. Despite the restriction stated here in the text divorce for desertion was approved in the Scottish Church from the earliest days and as such was embodied in an Act of Parliament of 1573. (*NSH*, 3.453; *CR*, 10.1.41ff, 110ff; Bucer, *De Regno Christi*, 2.22-42, *Opera Latina*, 15.165-220; *StAKSR*, 1.xxxvii ff; Ireland, 'Divorce, Nullity of Marriage and Separation', 94ff; Walton, 'The Courts of the Officials and the Commissary Courts 1512-1830', 146; Smith, 'The Reformers and Divorce', *SHR*, 9 (1911-12), 10ff; Smith, 'A Note on Divorce for Desertion' *Juridical Review*, 51 (1939) 254ff.)

⁶² This is in agreement with *Les Ordonnances Ecclésiastiques de 1561*: 'S'il est requis de prononcer quelque sentence iuridique, que les parties soyent renvoyees au Conceil, avec declaration l'avis du Consistoire, pour en donner la sentence diffinitive'. (*CR*, 10.1.114, cf. 44; Bergier, *Registres*, 1.47; see also *La Discipline ecclésiastique*, 1559; Niesel, *The Theology of Calvin*, 56; see further notes 63 and 64.)

⁶³ Leviticus 20.10, Deuteronomy 22.22. The Reformers on the basis of the Mosaic code held to the theory that the guilty person was legally 'dead' and consequently the innocent free to remarry. The St Andrews Kirk Session were acting on this basis in 1560. Winzet attacked the Reformers on the grounds that St Paul commanded the innocent woman to remain unmarried or be reconciled to her husband. Calvin advocated the death penalty for adultery and the Scottish reformers pressed for an Act of Parliament to enforce it. One was secured in 1563

spare the life of the offender, yet may not the Kirke be negligent in their office, which is to excommunicate the wicked and to repute them as dead members and to pronounce the innocent partie to be at freedome, be they never so honourable before the world.[64] If the life be spared, as it ought not to be, to the offenders, and if fruits[g] of repentance of long time appeare in them and if they earnestly desire to be reconciled with the Kirk, we judge they[h] may be received to the[i] participation of the Sacraments, and other[j] benefites of the Kirk. For we would not that the kirk should hold them excommunicate, whom God absolved, that is, the penitent.

If any demand whether that the offender after reconciliation with the kirk may not marry againe. We answer, that if they cannot live continently,[k] and if the necessity be such, as that they feare further offence of God, we cannot forbid them to use the remedy ordained of God.[65] If the partie offended, may be

[g] the fruits   [h] that they   [i] Not in Laing MS   [j] of the other
[k] continent

---

but Knox commented 'no law and such Acts were both alike'. In fact the penal part of this statute, which seems to one modern commentator 'severe enough', was not often enforced; a similar act was passed in 1564. In 1563 Randolph reported that two people in Edinburgh were executed for adultery; and in 1584 a man was executed in Perth. (*StAKSR*, 1.50f, 59f, 71; Smith, 'The Reformers and Divorce', *SHR*, 9 (1911-12), 22ff; Calvin, *Institutes*, 4.0.37; Calvin, *Commentaries on the Four Last Books of Moses*, 3.78; Bucer, *De Regno Christi*, 2.33, *Opera Latina*, 15.189ff; Dickinson, *Knox's History*, 2.49, 79f, 138; *APS*, 2.539; *CPS Scot.*, 2. no. 45, p. 33; no. 124, p. 100; Winzet, *Works*, 1.109; *RPC Scot.*, 1.298; 'Extracts from the Kirk Session Register of Perth', 242; and *supra*, p. 165 n.4.)

[64] That this was already taking place is demonstrated by the *St Andrews Kirk Session Register* (pp. xxxvii ff, xlv, and Index) from which it is also clear that the kirk session had, in addition to its powers as a court of ecclesiastical discipline, assumed the powers of the abolished Consistorial Court. Indeed kirk sessions continued to exercise such powers until the Commissary Courts were established by Royal Charter in February 1563 and that of Edinburgh given jurisdiction over all Scotland in cases of marriage, divorce and bastardy. (Walton, 'The Courts of the Officials and the Commissary Courts 1512-1830', *An Introductory Survey of the Sources and Literature of Scots Law*, 145f; Ireland, 'Divorce, Nullity of Marriage and Separation', 94f; Donaldson, 'The Church Courts', *An Introduction to Scottish Legal History*, 82f, 366f; Smith, 'The Reformers and Divorce', *SHR*, 9 (1911-12), 12ff; see also Bucer, *De Regno Christi*, 2.34, *Opera Latina*, 15.194ff.)

[65] It is not clear whether the text here permits marriage with the paramour, but from later action it would appear that the Reformers did not so intend; nevertheless, such marriages did take place. The General Assembly in 1566 decreed that superintendents 'admonisch all ministers within ther jurisdictiouns, that none joyne any partie separatit for adulterie in marriage, under paine of removeing from the ministrie' (*i.e.* the offending or guilty party) and in 1571 declared such marriages

reconciled to the offender, then we judge that on no wayes¹ it shall be lawfull to the offender to marry any other, except the partie that before hath been offended; and the solemnization of the latter marriage must be in the open face of the kirk, like as the former, but without proclamation of bands.

This we do offer as the best counsel that God giveth unto us in so doubtsome a case, but the most perfect reformation were, if your Honours would give to God his honour and glory, that yee would preferre his expresse commandment to your own corrupt judgements, especially in punishing of these crimes, which he commandeth to be punished with death.⁶⁶ For so should yee declare yourselves Gods true obedient ᵐ officiars, and your commonwealth should be rid of innumerable troubles.

We meane not that sinnes committed in our former blindnesse (which be almost buried in oblivion) shall be called again to examination and judgement.⁶⁷ But we require that the law may bee now and hereafter ⁿ so established and execute, that this un-

---

¹in nowyse   ᵐ and obedient   ⁿ now and heirafter be

---

unlawful. The matter continued to be raised in the Courts of the Church and in 1595 the Assembly declared 'thir two sorts to be unlawfull: first, when ane person marieth another quhom they have pollutit by adulterie; nixt quhen the innocent person is content to remaine with the [nocent and] guiltie, and the guiltie will have another or takis another'. This action did not end the matter for in 1600 the Generall Assembly again noted that the 'mariage of persons convict of adulterie is a great allurement to maried persons to committ the said cryme, thinking therby to be separate from their awin lawfull halfe marrowes, to injoy the persons with quhom they have committed adulterie' and thought it expedient 'that ane supplicatioun be givin in to the nixt Conventioun, craveand ane act to be made dischargeand all mariages of such persons as are convict of adulterie, and that the samein be ratified in the nixt Parliament'. As a result Parliament passed an Act that year annulling marriages contracted by persons divorced for adultery with the persons 'with quhome they are declarit be sentence of the ordinar judge to have commit the said cryme and fact of adulterie'. Of this Act, Ireland wrote; 'The general consensus of the institutional writers is, however, in favour of a strict interpretation of the Act, so that marriage may be contracted with any person other than the paramour actually named in the decree.' Bucer, who discussed at greater length than any of the other Continental reformers the subject of marriage and divorce, and with whose views the authors of this section of the Book of Discipline were clearly acquainted, advocated that divorced persons, if permitted to live, ought to be allowed to marry. (BUK, 1.91, 98. 171, 197, 308, 377, 3.885, 953; Calderwood, History, 2.331, 371; Winzet, Works, 1.74, 109f; APS, 4.233; StAKSR, 1.302; Smith, 'The Reformers and Divorce'. SHR, 9 (1911–12), 19f, 33ff; Ireland, 'Divorce, Nullity of Marriage and Separation', The Stair Society, 20.93f; Bucer, De Regno Christi, 2.44, Opera Latina, 15.225f.)

⁶⁶ See supra, p. 196 and n.63. This position is maintained by Bucer (De Regno Christi, 2.44, Opera Latina, 15.225) in virtually the same terms.

⁶⁷ i.e., prior to the acceptance of the Reformation.

godly impunity of sinne have no place within this Realme. For in the feare of God we signifie unto your Honours, that whosoever perswades you, that ye may pardon where God commandeth death deceives your soules and provokes you to offend Gods Majestie.[68]

Of Buriall[69]

Buriall in all ages hath bene holden in estimation to signifie that the same bodie which was committed to the earth should not utterly perish, but should rise againe,[70] and the same we would have kept within this realme, provided that superstition, idolatry and whatsoever hath proceeded of a false opinion, and for advantage sake may be avoided, and[o] singing of Masse, *placebo*,[71] and *dirige*,[72] and all other prayers over or for the dead, which[p] are not onely superstitious[q] and vaine, but also are idolatry and doe repugne to the plaine Scriptures of God. For plaine it is that every-one that dyeth, departeth either in the faith of Christ Jesus or[r] departeth in incredulity. Plain it is that they that depart in the true faith of Christ Jesus rest from their labours and from death doe[s] goe to life everlasting, as by our Master and his Apostles[t] we are taught. But whosoever departeth in unbeleefe, or in incredulitie, shall never see life, but the wrath of God abides upon him. And so we say that prayers for the dead are not onely superstitious[u] and vaine, but doe expressly repugne to the manifest

---

[o] *as*   [p] Not in Laing MS   [q] *superfluous*   [r] *or ellis*
[s] Not in Laing MS   [t] *Apostle*   [u] *superfluous*

[68] See the reference above to the Acts of Parliament and also Ireland, 'Divorce, Nullity of Marriage and Separation', 83, 93. The attitude of the authors of the Book of Discipline and of the reformers engaged in the struggle to have the law brought into line with their teaching and to have it enforced was fittingly summed up by Smith, 'The Reformers and Divorce', SHR, 9 (1911–12), 34: 'The long struggle of forty years shows clearly the functions which the General Assembly conceived it its duty to exercise; it conceived itself as a purifying and illuminating influence in the community, and as a consultative body like the old Lords of the Articles, suggesting legislation and urging its enforcement. Its attempt to enforce criminal penalties failed and it had to content itself with the infliction at its instance of civil disabilities. Its failure was, in fact the failure to induce the state to incorporate the disciplinary system of the Church in the penal code.'

[69] A similar but much shorter section is found in *Ordonnances Ecclésiastiques* of 1541 and 1561 and in *Forme of Prayers*, 1556, (*CR*, 10.1.27, 114; Niesel, *Theology of Calvin*, 59; Laing, *Knox's Works*, 4.203.)

[70] cf. Calvin, *Institutes*, 3.25.5.

[71] Vespers for the Dead.

[72] Matins in the Office of the Dead.

Scriptures and veritie thereof.⁷³ For avoiding of all inconveniences we judge it best, that neither singing nor reading be at⁰ buriall. For albeit things sung and read may admonish some of the living to prepare themselves for death, yet shall some superstitious⁰ think that⁰ singing and⁰ reading of the living may⁰ profite the dead.⁰ And therefore we think it most expedient, that the dead be conveyed to the place of buriall with some honest company of the kirk, without either singing or reading; yea without all kind of ceremony heretofore used,⁷⁴ other then that the dead be committed to the grave, with such gravity and sobriety, as those that be present may seeme to feare the judgements of God, and to hate sinne which is the cause of death.⁰ ⁷⁵

We are not ignorant that some require a Sermon at the buriall,⁷⁶

⁰ *at the*   ⁰ *superstitious and ignorant personis ever*
⁰ *the workis*   ⁰ *or*   ⁰ *do and may*
⁰ Margin, *Refers this article to the judgement of the Churche*
⁰ The following *additio* is found in the Laing MS only. *And yit, nochtwith-standing, we are not so precise, but that we ar content that particular Kirkis use thame in that behalf wyth the consent of the Ministerie of the same, as they will answeir to God and Assemblie of the Universall Kirk gathered within the Realme.*

⁷³ Prayers for the dead were regarded by Calvin as without warrant in Scripture. See *Institutes*, 3.5.10; *Psychopannychia, CR*, 5.177ff, 201ff; *Tracts*, 2.432ff, 449f; and *The True Method of Giving Peace and of Reforming the Church, CR*, 7.655ff; *Tracts*, 2.321ff.

⁷⁴ Cf. *Forme of Prayers*. 'The corps is reverently brought to the grave, accompagnied with the Congregation, withowte any further ceremonies.' The General Assembly in 1579 forbade what it regarded as 'superstitious rites' in connection with the burial of the Earl of Atholl. (Laing, *Knox's Works*, 4.203; *BUK*, 2.431, see also 539, 566 and 939; McMillan, *Worship*, 287ff.)

⁷⁵ The *additio* mentioned above (note *b*) which follows this paragraph in the Laing MS may represent the Church's judgment in the matter and may be regarded as an indication of its awareness of a different practice in some reformed congregations. This is witnessed by the 'Forme and Maner of Buriall in the Kirk of Montrois' which may be earlier than 1560. (*Miscellany of the Wodrow Society*, 1.291ff; McMillan, *Worship*, 45f.)

⁷⁶ The section in the *Forme of Prayers*, 1556 quoted in note 74 states that after burial 'the minister goeth to the church, if it be not farre of and maketh some comfortable exhortacion to the people towchying deathe and resurrection'. John à Lasco's *Forma ac Ratio* makes provision for a sermon if the funeral could not be held on a preaching day. The preaching of sermons at funerals, at least in the case of prominent persons, took place in Scotland throughout the remaining part of the sixteenth century and well into the seventeenth. That Knox preached on the text 'Blessed are these that dee in the Lord' at the burial of the Regent Moray was recorded by Calderwood: McMillan pointed out that a sermon was preached in 1618 at Stirling at the funeral of Patrick Simpson, an opponent of episcopacy, and that 'among the episcopalians the same custom was observed, the only funeral service being the funeral sermon'. It is worth noting, however, that in 1594 Lord Seton asked the Presbytery of Haddington to appoint someone to preach on a

or else some place^c of Scripture to be read, to put the living in
minde that they are mortall, and that likewise they must die. But
let these men understand that the Sermons which be daily made,
serve for that use, which if men despise, the^d funerall Sermons
shall rather nourish superstition, and a false opinion, as before is
said, then that they shall bring such persons to a^e godly consideration of their own estate. Attour either shall the Ministers for the
most part be occupied in^f funerall Sermons, or else they shall have
respect of persons, preaching at the burials^g of the rich and
honorable, but keeping silence when the poore and^h despised
departeth, and this with safe conscience cannot the Ministerⁱ
doe. For seeing that before God there is no respect of persons and
that their Ministrie appertaineth to all alike, whatsoever they doe
to the rich in respect of their Ministery, the same they are bound
to doe to the poorest under their charge.

In respect of divers inconveniences we think it neither seemly
that the Kirk appointed to preaching and ministration of the
Sacraments shall be made a place of buryall, but that some other
secret and convenient place, lying in the most free aire, be
appointed for that use, which place ought to be^j walled and
fenced about *and* kept for that use onely.[77]

^c *places*　　^d *the preaching of the*　　^e *any*　　^f *in preaching*　　^g *buriall*
^h *or*　　ⁱ *Ministeris*　　^j *be weill*

Sunday at the burial of his brother and that the Presbytery refused as funeral
sermons were forbidden by Act of Assembly and warned Lord Seton not to hold
the burial on a Sunday. Nevertheless, a funeral oration was made by the schoolmaster to Seton's children. Subsequently he was called before the Presbytery and
'was admonished on his submission to guard against transgressing in future'. (Laing,
Knox's Works, 4.203; J. à Lasco, *Opera*, 2.273ff; Calderwood, *History*, 2.525f;
McMillan, *Worship*, 284f; Register House MS CH 2.185.1 *sub* 13 June, 3 July,
13 July, 1594; Seton, *History of the Family of Seton*, 1.213).

[77] Burials within church buildings continued to be made despite repeated Acts
of General Assemblies strongly forbidding them. In 1588 severe penalties were
attached to the breaking of the Acts and it was agreed that 'ane ordinance may
passe be his Hieness and Counsell discharging the said buriall within kirks and
sicklyke erecting of tombis'. A similar 'crave' was agreed to in 1597. The matter
was raised again in 1638 and in 1643 when the Assembly ratified and approved the
former Acts. The decision in the early years was obviously taken on sanitary
grounds; in 1563 the Assembly decreed that in rural areas the body be buried 'saxe
foote under the eird'. (*BUK*, 1.43, 280, 378, 388, 2.603, 733, 3.937; *StAKSR*,
1.452; Pitcairn, *Acts*, 26, 79; on post-Reformation burial and monuments within
churches see Hay, *Architecture of Scottish Post-Reformation Churches*, 20, 29ff, 61ff,
201ff.)

O

For Reparation of the Kirkes[78]

Least that the word of God and ministration of the Sacraments by unseemlinesse of the place come in contempt, of necessity it is that the Kirk and place[k] where the people ought publickly to convene be with expedition repaired with[l] dores, windowes, thack, and with such preparation[m] within as appertaineth as well to the Magestie of[n] God, as unto the ease and commodity of the people.[o] And because we know the slouthfulnesse of men in this behalfe and in all other, which may not redound to their private commoditie, strait charge and commandement must be given, that within ane certaine day the reparation[p] must be begun and within another day to be affixed by your Honours, that it[q] may be finished. Penalties and summs of mony must be injoyned, and without pardon taken from the contemners.[79]

---

[k] *Churches and Places*   [l] *in*   [m] *preparationis*   [n] *of the word of*
[o] Margin *Aggreit on*   [p] *reparationis*   [q] *thei be*

---

[78] The ruinous state of many churches prior to the Reformation is well attested. Hay writes that 'long before Protestant propaganda become a significant force . . . many noble ecclesiastical buildings deprived of the means for their maintenance, were tottering in ruin'. Attempts had been made by the Provincial Council in 1559 to make amends by ordaining rectors and parishioners to fulfil their legal obligations. (Patrick, *Statutes*, 168, cf. 57f. For a general discussion see further Hay, *Architecture of Scottish Post-Reformation Churches*, 9ff, 18; Donaldson, *Scottish Reformation*, 21ff, and Fleming, *Reformation in Scotland*, 327ff, 358ff; McRoberts, 'Material destruction caused by the Reformation', in *Essays on the Scottish Reformation*, 415-462.)

[79] Parliament by a statute of June 1563 empowered the Privy Council to enact regulations for the repair and maintenance of Churches. Accordingly in September of that year the Council ordained that ruinous churches be repaired and maintained 'upoun the expenssis of the parishinaris and Persone'; two parts of the cost were to be provided by the parishioners and the third by the benefice holder. Parishioners were ordered to appoint someone to apportion the amount to be raised among themselves within a specified time and to have the sum paid over to the deacons; parishioners were also empowered to withhold from the parson 'the frutis, teindis and proffittis . . . so far as may extend to the Personis part' until such time as the parson put his part in the hands of the deacons. This enactment closely followed pre-Reformation canon law and the canons of the Scottish Provincial Councils. As the decision of the Privy Council proved ineffective, another, enjoining the same procedure, was passed by Parliament in January 1572, which provided that in the absence of deacons, the archbishop, bishop, Superintendent or commissioner of the kirks should appoint men to set and receive the tax by the following June. In March 1575 the Superintendent of Angus and the Commissioner for Aberdeen assured the General Assembly that 'taskmasters' within every parish had been appointed for this purpose. But 'the whole business, with little or no help from the lairds or magistrates proceeded most tardily'. (*APS*, 1.247f, 3.76f; *RPC Scot.*, 1.247f, 608ff, 677; *BUK*, 1.17, 23, 34, 53, 59f, 148,

The reparation would be according to the ability[r] and number of Kirks.[r] Every Kirk must have dores, close windowes of glasse, thack[s] able to withhold raine, a bell to convocate the people together, a pulpet, a basen for baptizing[t] and tables for[u] ministration of the Lords Supper.[80] In greater Kirks and where the congregation is great in number, must reparation be made within the Kirk, for the quiet and commodious receiving of the people.[81] The expenses are[v] to be lifted partly of the people[82] and partly of the teinds,[83] at the consideration of the Ministry.[84]

[r-r] *possibilitie and nomber of the Churche*   [s] *thak or sclait*   [t] *baptisme*
[u] *for the*   [v] Not in Laing MS

314, 316; Patrick, *Statutes*, 57f, 168; Duncan, *Parochial Ecclesiastical Law*, 101ff; Hay, *The Architecture of Scottish Post-Reformation Churches*, 20ff; Fleming, *Reformation in Scotland*, 418f.)

[80] Detailed information on all these items of furniture and fittings is given in Hay, *The Architecture of Scottish Post-Reformation Churches*, 178ff.

[81] On 19th June 1560 Edinburgh Town Council ordered the Dean of Guild to make 'saittis, furmes and stullis . . . for the people to syt upoun the tyme of the sermoun and prayarris within the Kirk and all uther thingis till do as salbe thocht gude for decoring of the said Kirk'. This was not, however, accomplished until much later. Scottish churches generally remained devoid of seating for the public 'for some time after the Reformation'. (*Extracts from the Records of the Burgh of Edinburgh, 1557–1571*, 67; see further Hay, *The Architecture of Scottish Post-Reformation Churches*, 195f.)

[82] In the statutes referred to in note 79 *supra* and in the canons of the Provincial Council 'parishioners' takes the place of 'people' here. Duncan (*Parochial Ecclesiastical Law*, 105) noted with reference to the statutes that the term 'parochiners' had 'been interpreted to mean not the inhabitants generally, but such of them distinctively as possessed landed property therein situated i.e. the heritors'. This interpretation is supported by the record of the action taken by John Winram against the Parson of Balingry in the summer of 1561. Winram required that the church be repaired 'conform to the Act of his visitacion and Book of Reformacione i.e. the Book of Discipline vidz., partlie upon the expensis of the parrochyn and partlie upon the expensis of the tendis'. (*StAKSR*, 85ff.)

[83] *i.e.*, out of the traditional income of the benefice holder which the authors of the Book of Discipline sought to have made available to the Protestant ministers (see *supra*, pp. 156f). The parson or benefice holder's liability to contribute to the repair and maintenance of the fabric of the church contained in the Canons and Statutes (*supra*, note 79) continued to be recognised in Scotland until the late seventeenth century. (Duncan, *Parochial Ecclesiastical Law*, 106; see also *supra*, note 82.)

[84] The Act of Privy Council of 1563 (see *supra*, note 79) ordained that parishioners were to elect 'certane of the maist honest qualifiit men within thair parochinnis to taxt every ane of thame efferand to thair substance, for furnessing of the tua part of the expenssis' and does not mention in this matter the 'ministry', *i.e.* the kirk session, but only the kirk maisters or deacons who were to collect the sums appointed. (*RPC Scot.*, 1.248.)

For the punishment of those that Profane the Sacraments and[w]
contemne the Word of God and dare to presume to minister
them not being thereto lawfully called[85]

As Satan hath never ceased from the beginning to draw mankind
in one of two extremities, to wit, that men should either be so
ravished with gazing upon the visible creatures, that forgetting
the cause wherefore[x] they are[x] ordained, they attributed unto
them a vertue and power, which God hath not granted unto them,
or else that men should so contemne and despise Gods blessed
Ordinance and holy Institutions, as if[y] that neither in the right
use of them there were any profite, neither yet in their pro-
phanations[z] there were any danger. As this way, we say Satan
hath blinded the most part of mankinde from the beginning, so
doubt we not, but that he will strive to continue in his malice
even to the end. Our eyes have seene and presently doe see the
experience of the one and of the other. What was the opinion of
the[a] most part of men of the Sacrament of Christs bodie and
bloud during the darknesse of superstition, is not unknowne?
How it was gazed upon, kneeled unto, borne in procession and
finally worshipped and honoured as Christ Jesus himselfe.[86] And
so long as Satan might then retaine men[b] in that damnable idolatrie, he was quiet, as one that possessed his Kingdome of darknes
peaceably. But since that it hath pleased the mercies of God to
reveale unto the unthankfull world the light of his Word, the
right use and administration of his Sacraments, he assayes man
upon the contrary part. For where not long agoe men stood in
such admiration of that idol the Masse,[87] that none durst have
presumed[c] to have said the Masse but the shaven sort,[d] [88] the
beasts marked men,[89] some dare now be so bold as, without all

[w] and do [x–x] why thai war [y] Not in Laing MS [z] prophanatioun
[a] Not in Laing MS [b] man [c] durst presume
[d] the foirsworne schavin sorte

[85] For the reformers' definition of a lawfully called minister see *supra*, p. 90
and n.3.

[86] A reference to the veneration of the Host on the altar at the Mass, or when
reserved in a sacrament house, or carried in a monstrance in processions both
inside and outside church buildings. (Cf. *Confession of Faith*, cap. XXII; Laing,
Knox's Works, 3.67; Calvin, *Institutes*, 4.17.37.)

[87] See *supra*, p. 94.   [88] The tonsured priests.

[89] In sixteenth-century Protestant polemical writings the Pope was frequently
identified with the beast of the Revelation of St John 13.4, 18, or the Antichrist.

vocation,ᵉ to minister, as they suppose, the true Sacraments in
open Assemblies;⁹⁰ and some idiots⁹¹ (yet more wickedly and
impudentlyᶠ) dare counterfeit in their house,ᵍ that which the true
Ministers doe in open Congregations.ʰ They presume, we say, to
doe it in houses without reverence, without word preached, and
without minister.ⁱ ⁹² This contempt proceeds, no doubt, from
the malice and craft of that Serpent, who first deceived man of
purpose to deface the glorie of Christ's Evangell,ʲ and to bring
his blessed Sacraments in a perpetuall contempt. And further,
your Honors may clearly see how stubbornly and proudly the
most part despisesᵏ the Evangellʲ of Christ Jesus offered unto you,
whom unles that sharply and stoutly ye resist, we mean as wel the
manifest despiser as the prophaner of the Sacraments, ye shal find
them pernicious enemies ereˡ it be long. And therefore in the
name of the eternall God and of his Son Christ Jesus, we require
of your Honours that without delay strait Lawes be made against
the one and the other.⁹³

ᵉ convocatioun   ᶠ more imprudentlie   ᵍ houses   ʰ congregatioun
ⁱ Minister, other then of companioun to companioun   ʲ See p. 87 n.b.
ᵏ despyse   ˡ or

⁹⁰ i.e., meetings of individuals to form congregations for worship.

⁹¹ Dickinson considered that this word was used here in the sense of private
persons or laymen, and not in the sense of uneducated individuals. (Knox's History,
2.321.)

⁹² The administration of the Sacraments by Protestants who were not lawfully
admitted to the ministry would appear to have been a matter of considerable
concern for the reformers at this time. Winzet upbraided them for contending
'tooth and nail' with 'sum Lordis and gentlemen' who had greatly failed the cause
by ministering 'your' communion in times past to their own household servants
and tenants, even although they had been permitted to do so by these servants
and tenants who claimed to be 'a Kirk of God'. See also the Mandate to John
Spottiswoode as Superintendent of Lothian in which he is charged 'to take
inquisitioun quhat persones sen the last parliament aganis the tenour of the actis
and statutis maid thairin hes said mess or hard mess or that ministrate the sacramentis nocht being admittit thairto and report the samin to the saidis lordis'. In
May 1561 the General Assembly petitioned the Privy Council that 'punischment
be appoynted for the abusairs of the sacramentis and for the contempnaris of the
same'. Winram was particularly active in his diocese in suppressing the unauthor-
ised administration of the Sacraments and as late as 1586 we find a layman being
heavily fined in the Kirk Session of St Andrews for usurping the office of a minister
by administering the Sacrament of baptism. (Winzet, Works, 1.16.100; Donaldson,
Scottish Reformation, 226f; BUK, 1.8, 276; Laing, Knox's Works, 2.161; Dickinson,
Knox's History, 1.360; StAKSR, xiv, 84, 176ff, 226f, 277, 282, 2.563, 567, 572;
Calderwood, History, 2.422, 3.293.)

⁹³ In the Act of the Parliament of August 1560 abolishing the Mass much of the
foregoing paragraph is reflected. The Act ordained that 'no maner of persone or
personis in ony tume cuming administrat ony of the sacramentis foirsaidis secreitlie,

We dare not prescribe unto you what penalties shall be required of such. But this we feare not to affirme, that the one and the other deserve death.[94] For if he who doth falsifie the seale, subscription or coine of a King is judged worthy of death,[95] what shall we think of him who plainly doth falsifie the Seales of Christ Jesus, Prince of the Kings of the earth?[96] If Darius pronounced that a balk [m] should be taken from the house of that man, and he him-selfe hanged upon it, that durst attempt to hinder the re-edifying[n] of the materiall Temple,[97] what shall we say of those that con-temptuously blaspheme God, and manifestly hinder the Temple of God, which is the soules and bodies of the elect[98] to be purged by the true preaching of Christ Jesus from the superstition and damnable idolatry in which they have bene long[o] plunged and holden captive? If ye, as God forbid, declare yourselves carelesse over the true Religion, God will not suffer your negligence unpunished. And therefore more earnestly we require that strait lawes may be made against the stuborne contemners of Christ Jesus, and against such as dare presume to minister his Sacraments, not orderly called to that office, least while that there be none found to gainstand impiety, the wrath of God be kindled against the whole.[99]

The Papisticall Priests have neither power nor authority to minister the sacraments of Christ Jesus, because that in their mouth is not the Sermon of exhortation; and therefore to them

[m] bauk   [n] re-edificatioun   [o] of long

---

or ony other maner of way but thai that ar admitted and havand power to that effect, and that na maner of person nor personis say messe, nor yet heir messe' under pain of confiscation of goods, punishment of their bodies, banishment and, for the third offence, death. (*APS*, 2.535; Laing, *Knox's Works*, 2.123f; Dickinson, *Knox's History*, 1.340; see also *supra*, p. 95.)

[94] See previous note. No separate statute was passed by Parliament against those Protestants who unlawfully attempted to exercise the ministerial sacramental functions, but if the St Andrews Kirk Session Register be typical of what happened we may conclude that severe penalties were imposed upon them as well as upon former priests who had conformed but had not been admitted as ministers and who yet were accused of administering baptism.

[95] Forgery was a capital offence at common law until the nineteenth century. (*Green's Encyclopaedia of Scots Law*, 6.41.)

[96] In Calvinist theology the Sacraments were commonly spoken of as 'seals' of the Christian faith. (cf. *Confession of Faith*, cap. XXI; Calvin, *Institutes*, 4.14.5; and *supra*, p. 90.)

[97] Ezra 6.11, 12.   [98] 1 Corinthians 3.16, 17, 6.19.

[99] See *supra*, notes 93 and 94.

must strait inhibition be made notwithstanding any usurpation they have had[p] in the time of blindnesse.[100] It is neither the clipping of their crownes, the greasing[q] of their fingers, nor the blowing of the dumb dogges[101] called the Bishops, neither the laying on of their hands that maketh Ministers[r] of Christ Jesus.[102] But the Spirit of God inwardly first moving the hearts to seeke Christs glorie, and the profite of his Kirk, and thereafter the nomination of the people, the examination of the learned, and publick admission (as before is said) make men lawfull ministers of the Word and Sacraments.[103] We speak of an ordinarie vocation;[s] and not of that which is extraordinary, when God by himselfe, and by his onely power, raiseth up to the Ministerie such as best pleaseth his wisdome.[104]

[p] *which they have had in that behalf*   [q] *crossing*   [r] *thame true ministers*
[s] *vocatioun, whare churches ar reformed or at least tend to reformatioun*

[100] According to Protestant theology the preaching of the Word was inseparably connected with the administration of the Sacraments and therefore the ability to preach was regarded as essential for admission to the ministry. (Calvin, *Institutes*, 4.17.39; *Confession of Faith*, cap. XXII; and *supra*, pp. 90ff, 96f, and p. 205 n.93.)

[101] See *supra*, p. 160 n.22.

[102] The ceremonies used in the ordination of priests – the tonsure, the anointing of the hands and the insufflation – were discussed and condemned by Calvin in *Institutes*, 4.19.25–29. On the imposition of hands see *supra*, p. 102 and n.25; also *Cath. Ency.*, 11.282ff, Law, *Catechism of John Hamilton*, 230ff.

[103] See *supra*, pp. 96ff. The inner call of the Spirit has not hitherto been mentioned in those sections which concern admission to the ministry. It nevertheless was reckoned an important element in Protestant thinking on the ministry. (Calvin, *Institutes*, 4.3.10, 11.)

[104] Extra-ordinary vocation, although recognised by the reformers, was not given an important place in their understanding of the ministry. Calvin, for example, considered that the Apostles had been extra-ordinarily called. In reply to a question about his own ordination from Ninian Winzet, Knox is reported to have claimed that 'he was extraordinarlie callit, euin as S. Johne the Baptist'. See also 'Ane letter written to the Quein's Grace and Regent be the Professouris of Christis ewangell in the Realme of Scotland – 6th May 1559', where we read 'gif it be Godis word that is spokin, we aucht to heir and resawe it, howbeit that the person that speiks hef na ordinarie wocatioun, forr howbeit God hes apointit in the Kirk ordinarie wocatioun to continew, yit is he nocht himself sa astrikit thairunto bot he may and dois send oft tymes personis callit be hymself extraordinarlie and that hapins mast commonlie quhen the ordinarie ministeris ar corrupt'. (*Institutes*, 4.3.13; Winzet, *Works*, 2.108f; *Misc. of the Spalding Club*, 4.90.)

The Conclusion

Thus have we in these few heads offered unto your Honours our judgements, according as we were commanded,[1] touching the reformation of things, which heretofore have altogether bene abused in this cursed Papistrie. We doubt not but some of our petitions shall appeare strange unto you at the first sight. But if your wisedomes deeply consider, that we must answer not onely unto man, but also before the throne of the eternall God, and of his Son Christ Jesus, for the counsell which we give in this so grave a matter, your Honours shall easily consider, that more assured it is to us to fall in the displeasure of all men in the*a* earth, then to offend the majestie of God, whose justice cannot suffer flatterers and deceitfull counsellers unpunished.

That we require the Kirk to be set at such liberty, that she neither be compelled to feed idle bellies,[2] neither yet to sustaine the tyrannie which heretofore hath been by violence maintained,[3] wee know we shall offend many, but if we should keep silence hereof, we are most assured to offend the just and righteous God, who by the mouth of his Apostle hath pronounced this sentence: 'He that laboureth not, let him not eate.'[4] If we in this behalfe or in any other require or aske any other*b* thing then by Gods expresse commandement, by equity and good conscience ye are bound to grant, let it be noted and after repudiate.[5] But if wee require nothing which God requireth not also, let your Honours take

a Not in Laing MS   *b* Not in Laing MS

[1] See *supra*, p. 85, and Introduction, pp. 3ff.

[2] *i.e.*, those who were drawing an income for their support from ecclesiastical revenue and who did nothing for it in return. Cf. p. 122.

[3] Probably a reference to the prominent place occupied in the government by leading churchmen such as Cardinal David Beaton and his successor Archbishop John Hamilton. Cf. p. 157.

[4] 2 Thessalonians 3.10; cf. Lindsay, *Works*, 2.91, who also quoted this verse in Latin in a similar context. See further, Donaldson, *Scottish Reformation*, 48f.

[5] See *supra*, p. 86, where a similar statement is made. In the Conclusion to the *De Regno Christi* Bucer had made the same point. (*Opera Latina*, 15.304.) Cf. *First Confession of Basel*, 1534, article XII. (Cochrane, *Reformed Confessions of the 16th Century*, 96.)

heed, how ye gainstand the charge of him whose hand and punishment yee cannot escape.

If blind affection rather lead you to have respect to the sustentation of these your carnall friends, who tyrannously have impyred above the*c* flock of Christ Jesus, then that the zeale of Christ*d* Jesus his glory*d* provoke and move you to set his oppressed Kirk at freedome and liberty, we feare your sharpe and suddaine punishments, and that the glory and honour of this enterprise be reserved unto others. And yet shall this our judgement abide to the generations following for a monument and witnesse how lovingly God called you and this nation*e* to repentance; what counsellours God sent unto you, and how ye have*f* used the same. If obediently ye heare God now calling, we doubt not but he shall heare you in your greatest necessitie. But if, following your own corrupt judgements, ye contemne his voyce and vocation, we are assured that your former iniquitie, and present ingratitude shall together crave great*g* punishment from God, who cannot long delay to execute his most just judgements, when after many offences and long blindnesse grace and mercy offered is contemptuously refused.[6]

God the Father of our Lord Jesus Christ, by the power of his holy Spirit so illuminate your hearts, that ye may clearly see what is pleasing and acceptable in his presence and*h* so bow the same to his obedience, that ye may preferre his reveiled will to your owne affections. And so strengthen you by the spirit of fortitude, that boldly ye may punish vice and maintaine vertue within this Realme, to the praise and glory of his holy name, to the comfort and assurance of your own consciences and to the consolation and the good example of the posterity*i* following. Amen.*j*

From Edinburg the 20   By your Honours
   of Maii 1560   most humble servitours.*k*

c the poor flock   *d–d* Goddis glorie   *e* Realme   *f* Not in Laing MS
g just   *h* Not in Laing MS   *i* posteriteis   *j* Amen. So be it   *k* etc.

[6] On the dating and historical background of this section see Introduction, pp. 3ff., 49.

P

Act of Secret Counsell

17ᵃ Januarii anno^b 1560¹

Wee which have subscribed thir presents, having advised with the Articles herein specified, as is above mentioned from the beginning of this book, thinkes the same good and conforme to Gods Word in all points, conforme to the notes and additions hereto eiked² : and promises to set the same forward to^c the uttermost of our powers. Providing that the Bishops, Abbots, Priors and other^d Prelates³ and benificed men which els have adjoyned them to us, bruik the revenues of their benefices during their liftimes,⁴ they sustaining and upholding the Ministry and Ministers, as herein is specified, for the^e preaching of the word and ministring of the sacraments.^f

sic subscribitur,

James^g Hamiltoun,⁵   Archbald, Argyle,⁶

^a xxvii   ^b anno etc.   ^c at   ^d otheris   ^e Not in Laing MS
^f Sacramentis of God
^g In Laing MS the list of subscriptions is headed James, and then James Hammyltoun, see note 5 infra.

¹ i.e., 1561; the new year was dated from 25th March. There is a gap in the Register of the Privy Council from 22nd January 1554 to 4th September 1561. On this 'Act' see Introduction, pp. 10ff; Laing, Knox's Works, 2.129ff; Dickinson, Knox's History, 1.344ff.

² See Introduction, pp. 11ff.

³ Apart from those mentioned the word 'prelate' was often used with a wider connotation and included various church dignitaries of high rank. (Cath. Ency., 12.386.)

⁴ For a discussion of this considerable limitation upon the financial proposals of the Book of Discipline see further Introduction, pp. 12ff, 74ff. Bucer, it may be noted, had made a similar recommendation for England in De Regno Christi, 2.13, Opera Latina, 15.136.

⁵ According to both accounts in Knox's History the first person to sign was James, Duke of Châtelherault (†1575), who had joined the Lords of Congregation at the end of June 1559 and was accepted as their titular head. He was never a staunch supporter of the cause, and later opposed the Regent Moray, and was regarded as chief of the Marian party. The disappearance of his name from the list of signatures in the 1621 edition was probably due to an error in the transmission of the manuscript. The second person to sign was his son and heir, James, third Earl of Arran (c. 1537–1609), who had become a Protestant in France and on his return to Scotland joined the Congregation. (Laing, Knox's Works, 2.129, 258; Dickinson, Knox's History, 1.344f, 2.324; DNB, 24.167ff, 173ff; Scots Peerage, 4.366ff, 4.368.)

⁶ Archibald, fifth Earl of Argyll (c. 1538–1573), had been active in the Protestant

James Stewart[7]
Rothes[8]
Boid[9]
William Lord Hay[10]
Alexander Cambell[h] [11]
M. Alexander Gordoun[12]

Glencarne[13]
Uchiltrie[14]
Sanquhare[15]
S. Jhones[16]
William of Culrosse[17]
Drumlangrig[18]

[h] Adds *Dene of Murray* which the editor of the 1621 edition places at the end of the list as if it were a separate signature. See note 11 *infra*.

---

cause since 1557 and was one of the leaders from the end of May 1559; from 1561 he supported Queen Mary until her flight to England; in 1571 he submitted to King James VI's party. (*DNB*, 8.314ff; *Scots Peerage*, 1.340ff.)

[7] Lord James Stewart, half brother of the Queen and subsequently Earl of Moray, joined the Lords of the Congregation at the end of May 1559 and was from that day a prominent leader of the Protestant movement. (Lee, *James Stewart, Earl of Moray*.)

[8] Andrew, fifth Earl of Rothes (†1611), joined the Lords of the Congregation in June 1559 but supported the Queen from 1566. (*DNB*, 33.76ff; *Scots Peerage*, 7.292ff.)

[9] Robert, fifth Lord Boyd (*c.* 1517–90), joined the Lords of the Congregation at the end of May 1559 and became an active supporter of the reformers, but subsequently entered the service of the Queen, to whom he remained loyal until 1571. (*DNB*, 6.96ff; *Scots Peerage*, 5.152ff; Burton and Haig, *Senators of the College of Justice*, 155.)

[10] William, fifth Lord Hay of Yester (*c.* 1537–86), joined the Lords of the Congregation in May 1560, but supported the Queen after her marriage to Darnley and until 1571. (*DNB*, 25.276ff; *Scots Peerage*, 8.438ff.)

[11] Alexander Campbell, Dean of Moray from 1557 until his resignation in 1563. He was a brother of the fourth Earl of Argyll. (Watt, *Fasti Eccl. Scot.*, 221; Laing, *Knox's Works*, 2.259; *Scots Peerage*, 1.338.)

[12] Alexander Gordon, Bishop of Galloway, see *supra*, p. 121 note 17.

[13] Alexander, fourth Earl of Glencairn (†1574), one of the earliest and foremost supporters of the Protestant cause. (*DNB*, 13.303ff; *Scots Peerage*. 4.239ff.)

[14] Andrew Stewart, second Lord Ochiltree (†*c.* 1592), an early and consistent supporter of the Protestant movement (*DNB*, 54.271ff; *Scots Peerage*, 6.512f.)

[15] Robert, sixth Lord Crichton of Sanquhar (†1561), is not recorded as having played a significant part in the Protestant movement. His name occurs in a list of the lords and nobles dated 1560, whose position was 'dowptfull'. (*Scots Peerage*, 3.229; Hamilton *Papers*, 2.748.)

[16] James Sandilands, second son of Sir James Sandilands of Calder (†1579), Preceptor of Torphichen and head of the Order of St John of Jerusalem in Scotland, was made Lord Torphichen in 1564; had joined the Lords of the Congregation in 1559; he is not recorded as having played a significant part in the Protestant movement. (*DNB*, 50.278ff; *Scots Peerage*, 8.386f.)

[17] William Colville (†1567), Abbot *in commendam* of Culross, joined the Protestant movement but retained his commendatorship until his death. (*Scots Peerage*, 2.545f.)

[18] Sir James Douglas of Drumlanrig (1498–1578) joined the Protestant movement in March 1560, and opposed the Queen after the murder of Darnley. (*Scots Peerage*, 7.119–125.)

Bargannie yonger[19]	Scot of Haning[25]
Lochinvar[20]	James[j] Maxwell[26]
Cunninghamhead[21]	George Fentoun[k] of that ilk[27]
James Haliburtoun[i] [22]	Andro Ker of Fadounside[28]
Jhone Lochart of Bar[23]	Andro Hamiltoun of Lethane[29]
Johne Schaw of Halie[24]	Deane of Murray[l] [30]

[i] Not in Laing MS   [j] John   [k] *George Setoun of that Ilk* See note 27 *infra*.
[l] This list has some of the names in a slightly different order from that of the MS; it also omits that of George Corrie of Kelwood. (See further Laing, *Knox's Works*, 2.258ff, and Dickinson, *Knox's History*, 2.325f.)

[19] Thomas Kennedy of Bargany (†1564). (Laing, *Knox's Works*, 2.259.)

[20] Sir John Gordon of Lochinvar (†1604) does not appear to have strongly supported the reformers; he sided with the Queen. (*Scots Peerage*, 5.110f.)

[21] William Cunningham of Cunninghamhead (†1576), a loyal and active supporter of the Protestant movement. (Laing, *Knox's Works*, 2.260.)

[22] James Haliburton (†1588), Tutor of Pitcur, and Provost of Dundee for thirty-three years and a prominent supporter of Protestantism. (Laing, *Knox's Works*, 5.678f; Maxwell, *Old Dundee*, 196ff.)

[23] John Lockhart of Bar (†c. 1575) a supporter of the Protestant movement from the time of George Wishart. (Laing, *Knox's Works*, 2.259.)

[24] John Shaw of Haily.

[25] Thomas Scott of Haining (†c. 1576). (Laing, *Knox's Works*, 2.259.)

[26] Sir John Maxwell of Terregles, fourth Lord Herries (c. 1512–1583) supported the Lords of the Congregation from 1559 but became a devoted partisan of the Queen and his subsequent attitude to the Reformation was uncertain. (*DNB*, 37.121ff; *Scots Peerage*, 4.410ff.)

[27] The text presents a difficulty here; Laing pointed out that there was no Seton of that Ilk; and George Fenton of the Ilk is the most likely alternative rendering. (Laing, *Knox's Works*, 2.260; Dickinson, *Knox's History*, 2.324 n.31.)

[28] Andrew Ker of Fawdonside (†1598), a supporter of the Protestant movement and opponent of the Queen. He took a leading part in the murder of Riccio. Subsequently he married the widow of John Knox. (Ridley, *John Knox*, 521; Laing, *Knox's Works*, 2.259.)

[29] Andrew Hamilton of Lethan (†c. 1585). (Laing, *Knox's Works*, 2.260.)

[30] See *supra* p. 211 nn. *h* and 11.

BIBLIOGRAPHY AND REFERENCES

Anderson, *Early Records*: ANDERSON, J. M., ed., *Early Records of the University of St Andrews: the graduation roll 1413–1579 and the matriculation roll 1473–1579*, Scottish History Society, 3rd series, vol. 8, Edinburgh, 1926.

ANDERSON, J. M., 'The Beginnings of St Andrews University', *Scottish Historical Review*, vol. 8, pp. 333–360, 1910–11.

APS: *The Acts of the Parliament of Scotland (1127–1707)*, 12 vols., 1844.

Bannatyne, *Memorials*: BANNATYNE, R., *Memorials of transactions in Scotland, A.D. MDLXIX–MDLXXIII*, Bannatyne Club, Edinburgh, 1836.

Bergier, *Registres*: BERGIER, J.-F. and R.-M. KINGDOM, eds., *Registres de la Compagnie des Pasteurs de Genève au temps de Calvin*, vol. 1, 1546–1553, vol. 2, 1553–1564, Travaux d'humanisme et renaissance, vol. 55, Geneva, 1964, 1962.

BORGEAUD, C., *L'Académie de Calvin 1559–1798*, Geneva, 1900.

BOURCHENIN, P.-D., *Etude sur les Académies Protestantes en France au XVIᵉ et au XVIIᵉ siècle*, Paris, 1882.

BOYD, W., *Education in Ayrshire Through Seven Centuries*, London, 1961.

BROWN, P. H., *John Knox*, London, 1895, 2 vols.

BRUCE, F. F., *The English Bible: A History of Translations*, London, 1961.

BRUNTON, G. and D. HAIG, *An Historical Account of the Senators of the College of Justice*, London, 1832.

BUCER, M., *Martini Buceri Opera Latina*, vol. 15, *De Regno Christi*, edited by F. Wendel, Gütersloh, 1955.

BUIST, R. C., 'Medicine' in *Votiva Tabella; A Memorial Volume of St Andrews University*, 197ff, St Andrews, 1911.

BUK: *The Booke of the Universall Kirk, Acts and Proceedings of the General Assemblies of the Kirk of Scotland, 1560–1618*, Bannatyne and Maitland Clubs, 3 vols., and Appendix vol., Edinburgh, 1839.

Calderwood, *Kirk of the Canagait*: CALDERWOOD, A. B., ed., *The Buik of the Kirk of the Canagait 1564–1567*, Scottish Record Society, Edinburgh, 1961.

Calderwood, *History*: THOMSON, T., ed. *The History of the Kirk of Scotland, by Mr David Calderwood*, The Wodrow Society, 7 vols., Edinburgh, 1842.

CALVIN, JOHN, *Commentary upon the Acts of the Apostles*, vol. 2, Calvin Translation Society, Edinburgh, 1844.

CALVIN, JOHN, *Commentary on the Epistles of Paul the Apostle to the Corinthians*, Calvin Translation Society, vol. 1, Edinburgh, 1848.

CALVIN, JOHN, *Commentaries on the Four Last Books of Moses*, vol. 3, Calvin Translation Society, Edinburgh, 1854.

CALVIN, JOHN, 'Psychopannychia', in *Tracts*, vol. 3, Calvin Translation Society, Edinburgh, 1851.

Calvin, *Institutes*: BENOIT, J.-D., ed., *Institution de la Religion Chrestienne*, 5 vols., Paris, 1957–63.

Calvin, *Institutes*: McNEILL, J. T. and F. L. BATTLES, eds., *Calvin: Institutes of the Christian Religion* (The Library of Christian Classics, vols. 20 and 21), London, 1961.

CANT, R. G., *The College of St Salvator*, St Andrews University Publications, No. 47, Edinburgh, 1950.

CANT, R. G., *The University of St Andrews: a short history*, Edinburgh, 1946.

Cath. Ency.: *The Catholic Encyclopedia*, 15 vols., London, 1907.

COCHRANE, A. C., *Reformed Confessions of the 16th Century*, London, 1966.

CONNELL, J., *A Treatise on the Law of Scotland Respecting Tithes*, 2 vols., 2nd edn., Edinburgh, 1830.

Corpus Iuris Canonici, ed. A. L. Friedberg, 2 vols., Leipzig, 1881.

COURVOISIER, J., *La Notion d'Eglise chez Bucer dans son développement historique*, Paris, 1933.

COUTTS, J., *A History of the University of Glasgow*, Glasgow, 1909.

COWAN, I. B., 'The Five Articles of Perth' in D. Shaw, ed., *Reformation and Revolution*, Edinburgh, 1967.

CR: Corpus Reformatorum, Ioannis Calvini Opera . . . omnia, eds. G. Baum, E. Cunitz, and E. Reuss, vol. 10, Brunswick, 1871–72.

CSP Foreign 1560–1561: Calendar of State Papers, Foreign Series, of the Reign of Elizabeth, 1560–1561, ed. J. Stevenson, London, 1865.

CSP Scot: Calendar of the State Papers relating to Scotland and Mary, Queen of Scots 1547–1603, ed. Joseph Bain, vol. 1 (1547–1563) and vol. 2 (1563–69), Edinburgh, 1891, 1898.

DALY, L. J., *The Medieval University 1200–1400*, New York, 1961.

DARLOW, T. H. and H. F. MOULE, eds., *Historical Catalogue of the Printed Editions of Holy Scripture*, London, 1903.

Dickinson, *Knox's History*: DICKINSON, W. C., ed., *John Knox's History of the Reformation in Scotland*, Edinburgh, 1949.

Dictionnaire de Droit Canonique, ed. R. Naz, 7 vols., Paris, 1935–1965.

La Discipline ecclésiastique: in W. Niessel, *Bekenntnisschriften und Kirchenordnungen der nach Gottes Wort reformierten Kirche*, 2nd edn., 75ff, Zurich, [1938].

Diurnal: A Diurnal of Remarkable Occurrents that have passed within the Country of Scotland since the death of King James the Fourth till the year M.D. LXXV, Bannatyne Club, Edinburgh, 1833.

DNB: Dictionary of National Biography, ed. L. Stephen, London, 1885–1912.

DONALDSON, G., 'Alexander Gordon, Bishop of Galloway (1559–1575) and his work in the Reformed Church', *Transactions of the Dumfriesshire and Galloway Natural History and Antiquarian Society*, 3rd series, vol. 24, pp. 111–128, 1945–46.

DONALDSON, G., 'Bishop Adam Bothwell and the Reformation in Orkney', *Scottish Church History Society Records*, vol. 13, pp. 85–100, 1959.

DONALDSON, G., 'The Church Courts' in *An Introduction to Scottish Legal History*, The Stair Society, vol. 20, pp. 363–373, Edinburgh, 1958.

DONALDSON, G., ' "The Example of Denmark" in the Scottish Reformation', *Scottish Historical Review*, vol. 27, pp. 57–64, 1948.

DONALDSON, G., *James V to James VII*, The Edinburgh History of Scotland, vol. 3, Edinburgh, 1965.

DONALDSON, G., *The Making of the Scottish Prayer Book of 1637*, Edinburgh, 1954.

DONALDSON, G., 'The Polity of the Scottish Church 1560–1600' in *Scottish Church History Society Records*, vol. 11, pp. 212–226, Glasgow, 1955.

DONALDSON, G., *The Scottish Reformation*, Cambridge, 1960.

Donaldson, 'Scottish Episcopate', *EHR*: DONALDSON, G., 'The Scottish Episcopate at the Reformation', *English Historical Review*, vol. 60, pp. 349–364, 1945.

Donaldson, *Thirds*: DONALDSON, G., *Accounts of the Collectors of Thirds of Benefices 1561–1572*, Scottish History Society, Edinburgh, 1949.

Doumergue, *Calvin*: DOUMERGUE, E., *Jean Calvin. Les Hommes et les choses de son temps*, 7 vols., Lausanne, 1899–1928.

DUNCAN, J. M., *The Parochial Ecclesiastical Law of Scotland*, revised ed. C. N. Johnston, Edinburgh, 1903.

DUNKLEY, E. H., *The Reformation in Denmark*, London, 1948.

DUNLOP, A. I., ed., *Acta Facultatis Artium Universitatis Sanctiandree 1413–1588*, St Andrews University Publications, No. 56, Edinburgh, 1964.

DUNLOP, A. I., *The Life and Times of James Kennedy*, St Andrews University Publication, No. 46, Edinburgh, 1950.

DURKAN, J., 'Care of the Poor: Pre-Reformation Hospitals' in D. McRoberts, ed., *Essays on the Scottish Reformation, 1513–1625*, pp. 116–128, Glasgow, 1962.

DURKAN, J., 'Education in the century of the Reformation' in D. McRoberts, ed., *Essays on the Scottish Reformation*, pp. 145–168, Glasgow, 1962.

EASSON, D. E., *Medieval Religious Houses, Scotland*, London, 1957.

EDGAR, J., *History of Early Scottish Education*, Edinburgh, 1893.

Edinburgh Burgh Records: Extracts from the Records of the Burgh of Edinburgh, A.D. 1557–1571, The Scottish Burgh Records Society, Edinburgh, 1875.

ESMEIN, A., *Le mariage en droit canonique*, 2nd ed., edited by R. Génestal and J. Dauvillier, 2 vols., Paris, 1929, 1935.

Evidence: Evidence, Oral and Documentary, taken and received by the Commissioners appointed for visiting the Universities of Scotland, vol. 3, *University of St Andrews*, London, 1837.

'Extracts from the Kirk Session Register of Perth', *The Spottiswoode Miscellany*, vol. 2, pp. 225–311, Edinburgh, 1845.

Fasti Aberdonenses, Selections from the Records of the University and King's College of Aberdeen 1494–1854, The Spalding Club, Aberdeen, 1854.

FLEMING, D. H., *The Reformation in Scotland*, London, 1910.

FRASER, P., *Treatise on Husband and Wife according to the Law of Scotland*, 2 vols., Edinburgh, 1876, 1878.

GAUFRÈS, M.-J., *Claude Baduel et la réforme des études au XVIe siècle*, Paris, 1880; Slatkine Reprints, Geneva, 1969.

GAULLIEUR, E., *Histoire de Collége de Guyenne*, Paris, 1874.

GEE, H., and W. J. HARDY, *Documents illustrative of English Church History*, London, 1896.

Grant, *Burgh Schools*: GRANT, J., *History of the Burgh Schools of Scotland*, London and Glasgow, 1876.

Green's Encyclopaedia of the Law of Scotland, ed. J. Chisholm, 14 vols., Edinburgh, 1896–1904.

GREENSLADE, S. L., ed., *The Cambridge History of the Bible*, [vol. 3], The West from the Reformation to the Present Day, Cambridge, 1963.

Hamilton Papers, ed. J. Bain, vol. 2, 1543–1590, Edinburgh, 1892.

HANNAY, R. K., 'Early University Institutions at St Andrews and Glasgow: A Comparative Study', *Scottish Historical Review*, vol. 11, pp. 266–283, 1913–1914.

Hannay, *Statutes*: HANNAY, R. K., ed., *The Statutes of the Faculty of Arts and the Faculty of Theology at the Period of the Reformation*, St Andrews University Publications, No. 7, St Andrews, 1910.

HAY, G., *The Architecture of Scottish Post-Reformation Churches, 1560–1843*, Oxford, 1957.

HENDERSON, G. D., 'The Exercise' in *The Burning Bush*, Edinburgh, 1957.

HENDERSON, G. D., *The Founding of Marischal College Aberdeen*, Aberdeen University Studies No. 123, Aberdeen, 1947.

HENDERSON, G. D., *The Scottish Ruling Elder*, London, 1935.

HENDERSON, J. M., *Scottish Reckonings of Time, Money, Weights and Measures* (Historical Association of Scotland Pamphlets N.S. No. 4), Edinburgh, 1926.

HERKLESS, John and R. K. HANNAY, *The Archbishops of St Andrews*, vol. 5, Edinburgh, 1915.

HERKLESS, J. and R. K. HANNAY, *The College of St Leonard*, Edinburgh and London, 1905.

HERMINJARD, A. L., *Correspondance des Réformateurs dans les Pays de la langue française*, vol. 4, Geneva and Paris, 1872.

HEYER, H., *L'Eglise de Genève: Esquisse historique de son organisation*, Geneva, 1909.

HOLL, K., *The Cultural Significance of the Reformation*, New York, 1959.

HORN, D. B., *A Short History of the University of Edinburgh 1556–1889*, Edinburgh, 1967.

HUME, D., *Commentaries on the Law of Scotland, respecting Trial for Crimes*, 2 vols., Edinburgh, 1800.

IRELAND, R. D., 'Divorce, Nullity of Marriage and Separation' in *An Introduction to Scottish Legal History*, The Stair Society, vol. 20, pp. 90–98, Edinburgh, 1958.

IRELAND, R. D., 'Post-Reformation Canon Law of Marriage of the Commissaries' Courts' in *An Introduction to Scottish Legal History*, The Stair Society, vol. 20, pp. 82–89, Edinburgh, 1958.

JUNOD, L. and H. MEYLAN, *L'Académie de Lausanne au XVIe siècle* (*Leges Scholae Lausannensis 1547, Lettres et documents inédits*), Lausanne, 1947.

Keith, *History*: KEITH, R., *History of the Affaires of Church and State in Scotland from the beginning of the Reformation to the year 1568*, The Spottiswoode Society, 3 vols., Edinburgh, 1844–1850.

KERR, J., *Scottish Education, School and University, from early times to 1908*, Cambridge, 1910.

KIBRE, P., *The Nations in the Mediaeval Universities*, Mediaeval Academy of America Publications, No. 49, Cambridge, Mass., 1948.

KIBRE, P., *Scholarly Privileges in the Middle Ages*, Mediaeval Academy of America Publications, No. 72, London, 1961.

KRAMM, H. H. W., *The Theology of Martin Luther*, London, 1947.

Laing, *Knox's Works*: LAING, D., ed., *The Works of John Knox*, 6 vols., Edinburgh, 1846.

LASCO, Joannes A., *Opera*, ed. A. Kuyper, 2 vols., Amsterdam, 1866.

LAW, T. G., ed., *The Catechism of John Hamilton . . . 1552*, Oxford, 1884.

LCC: *The Library of Christian Classics*.

LE COULTRE, Jules, *Maturin Cordier et les origines de la pédagogie protestante dans les pays de langue française*, Neuchâtel, 1926.

LEE, J., *Lectures on the History of the Church of Scotland from the Reformation to the Revolution Settlement*, 2 vols., Edinburgh, 1860.

LEE, M., *James Stewart, Earl of Moray: a political study of the Reformation in Scotland*, New York, 1953.

Lindsay, *Works*: *The Works of Sir David Lindsay 1490–1555*, ed. D. Hamer, 4 vols., The Scottish Text Society, 1931–36.

McCRIE, T., *Life of Andrew Melville*, new ed., Edinburgh, 1856.

MACGREGOR, J., *The Scottish Presbyterian Polity*, Edinburgh, 1926.

McKAY, D., 'The Election of Parish Clerks in Medieval Scotland', *Innes Review*, vol. 18, pp. 25–35, Glasgow, 1967.

MACKIE, J. D., *The University of Glasgow 1451–1951*, Glasgow, 1954.

McMillan, *Worship*: McMILLAN, W., *The Worship of the Scottish Reformed Church, 1550–1638*, London, 1931.

McNeill, *Calvinism*: McNEILL, J. T., *The History and Character of Calvinism*, New York, 1954.

McROBERTS, D., ed., *Essays on the Scottish Reformation 1513–1625*, Glasgow, 1962.

Marwick, *Records*: MARWICK, J. D., ed., *Records of the Convention of the Royal Burghs of Scotland, 1295–1597*, Edinburgh, 1864.

MATHESON, A., 'Bishop Carswell', *Transactions of the Gaelic Society of Inverness*, vol. 42 (1953–59), pp. 182–205, Stirling, 1965.

MAXWELL, A., *The History of Old Dundee*, Edinburgh and Dundee, 1884.

MAXWELL, W. D., *A History of Worship in the Church of Scotland*, London, 1955.

MAXWELL, W. D., *The Liturgical Portions of the Genevan Service Book*, Edinburgh, 1931.

MAXWELL, W. D., *An Outline of Christian Worship*, London, 1936.
Melvill, *Diary*: PITCAIRN, R., ed., *The Autobiography and Diary of Mr James Melvill*, The Wodrow Society, Edinburgh, 1842.
MIGNE, P.L., *Patrologiae cursus completus, series Latina*, Paris, 1878–90.
The Miscellany of the Spalding Club, vol. 4, Aberdeen, 1849.
The Miscellany of the Wodrow Society, ed. D. Laing, vol. 1, Edinburgh, 1844.
MITCHELL, A. F., ed., '*Livre des Anglois*' *or Register of the English Church at Geneva under the pastoral care of Knox and Goodman*, 1555–1559, [n.p.] 1889.
Munimenta Alme Universitatis Glasguensis, 1450–1727, Maitland Club, 2 vols., 1854.
NIESEL, W., *The Theology of Calvin*, London, 1956.
NSH: *New Schaft-Herzog Encyclopedia of Religious Knowledge*, 22 vols., New York and London, 1908–1912.
Patrick, *Statutes*: PATRICK, D., ed., *Statutes of the Scottish Church*, *1225–1559*, Scottish History Society, vol. 45, Edinburgh, 1907.
Pitcairn, *Acts*: *Acts of the General Assembly M.DC.XXXVIII–M.DCCC.XLII*, ed. T. Pitcairn, Edinburgh, 1843.
PRYDE, G. S., ed., *Ayr Burgh Accounts, 1534–1624*, Scottish History Society, vol. 28, Edinburgh, 1937.
RAIT, R. S., *The Universities of Aberdeen*, Aberdeen, 1895.
RANKIN, W. E. K., 'Scottish Burgh Churches in the 15th Century', *Scottish Church History Society Records*, vol. 7, pp. 63–75. 1941.
Rashdall, *Medieval Universities*: RASHDALL, H., *The Universities of Europe in the Middle Ages*, eds. F. M. Powicke and A. B. Emden, 3 vols., Oxford, 1936.
RICHTER, A. L., ed., *Die evangelischen Kirchenordnungen des XVI. Jahrhunderts*, 2 vols., [reprint of 1864 Weimar edition,] Nieukoop, 1967.
Ridley, *Knox*: RIDLEY, Jaspar, *John Knox*, London, 1968.
ROGER, C., *History of St Andrews*, 2nd ed., 1849.
ROW, JOHN, *The History of the Kirk of Scotland from the year 1558 to August 1637*, The Wodrow Society, Edinburgh, 1842.
RPC: MASSON, D., ed., *The Register of the Privy Council of Scotland*, vol. 1, Edinburgh, 1882.
RSCHS: *Records of the Scottish Church History Society*.
RUCHAT, A., *Histoire de la Réformation de la Suisse*, Geneva, 1727.
RUPP, G., *The Righteousness of God: Luther Studies*, London, 1953.
StAKSR: FLEMING, D. H., ed., *Register of the Minister, Elders and Deacons of the Christian Congregation of St Andrews 1559–1600*, Scottish History Society, 2 vols., Edinburgh, 1889, 1890.
SCANLAN, J. D., 'Husband and Wife: Pre-Reformation Canon Law of Marriage of the Officials' Courts' in *An Introduction to Scottish Legal History*, The Stair Society, vol. 20, pp. 69–81, Edinburgh, 1958.
SCHMIDT, C., 'Mémoire de Jean Sturm sur le projet d'organisation du Gymnase de Strasbourg (Fév. 1538)', *Bulletin Historique et Littéraire, Société de l'Histoire du Protestantisme Français*, vol. 25, pp. 499–505, Paris, 1876.
Scots Peerage, ed. J. Balfour Paul, 9 vols., Edinburgh, 1904.
SETON, G., *A History of the Family of Seton*, 2 vols., Edinburgh, 1896.
SHAW, D., *The General Assemblies of the Church of Scotland 1560–1600*, Edinburgh, 1963.
SHAW, D., 'The Inauguration of Ministers in Scotland 1560–1620' in *Scottish Church History Society Records*, vol. 16, pp. 35–62, Edinburgh, 1966.
SHAW, D., 'John Willock' in D. Shaw, ed., *Reformation and Revolution*, pp. 42–69, Edinburgh, 1967.
SMITH, D. B., 'A Note on Divorce for Desertion', *Juridical Review*, vol. 51, pp. 254–259, Edinburgh, 1939.
SMITH, D. B., 'The Reformers and Divorce' in *Scottish Historical Review*, vol. 9, pp. 10–36, Glasgow, 1911–12.

SMITH, J. I., 'The Transition to Modern Law 1532–1660' in *An Introduction to Scottish Legal History*, The Stair Society, vol. 20, pp. 25–43, Edinburgh, 1958.

SYKES, N., *Old Priest and New Presbyter*, Cambridge, 1956.

TORRANCE, T. F., *The School of Faith: The Catechisms of the Reformed Church*, London, 1959.

VUILLEUMIER, H., *Histoire de l'Eglise Réformée du Pays de Vaud*, 4 vols., Lausanne, 1927–33.

WALLACE, R. S., *Calvin's Doctrine of the Christian Life*, Edinburgh, 1959.

WALLACE, R. S., *Calvin's Doctrine of the Word and Sacrament*, Edinburgh, 1953.

WALTON, F. P., 'The Courts of the Officials and the Commissary Courts 1512–1830' in *An Introductory Survey of the Sources and Literature of Scots Law*, The Stair Society, vol. 1, pp. 133–153, Edinburgh, 1936.

WATT, D. E. R., *Fasti Ecclesiae Scoticanae Medii Aevi ad annum 1638*, second draft, St Andrews, 1969.

Winzet, *Works*: HEWISON, J. K., ed., *Certain Tractates together with the Book of Four Score Three Questions*, by Ninian Winzet, The Scottish Text Society, Edinburgh, 1888, 1890.

Zürich Letters: ROBINSON, H., ed., *The Zürich Letters (Second Series) A.D. 1558–1602*, The Parker Society, Cambridge, 1845.

INDEX